60 READY-TO-USE CODING PROJECTS

ALA Editions purchases fund advocacy, awareness, and accreditation programs for library professionals worldwide.

60 READY-TO-USE CODING PROJECTS

EDITED BY
Ellyssa Kroski

ELLYSSA KROSKI is the director of information technology at the New York Law Institute as well as an award-winning editor and author of 37 books. She is a librarian, an adjunct faculty member at Drexel University and San Jose State University, and an international conference speaker. She received the 2017 Library Hi Tech Award from the ALA/LITA for her long-term contributions in the area of library and information science technology and its application. She can be found at: http://amazon.com/author/ellyssa/.

ISBN: 978-0-8389-1872-2 (paper)

Library of Congress Cataloging-in-Publication Data

Names: Kroski, Ellyssa, editor.
Title: 60 ready-to-use coding projects / edited by Ellyssa Kroski.
Other titles: Sixty ready-to-use coding projects
Description: Chicago : ALA Editions, 2020. | Includes bibliographical references and index. | Summary: "This book provides 60 ready-to-use coding projects that can be implemented in libraries"—Provided by publisher.
Identifiers: LCCN 2019029389 | ISBN 9780838918722 (paperback)
Subjects: LCSH: Libraries—Activity programs—United States. | Computer programming—Study and teaching. | Computer literacy—Study and teaching.
Classification: LCC Z716.33 .A145 2020 | DDC 025.5—dc23
LC record available at https://lccn.loc.gov/2019029389

Cover design by Kimberly Thornton. Cover illustration © Nizwa Design/Adobe Stock.

Text design and composition by Dianne M. Rooney using Archer and Univers typefaces.

♾ This paper meets the requirements of ANSI/NISO Z39.48-1992 (Permanence of Paper).

Printed in the United States of America

24 23 22 21 20 5 4 3 2 1

Contents

Acknowledgments

I would like to sincerely thank all of the knowledgeable experts who contributed programs to this book for generously donating their time to making this an outstanding resource for libraries.

Preface

Coding or computer programming is an integral part of digital literacy and has become of paramount importance for libraries committed to providing computational thinking skills to their patrons. These types of programs offered by libraries can provide patrons of all ages with valuable STEM skills as well as problem-solving, critical thinking, and computational thinking abilities and practical career-building proficiencies. For these reasons, the interest in providing such technical programs in libraries continues to grow. ALA's Libraries Ready to Code initiative, funded by Google, provided "more than $500,000 in grants for 28 libraries in 21 states . . . to design and implement coding programs for young people." This was the first time ALA dedicated funds for computer science-related programming in libraries. The introduction shares findings from the Libraries Ready to Code program and shows how your coding projects can contribute to the larger goal of developing computational thinking.

While the benefits of coding programs in libraries is clear, these types of events and workshops can be quite intimidating for librarians who don't have a computer science background. And that's where this book comes in. Each chapter in this book is a complete start-to-finish recipe for how to plan and run an effective coding program in your library, including learning outcomes and recommendations for future programs, even for librarians without any technical background or previous experience.

The programs and workshops in this book have been organized by age group and cover a variety of challenging and engaging topics that run the gamut from choreographing music videos with Ozobots to programming Mad Libs games with Python to animation with Scratch. All age ranges and skill levels are represented—from the youngest kids who can take part in storytime coding activities to tweens who can learn to program robots and develop video games to hacker clubs for young adults and physical computing for adults.

60 Ready-to-Use Coding Projects is an all-in-one guide book for creating innovative coding and computer-related programming that is chock-full of practical project ideas for libraries. It provides real-world programming ideas for public, school, and academic libraries. The programming projects herein have been contributed by librarians and library professionals, and each chapter is specifically geared toward how to implement these projects in libraries.

Introduction

From Coding to Computational Thinking Literacy: A Library Call to Action

LINDA BRAUN and MARIJKE VISSER

Taylor, a teen girl from a rural community, took part in her library's Ready to Code–sponsored activities. She got involved because the school librarian talked with her about her interests and learned that Taylor is very interested in fashion. The librarian then introduced Taylor to Ready to Code programming by working with her on learning how to code and produce e-textiles. Taylor may not pursue a career in fashion or become a coder, but through the exposure to coding through the library, she is more aware of how coding can enhance her interests and even open up opportunities for her.

We often hear that children entering school now will work in jobs or pursue careers not yet imagined. Statistics tell us in the United States today, more than 500,000 computing jobs are not being filled and yet are the fastest growing type of science, technology, engineering, and mathematics (STEM) job available. Along with that, the majority of these jobs are outside the tech sector. Moreover, technology infuses all aspects of learning and human interaction. This will continue to change the nature of how we communicate, how we work, and how we live. There is tremendous opportunity for innovative approaches to solving complex social and economic problems that challenge local communities and around the globe.

Today's workforce requires technical and digital skills. As technologies continue to advance and as emerging technologies are embedded across work sectors and in daily life, the demand for specific sets of cognitive skills will increase in order to integrate these technologies into a variety of areas related to work and life. In response, recent reports from McKinsey & Company and Harvard Business Review have called for more attention to developing social and emotional (SE) skills such as taking initiative and collaboration as well as creativity and problem-solving skills. Coding and computer science (CS) activities help youth develop SE skills, which are at the heart of the concepts in computational thinking (CT).

Libraries Ready to Code CT Definition

"Computational thinking (CT) refers to thought processes used to formulate problems and their solutions.* These include breaking down problems into smaller parts, looking for patterns, identifying principles that generate these patterns, and developing instructions that computers—machines and people—can understand. It is an approach to critical thinking that can be used to solve problems across all disciplines.† Along with leaders in education and industry, the Libraries Ready to Code initiative considers CT to be a critical literacy for all ages of learners."

*Wing, Jeannette. "Computational Thinking." Communications of the ACM. March 2006. https://www.cs.cmu.edu/~15110-s13/Wing06-ct.pdf.

†"Google for Education: Exploring Computational Thinking." Google Expeditions. Accessed October 2, 2018. https://edu.google.com/resources/programs/exploring-computational-thinking/.

When libraries prepare youth for college and career or design programs for adult learners, they expose learners and connect their interests to the opportunities made available through technology. This is the first step in making sure youth and adults are equipped with essential work and life skills. More importantly, libraries that provide coding programs help their patrons develop a mindset to seek new or alternative strategies for using technology to find information, think critically, as well as create and share knowledge and ideas. As librarians and library staff embrace the emerging role of facilitators of coding and CS programs based in CT, they propel youth and adults to think differently. Library staff help build a community of thinkers and doers who create and share new ideas or use digital tools to imagine and put into place innovative solutions to community challenges.

Research also tells us that the educational and career opportunities technology brings are not equally available to young people. There are structural and social barriers that create disparities for some groups underrepresented in technology, including Hispanics, African American youth, and girls generally. Even when formal CS education is available, not all students are equally encouraged or individually inclined to pursue the options. Students in rural communities are also less likely to have access to CS courses or be exposed to computers at home. Nor do all uses of technology lead to the skills and fluency necessary to know how to most effectively use it.[1]

The library community—information professionals dedicated to ensuring equitable access to information—must take an active role in ensuring such opportunities are available to everyone regardless of zip code, cultural or ethnic background, gender identity, or age and ability. They can actively serve children and teens who are less likely to have access to or be exposed to technology, CS curriculum in school, or extended learning opportunities. To support all youth as they journey through the technology-rich educational and career landscape, libraries need to consider how effectively their coding and CS programs connect to youth interests and broaden participation. Coding and CT through the library are catalysts for youth to pursue their interests and discover new ones and ensure they have a portfolio of skills and literacies to meet life challenges and opportunities head-on.

ALA and Google Inc. are collaborating on the Libraries Ready to Code (RtC) initiative to build capacity, provide resources, and create a space for peer-to-peer learning so any library can design and implement coding and CS activities that promote CT literacies among children and youth. The initial RtC report, "Ready to Code: Connecting Youth to CS Opportunity through Libraries," found that librarians and library staff in school and public libraries are essential community resources ensuring youth have access to technology and are equipped with the skills and competencies required for full participation in today's and tomorrow's global economy and society.

IS IT CODING, COMPUTER SCIENCE, OR COMPUTATIONAL THINKING?

While the RtC initiative began with a scan of coding and computer science programs in libraries, it did not take the project team long to realize libraries are at varying levels of understanding why they should be part of the CS educator community and how best to do so. Evaluation data collected from a small cohort of faculty from library and information science schools and the RtC cohort libraries reveals a shift over the course of the projects from focusing on coding for coding's sake to a more nuanced approach that places computational thinking literacies at the center for library engagement. Whether cohort libraries view CT as necessary for workforce or early learning, or equitable access to opportunity, the cohort was in general agreement that CT is a fundamental literacy for children and youth.

WHY LIBRARIES AND CODING?

From early-learning activities with families, caregivers, and young children, to in and out of school time learning for youth, to college or career activities for young adults and activities for professionals already in the workforce, library programs are designed to address community needs. Libraries are key places for inclusive informal and lifelong learning experiences. Over the course of the RtC initiative (2015–2018), through focus groups, interviews, site visits, work with faculty at library and information science schools and iSchools, and the collaborative work of the 30 libraries (members of a cohort) selected to participate in the RtC project, evaluation and assessment data (both qualitative and quantitative) highlights how the library value of meeting community needs fits into CT programing for children and teens. Further, the RtC initiative identifies the contributions libraries that offer CT make for the youth they serve, their communities, and CS education stakeholders more broadly.

The RtC cohort libraries developed coding and CS programs while exploring and refining the skills and mindsets library staff need to ensure such programs foster CT literacies. Through a vibrant community of practice that developed among the cohort, participants gained confidence in developing CT programs while shifting from viewing coding-specific skills as the endgame of their programs. The cohort also contributed to the initiative's understanding of just what the library's role could be in addressing the gaps in access to CT programs among children and youth. Libraries are essential partners and, given a full array of support and resources, excel at designing CT programs that range from one-time events to multi-week sessions.

> "Ultimately, when youth practice CT, they find new ways to communicate their ideas, express themselves, and practice problem solving. Library staff can embed CT in addition to traditional literacy in their work with children and teens, empowering them with the literacies they need to be lifelong learners and to succeed in college and career."
>
> —Claudia Haines, RtC cohort member and youth services librarian, Homer (Alaska) Public Library; see chapter 8 for more from Claudia

FACILITATING CT LITERACIES THROUGH THE READY TO CODE THEMES

RtC research uncovered 5 themes that are integral to successful acquisition of CT literacies through libraries. These themes take into account the needs of youth, families, adults, communities, and libraries. They are organized in the RtC Facilitation Pathway, designed to help libraries find a good fit with CT activities offered in the Ready to Code website's collection of resources. See the facilitation pathway at www.ala.org/tools/readytocode/pathway/. See the Libraries Ready to Code website for more examples illustrating the themes along with tools and resources: https://www.librariesreadytocode.org.

Broadening Participation

The Leaky Tech Pipeline highlights 3 reasons why addressing underrepresentation in technology careers is important:

- The growing diversity of the U.S. population and need for a robust future workforce,
- The benefits associated with having a diverse workforce, and
- The detrimental impact of underrepresentation on exacerbating economic inequality for diverse communities.[2]

Through expanding their reach, working with community organizations and members, and developing recruitment and retention efforts that specifically focus on diverse youth and diverse learning environments, libraries play a role in addressing technology underrepresentation.

Connecting Youth Interests and Emphasizing Youth Voice

The connected learning framework emphasizes creative and social learning experiences that are driven by learners' personal interests. The framework's core principles include learning contexts that are peer supported, interest powered, and academically oriented along with experiences that are production centered, openly networked, and bring together learners and adults around a shared purpose.[3]

Engaging with Communities

In an RtC strategy brief, Susan Baier, library director for the McCracken County (Kentucky) Public Library, notes how she began learning about the community: "When I started out as a library director, I spent my first few months in meetings with community stakeholders. A common thread soon became evident—preparing a workforce for the future was a key concern for local employers with technology jobs they couldn't fill. Companies were approaching schools asking how they could attract youth to their industries. I saw an opportunity for us to better position the library as a partner in education and workforce development by offering CS/CT programs for youth."[4]

Engaging with Families

Families that take part in library CT literacy activities have the chance to become familiar with these skills and gain an understanding of the role these skills play in young people's lives.

Demonstrating Outcomes Through Impact

It should be expected that not all CT literacy activities that a library provides will be successful. However, there is extreme value in recognizing at the planning stage of a CT library activity what success will look like and how the library will measure that success.

THERE IS AN ENTRY POINT AT YOUR LIBRARY

For many library staff, the idea of including coding and CT activities in the services provided to youth and families may seem daunting and even a little bit scary. There are ways to start small and build as skills and knowledge are gained.

These tips and resources from the Libraries Ready to Code Collection can help you take first steps into this work:

- If you need to gain support from others within the library, such as colleagues or administrators, take a look at the slide deck—http://bit.ly/rtc_waseca_deck/—created by the Waseca (Minnesota) Public Library. It provides an overview of why libraries play a vital role in bringing coding and CT literacies to youth and families.
- Unplugged activities that don't require any technology to help youth gain CT skills are a great way to get started in this work. To learn more about designing and implementing these types of activities, take a look at the unplugged lesson plan from the Homer (Alaska) Public Library—http://bit.ly/homer_rtc_unplug ged. (You can see more about Claudia Haines's work in this area in chapter 8.)
- Looking for ways to get started with bringing community partners into coding and CT library activities? Take a look at the community partner invitation—http://bit.ly/rtc_kent_recruitment/—developed by the Kent County (Maryland) Public Schools.

No matter the entry point and resources you use to get started with this work, don't forget that every community is different. When using materials from other libraries, think about what should stay the same and what needs to change based on your community makeup. Ask yourself about the audience you serve, the partners you may work with, and the materials and resources available for the activity.

NOTES

1. Google Inc. & Gallup Inc. "Diversity Gaps in Computer Science: Exploring the Underrepresentation of Girls, Blacks and Hispanics." Gallup Inc., 2016, "Diversity Gaps in Computer Science: Exploring the Underrepresentation of Girls, Blacks and Hispanics," services.google.com/fh/files/misc/diversity-gaps-in-computer-science-report.pdf; Google Inc., and Gallup Inc. "Computer Science Learning: Closing the Gap Rural and Small-Town School Districts." Gallup Inc., 2017, "Computer Science Learning: Closing the Gap Rural and Small-Town School Districts," services.google.com/fh/files/misc/computer-science-learning-closing-the-gap-rural-small-town-brief.pdf.
2. Scott, Allison, et al. The Leaky Tech Pipeline. Kapor Center for Social Impact, 2018, The Leaky Tech Pipeline, www.leakytechpipeline.com/wp-content/themes/kapor/pdf/KC18001_report_v6.pdf.
3. Hoffman, Kelly M., et al. Connected Libraries: Surveying the Current Landscape and Charting a Path to the Future. The Connected Lib Project, 2016, Connected Libraries: Surveying the Current Landscape and Charting a Path to the Future, connectedlib.ischool.uw.edu/wp-content/uploads/2016/02/ConnectedLibraries-SurveyingtheCurrentLandscape-and-ChartingthePathtotheFuture.pdf.
4. Baier, Susan. "Strategy Brief: Making the Case to Your Community That Libraries Are Ready to Code." Libraries Ready to Code. 2018. Accessed October 2, 2018. https://drive.google.com/file/d/14ANpQaU4ptgJpeWsB9ElAKA_KNN157N2/view/.

PART I

PROGRAMS FOR KIDS

(AGES 3–7)

1

Make Your Own Cartoon with PBS Kids ScratchJr

JOANNA SCHOFIELD

Branch Services Librarian-Generalist | Cuyahoga County (Ohio) Public Library

PROJECT DESCRIPTION

What if I could make a cartoon story where my rocket can fly? What if I could make my pigs dance? What if my characters could sing "Happy Birthday"? These are just some of the things young children may want to do if they knew how to code. So how can we introduce coding to the youngest of children? One great resource for engaging and motivating young coders is PBS Kids ScratchJr. PBS has developed an entire curriculum for introducing the app and making fundamentals in their Family Creative Learning Project. This project is designed to teach young children the meaning of coding and making and how to use PBS Kids ScratchJr to create their own stories and images.

Age Range

- Kids (Ages 3–7)
- Adults

Type of Library Best Suited For

- Public Libraries
- School Libraries

Cost Estimate

- $0
  PBS ScratchJr is a free app for iPads and Android devices.

OVERVIEW

The PBS Family Creative Learning Project is a free guide and slideshow for libraries looking to teach coding to families with young children. It is designed to be a 4-week program with families meeting once a week for 2 hours. Each week covers a slightly different topic. Adults and children are split into 2 different rooms for instruction, and the program concludes with participants working together on the app and sharing their experiences. The PBS Family Creative Learning Project walks you step by step through the process and provides information for facilitators. You can access the documents at https://ideastream.pbslearningmedia.org/resource/fcl-scratchjr-rtl-2015-2020/family-community-learning-with-scratchjr-rtl-2015-2020/.

The program requires 2 staff facilitators. The program should be limited to no more than 10 families.

Software/Hardware Needed

Each family requires:

- A tablet with the PBS Kids ScratchJr application installed

Materials List

- Printed activity cards from facilitator website
- Peanut Butter
- Jelly
- Plastic knife
- Plates
- Food for dinner
- Napkins
- Cups for Water
- Water source (water fountain, water cooler, water tower)

STEP-BY-STEP INSTRUCTIONS

Eat

A major component of this series is community building. To encourage participants to get to know each other better, the session always begins with a communal dinner. For our program, we ordered pizza. You can order anything you like for the meal or even reach out to local restaurants to see if they would be willing to donate food. This portion usually takes up the first 20 minutes or so of the program.

Explore

- This is the time when adults and children are encouraged to split into different groups. The "Explore" time is for creative discussions and experiences.
- During the first week, the facilitator opens with a discussion of why adults are separated from children at this point (adults are having facilitated conversations about the maker movement while children are conducting maker activities). During the first week, adults discuss the use of technology in their children's lives and the pros and cons of technology usage.

FIGURE 1.1

The PBS ScratchJr interface

- Adults are also introduced to the PBS Kids ScratchJr app (figure 1.1) and given a few minutes to explore its contents. Children are discussing "what is a maker?" and creating maker hats.
- The second week, adults and children are separately introduced to coding and play a game called Robot Chef. The purpose of Robot Chef is to program a person to make a peanut butter and jelly sandwich. This teaches the complexity of a simple task and how important it is to give specific instructions. After playing Robot Chef, the groups are able to play Robot Dancer, which utilizes dance cards to program an individual dancer.
- The third week, everyone explores the engineering design process. Adults begin with a brief discussion of the engineering design process and engineering as a profession. Next, they break up into groups of 2–4 individuals and are challenged to create a paper airplane that will fly the farthest. In the other room, the children talk about designing and engineering. Next, they participate in a paper airplane challenge similar to what their parents did.
- The fourth week, adults engage in a short discussion about how to extend these engineering and making facets into their home life with their children. The children read the book *Rosie Revere Engineer* by Andrea Beaty.

Make

Each week the families are reunited for creative play on the PBS Kids ScratchJr app. There are note cards available on the facilitator's page that can be printed to show participants how to do basic functions, such as creating a sprite, moving the sprite around the screen, or having the sprite make noise. This time is really meant to engage children with their parents and work through creating images and stories on the PBS Kids ScratchJr app. The facilitator is there to help troubleshoot, but the emphasis should be on the family's exploration of the app.

Share

Each day students are encouraged to share their progress with the whole group. On the last day, groups are encouraged to share their final projects and explain how they developed their ideas.

LEARNING OUTCOMES

Participants will:

- Gain an understanding of engineering and the maker movement.
- Become familiar with PBS Kids ScratchJr.
- Work together with their parents to create something in PBS Kids ScratchJr.
- Gain an understanding of basic coding.

RECOMMENDED NEXT PROJECTS

- There are numerous iterations of Scratch that participants can master. After PBS Kids ScratchJr, participants can work in ScratchJr. After ScratchJr, participants can move into Scratch (https://scratch.mit.edu).
- There are other coding activities that participants can use, such as Codecademy, Code.org, and Khan Academy.

2

Before You Plug In, Analog Games to Play with Young Children

Story Mapping

STACY HURT

Librarian of Practice—Early Literacy | Evansville Vanderburgh (Indiana) Public Library

PROJECT DESCRIPTION

One of the first things I ask when doing a STEM program is, "Where are all the electrical outlets?" Fortunately, you don't need to "plug in" to turn kids on to coding. The first time that I did an analog coding program, the reason was quite simple: I didn't have any fancy technology equipment. (If you turned to this chapter first, you are probably in the same boat.) A computer is not required to begin teaching children to code. Coding is more than just getting technology to "do stuff." Coding is a way of thinking and creative problem solving. If you present the material effectively, even very young children can be taught coding. For example, the concept of binary on/off can be taught with a simple game of Red Light, Green Light. This chapter features some unplugged or analog games that kids can play to gear up to learn to code.

In Story Mapping, we start with the most basics concepts, such as following special directions. While the child is having fun with a story, you are introducing computational thinking. Story Mapping can be done as part of a regular storytime or as part of a preschool STEAM class. This game is excellent for the youngest of coders, but you can easily modify it for use as a warm-up activity with older students.

Age Range

- Kids (Ages 3–7)
- Can be modified for other ages

Type of Library Best Suited For

- Public libraries
- School libraries

Cost Estimate

- $0–$15

OVERVIEW

While children tell a well-known story, they place arrows on a grid to get from the beginning to the middle to the end. It is that simple. In fact, for the really young, you may even want to make it as easy as 1 arrow up or 1 arrow to the side. Once they understand that 1 arrow can point in different directions (and they are paying attention to those differences), then you can move on to actual Story Mapping. The computational thinking element is in how you present it to students. An algorithm is breaking a task into a series of instructions to accomplish a goal. Coding is the process of transforming actions into a symbolic language. Both of these concepts are introduced in Story Mapping.

Software/Hardware Needed

- None

Materials List

- Masking tape
- Arrows
- Old magazines or withdrawn books
- Your imagination

Optional Materials

- Grid paper
- Paper and pencils

STEP-BY-STEP INSTRUCTIONS

Preparation

- Print out and laminate about 40 arrows [↑]. You can print out more for longer stories or larger groups of children.
- Select the story. Try to pick a story that you know is familiar to kids. Don't assume they know classic fairy tales. If you are introducing the story for the first time or playing with young children, you may want to read the story to them first.
- Pre-select at least 1 story and find some pictures to match. I recommend a minimum of 3: 1 for the beginning, 1 for the middle, and 1 for the end of the story.
- Use masking tape to make a grid on the floor.

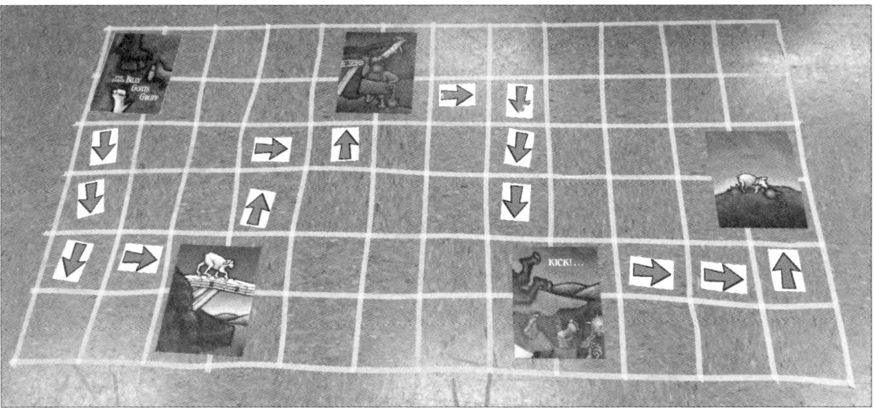

FIGURE 2.1

Story Mapping with Three Billy Goats Gruff

- Place the pictures on the grid so kids can travel through them sequentially. (See figure 2.1.)

PROJECT INSTRUCTIONS

The Game

- Have students place the arrows on the grid to connect the different story elements.
- The arrows need to be in the proper order/direction to be able to retell the story.
- Once kids have played through the game and understand the goal, let them pick a story. They can draw pictures or cut out images from magazines. I have even used withdrawn library books.

Variations

- Allow children to create the Story Map while you tell the story.
- Older kids can make up their own stories and take turns sharing with the group.
- Use grid paper and draw your own pictures and arrows. This is a useful alternative if you are limited on space.
- Make things more challenging by adding elements on the map that children must avoid.

LEARNING OUTCOMES

Participants will:

- Be introduced to the concepts of spatial reasoning and logic.
- Be introduced to algorithms and coding.
- Utilize skills such as sequencing, following directions, and storytelling.
- Learn about the elements of a story, which will strengthen their narrative skills.

RECOMMENDED NEXT PROJECTS

- Chapter 3: Before You Plug In, Analog Games to Play with Young Children: The Human Robot by Stacy Hurt
- Chapter 11: Program the Human Robot: Decomposition Activities for Preschoolers and Families by Paula Langsam
- Graph Paper Coding from the unplugged part of Code.org

3

Before You Plug In, Analog Games to Play with Young Children

The Human Robot

STACY HURT

Librarian of Practice—Early Literacy | Evansville Vanderburgh (Indiana) Public Library

PROJECT DESCRIPTION

Analog games in a book on coding? Yes! Analog coding can function as a stand-alone program or be easily incorporated into other activities. Many students are itching to get started with the robots or other tech you are using, but before the shiny lights distract them, unplugged games are a great introduction to the core concepts. Additionally, if you find yourself in the unfortunate position of having more kids than equipment, splitting kids into groups and using an analog backup activity can save the day. You can also play simple games as a brain break if kids become too intensely focused. Unplugging is also great for outreach, when you're dealing with unknown variables such as the environment, materials, or number of children who will be present. And they are great to have as an emergency backup—you never know when technology will fail or when someone (not you) will forget to bring the batteries.

The Human Robot game is an effective way to introduce the mechanisms of coding to students. It can be modified to fit the needs of nearly any age group, number of kids, or environment. To play the game, children must write code for someone else to act out using simple symbols. Students acquire an understanding of what an algorithm is and how computers "think." This game is a composite of My Robotic Friends from Hour of Code/Thinkersmith, Fuzz Family Frenzy from Kodable, and DrTechniko from Nikolaos Michalakis.

Age Range

- Kids (Ages 3–7)
- Tweens (Ages 8–12)

Type of Library Best Suited For

- Public libraries
- School libraries

Cost Estimate

- $0–$10

OVERVIEW

Playing My Robotic Friends can be used as introduction to algorithms at the beginning of a class. This helps students learn the coding concepts before you bring out the computers. It can also be used as an icebreaker game to get kids to work in pairs. Some of the concepts can be a little tricky for very young students.

Software/Hardware Needed

- Paper and pencils
- Other props as needed to make a simple obstacle course

STEP-BY-STEP INSTRUCTIONS

Preparation

- Before you begin, select some basic symbols you want to use. I recommend letting students create their symbols as needed. Samples: Ⓘ Left foot, Ⓘ Right foot, →Turn
- In your room, have space for the obstacle course.

PROJECT INSTRUCTIONS

- Set up a simple obstacle course. It can be a chair to walk around or a bean bag to pick up. I recommend having 2 or more options. That way the "robot" can't anticipate the commands.

- With a young group, you might want to have a few samples pre-made and go through it together. Better yet, have kids partner with their parent or caretaker and let the adult be the robot.
- Ask kids to find a partner. Each partner writes a code for his partner to follow.
- The instructions can be handed to the robot or given as oral commands. The "Human Robot" must follow the instructions explicitly. This is where it can get fun: If the robot follows the instructions exactly and does not complete the intended task, then it is time to debug the software.

Variations

- Start with only verbal commands. This lets children make corrections as they go along.
- Or have children write the code, but read out the instructions. Have them write their corrections as they go.

LEARNING OUTCOMES

Participants will:

- Obtain an understanding of the basic principles of computer programming.
- Exercise active listening skills.
- Learn to be succinct in their communication.
- Learn to break an action down into smaller steps through algorithms and coding.
- Potentially discover looping, patterns, and other coding shortcuts.
- Utilize skills such as encoding, decoding, conditionals, and problem solving.

RECOMMENDED NEXT PROJECTS

- LightBot
- ScratchJr

4

Mommy and Me Coding

Learning Coding Concepts Together with Code-a-Pillar

BIANCA RIVERA

Youth Librarian | Long Beach (New York) Public Library

PROJECT DESCRIPTION

Preschoolers and their moms can learn authentic coding concepts together using Fisher-Price's Think & Learn Code-a-pillar. Code-a-pillar is a fun and exciting robot that utilizes motorized parts, colorful glowing lights, and silly sounds to provide feedback to the youngest of coders. Bona fide coding concepts can be introduced to children as young as 3 years old.

Working alongside their moms (or another trusted grown-up), children can learn:

- To create and follow step-by-step instructions to complete a task (**algorithms**).
- To break down big problems into small steps (**modular programming**).
- To devise a series of steps to implement their program (**planning and sequencing**).
- To use symbols to represent values (**variables**).
- To repeat sequences of code multiple times (**loops**).
- To tell the computer what to do based on an "if, then" decision-making process (**conditions**).
- To identify and fix errors in programs (**debugging**).

In addition to the learning opportunities presented, perhaps the most important part of Mommy and Me Coding is the opportunity for parents and children to build familial bonds while working on a novel project. Children working alongside their adults learning new and exciting skills can receive the same benefits to the family unit as exercising, cooking together, or sharing bedtime stories as a family.

Age Range

- Kids (Ages 3–7): This activity is geared toward preschoolers working alongside an adult family member.

Type of Library Best Suited For

- Public libraries
- School libraries

Cost Estimate

- $40–$200

Required Costs

- $49.99 for each Code-a-pillar (Based on the size of your group, it is highly suggested *1* Code-a-pillar is purchased for *each* group of 2–3 children. For example, if you have 9 children in your program, we recommend purchasing at least 3 Code-a-pillars.
- $0 (Each Code-a-pillar comes with 1 green disc and 1 red disc. Green is the start point and red is the target.)
- $4 for a package of 4 AA batteries required for each Code-a-pillar.

Optional Costs

- $15 for each of the 3 Command Segment Expansion add-on sets (Each Code-a-pillar comes with 8 segments attached, each having its own function—1 sound piece, 3 straight pieces, 2 right turn pieces, and 2 left turn pieces.):
  - $15 for the Basic Expansion Pack (3 pieces for "Go forward," "90° right turn," "90° left turn"—this is the same set that comes with the Code-a-pillar)
  - $15 for the Silly Sounds & Lights Expansion Pack (3 pieces for "Wacky," "Sleepy ZZZs," "Happy"—this set has additional silly sounds and lights)
  - $15 for the Master Moves Expansion Pack (3 pieces for "180° left turn," "45° right turn," "Repeat"—this set gives children the opportunity to work on more complex moves)
  - Free Code-a-pillar app (The app can only be downloaded from the Apple App Store, Google Play Store, and the Amazon Appstore onto tablets and phones. It cannot be installed on personal computers or Chromebooks.)

OVERVIEW

Fisher-Price has invented an affordable and accessible coding robot for its Think & Learn series intended to encourage the acquisition of early childhood problem solving, planning, sequencing, and critical thinking skills.

First showcased at the 2016 Consumer Electronics Show, the anxiously awaited Code-a-pillar (figure 4.1) had been advertised as a leading early childhood robot. It has been promoted as the tool geared toward children ages 3–7 who will be the future coders of the year 2035.

Working as a children's librarian, I have seen firsthand how parental requests for more technology programs has increased over the last few years. The demand for instruction in coding, programmable robots, and 3-D printing has become a common request right alongside our story time, craft, movement and music, and cooking classes that we have historically offered.

I have found from experience that early childhood tech programs should run 30–45 minutes. Regardless of the size of the group of children, at least 1 parent must be available to work alongside their children. In addition, at least 1 staff member must be on hand to lead the session and be available to answer questions about the technology.

After leading this program several times, I recommend the following:

- To encourage adequate sharing of the Code-a-pillars and an orderly program, I would not admit more than 10–12 children at a time during

FIGURE 4.1

Three year olds considering symbols on segments

the session. Not only is this a safety issue, but you also want to avoid having the children fight over and damaging the Code-a-pillars. This can turn into quite an active program, and we want to ensure everyone has a turn.

- The maximum number of children per group is 2–3 children for 1 Code-a-pillar (2 children is optimal but, of course, not always feasible). This means if you wind up with 4 groups of children, you need 4 Code-a-pillars on hand (for the 12 children). At our library, we own 4 Code-a-pillars.
- Before the program starts, take a moment to speak directly to parents or caregivers about your expectations for running a smooth session, including keeping watch over the behavior of their children, ensuring the Code-a-pillars are not treated roughly, and reminding their children to take turns with their group's Code-a-pillar.
- Additionally, remind adults that this is a Mommy and Me/Family Program, and they need to actively engage with children during the activity. Children often need guidance when facing new challenges to feel successful, and some of the activities can be surprisingly difficult.
- Depending on how much gets accomplished during the workshop, activities will become more complex. Explain to parents that it is welcome and acceptable to assist their children with discovering solutions. However, it is always preferable to allow children to come up with their own solutions.

Software/Hardware Needed

Necessary Equipment

- Code-a-pillar (You will need multiple sets when there are multiple groups.)
- Ample room space (A flat surface such as tile, laminate, or hardwood flooring is highly recommended; avoid carpeting because it does not work well and can damage the Code-a-pillar's wheels.)

Recommended Equipment

- Code-a-pillar Expansion Sets
- For Code-a-pillar app
  - iOS, Android, and Kindle tablets (not available for personal computers or Chromebooks)
  - Interactive whiteboard to display app and allow children to drag and drop command segments

STEP-BY-STEP INSTRUCTIONS

Preparation

- Before the start of the first program, put new batteries in the Code-a-pillar.
- Each time you use Code-a-pillar for a program, check the batteries before you begin. Make sure the GO! button is working and the segments are lighting up.
- At the end of each session, remind children and their parents that it is important to slide the power switch off. We have discovered that the battery will continue to drain even if the Code-a-pillar is not being actively used but is still turned on.
- Plan your workspace a half hour before the program takes place. Remember you need a flat surface (avoid carpet). The Code-a-pillars tend to drive along quickly and at quite a distance, so a small corner of a room will not suffice. I recommend a full-size area.
- Keep in mind that the Code-a-pillars (although they possess quite charming, chirpy sounds) are loud and there is no volume control. Ensure they are far removed from those who need a quiet space.
- When working with older children (ages 6–7), design the obstacle course ahead of time. Be sure to have the green and red discs and any barriers you want to include readily available. You may also want to have your homemade coding cards in place.

PROJECT INSTRUCTIONS

- Begin by sparking participant interest—show a preplanned demo of what the Code-a-pillar is capable of. At this beginning stage, do something basic like mix up the pieces of the Code-a-pillar and have a child hit the GO! button to see what happens.
- Next, disassemble the pieces and put the segments in a different order. After children watch him move in a different path, ask them to take a moment to think about why that may have happened.
- Parents will already have an idea of how Code-a-pillar works, but remind them to hold their thoughts and let children answer on their own.
- Next, have a parent break Code-a-pillar down into pieces. Have her hold up the individual pieces and ask children what they think the symbols represent on the segments. Depending on the age of the children, they may not know what left or right is, so they could be asked to visually show what direction the symbols represent.

- Next, select a child volunteer to take all 7 segments of the Code-a-pillar and connect them to the head. After the pieces are connected securely and the robot is turned on, the child can put Code-a-pillar on the floor and push the GO! button. At this point, it is a good time to mention to children that the Code-a-pillar will take a few moments before starting up because it takes a few seconds for him to process a "program." He has to think about the path he's going to take based on a human's commands.
- Instruct everyone to watch the robot closely. When the robot stops, ask children if the order of the pieces impacted the direction of the Code-a-pillar's path. See if they can elaborate on their answer.
- After that conversation, another child can volunteer to take apart and reassemble the robot in the order of their choosing. A library staff member or parent volunteer can place the green and red discs on the floor and explain how these will be the beginning and end targets. The child can then place the robot on the floor and push the GO! button.
    - After watching the robot travel, children should be asked to consider how they can estimate the length of time it takes for each piece to move. (Hint: counting seconds will be helpful!)
    - They can also consider what strategies they could use to guess how to reach a predetermined target (the red disc). As this is a more complex question, parents can assist children with brainstorming the answers.
- Once the adult staff members are satisfied children are ready to start using the Code-a-pillars on their own (with their parents watching nearby), the fun begins! Children can now be broken into groups of 2–3 per group. At least 1 parent will be assigned to be the adult observer of a team.
- One last final warning for children and parents is that they must understand that the Code-a-pillars have electronic parts that can break if children are not careful. The library staff member should take time to show children and parents how to carefully put the pieces together. Most important is that they gently but firmly connect the prongs in the head to the first segment of the body. After that, they need to be careful about connecting the USB ports of the body segments. Once a prong or port is bent, it is nearly impossible to fix. Obviously, the Code-a-pillar was built for rough-and-tumble children, but they still need to be mindful of how they treat the robot. It is very important to model the handling of the Code-a-pillar to each group of children and ask the adult assistants to remind children of their responsibilities to treat the robot with respect.
- Lay out the green and red discs and ask children if they can work on a plan to make Code-a-pillar go from start to finish. Explain that there is no right or

wrong strategy—the goal is for the robot to end up at the finish line. There are many ways to achieve this goal.

- Show children how rooms can become obstacle courses in themselves. A chair or table can be an obstacle for the robot. Children can be challenged to estimate how to work past the obstacles to reach the red disc. They can also attempt to hand draw a "treasure hunt" map, including drawings of the segment directional arrows before they run their program.

ADDITIONAL TIPS AND TRIPS FROM FISHER-PRICE

Fisher-Price recommends the following tips that we have found to be especially useful:[1]

- Use Code-a-Pillar on hard floors. Avoid using Code-a-pillar on carpets as the wheels cannot move as easily and the carpet fabric can get stuck in the wheels.
- Code-a-pillar will not move if no pieces are connected to his head. His eyes will blink, and he will make a distinctive sound. This does not mean he's broken—it's just a reminder to connect pieces to his head.
- If a piece does not light up when connected, check to make sure the USB port is fully connected. If it is not, gently push it in.
- If you notice Code-a-pillar is moving slowly, it's possible the wheels are dirty. Have an adult clean off the wheels with a clean, dry cloth.
- If Code-a-pillar runs into an object and stops moving, simply clear his path and press the GO! button to resume moving. He will continue the path he started.
- Although you can add additional pieces to make Code-a-pillar grow, he will not recognize more than 15 pieces at a time. Adding more than 15 pieces could even permanently damage the prongs in his head and body.
- If Code-a-pillar's eyes are flashing red and he is not moving, this means the prongs in his head have most likely been permanently damaged. As of this writing, replacement heads cannot be purchased, so take care to avoid damaging the prongs in his head.
- Regarding health, note that Code-a-pillar emits flashing lights at 5–30 cycles per second. Be sure to make patrons aware of this before they interact with him.

LEARNING OUTCOMES

Participants will:

- Select individual segments and predict the impact they will have when executing a program.
- Plan successful sequences to achieve their end goal.
- Predict the distance each code segment will cover when approximating total distance needed to reach a target.
- Further develop their computational thinking skills by attempting more complex tasks.

RECOMMENDED NEXT PROJECTS

- Take Code-a-pillar's abilities to the next level. Learn math concepts such as rotation by degrees and the coding concept **loops** by purchasing the Master Moves Expansion Pack (3 pieces for "180° left turn," "45° right turn," "Repeat"). As these are more complicated moves, parents of older children may want to provide assistance when children are devising their plan.
- If your library owns an interactive whiteboard, connect a tablet to the board (either wired using an adapter or wirelessly using Apple TV) to display the free Code-a-pillar app. Children can take turns helping Code-a-pillar work through obstacles to reach his target by using the drag-and-drop command segments. Parents can assist children if they don't know how to use the drag-and-drop features of an interactive whiteboard. In addition, the obstacles become increasingly challenging as children "level up," and parents may want to coach children through complex levels.
- Parents and children can use library supplies to create their own DIY coding cards by simply using paper and markers or by downloading images off the Internet. The adult can print the cards in color and cut down the cards to a reasonable size so kids can easily see them. The coding cards should include the colored symbols found on the Code-a-pillar—this includes green forward arrows, yellow left turn arrows, orange right turn arrows, and purple audio symbols. An activity to utilize these cards is to lay out 8 cards on a table and have children and their adults take turns grabbing 1 card and attaching the matching segment to Code-a-pillar's head. After all the correlating segments have been attached to his head, push the GO! button and watch him take off. An alternative challenging activity is to place the green and red discs on the floor and plan which coding cards would help the coders achieve the goal

of getting Code-a-pillar to the red disc. This activity will really force coders to plan their sequence ahead of time.

- A fun and convenient way to create a DIY obstacle course is by utilizing any room in your library or house. Any room that has flat flooring and some furniture makes a perfect obstacle course for your Code-a-pillar. By placing the green and red discs a few feet away, parents can challenge children to plan a path while trying to avoid the obstacles (such as a living room chair, a desk, or even your pet). Explain that there is no right or wrong plan—the goal is for Code-a-pillar to end up at the finish line. There are many ways to achieve this goal. Note: Code-a-pillar does not have sensors on his face, so he will not know to stop when he's about to run into an object. When he hits the object, he will stop moving and make a sound. Simply move him in the correct direction and he will continue on his path.

ADDITIONAL RECOMMENDED NEXT PROJECTS

- Code.org's Pre-reader Express (ages 4–8): Pre-reader Express require screen time however they also include several "unplugged" activities when you want your child to take a break from the computer.
- The free ScratchJr app (ages 5–7) is available on iOS, Android, Chromebook, and Kindle (ScratchJr is not available on PCs).

And, although not a project, I would recommend a book—yes, an actual hardcover book (grades K–2)! *My First Coding Book,* authored by Kiki Prottsman, is a fun, interactive, and practical book explains coding concepts to young children.

NOTE

1. "Fisher-Price Think & Learn Code-a-pillar." Mattel and Fisher-Price Customer Service. 2016. Accessed October 16, 2018. https://service.mattel.com/us/productDetail.aspx?prodno=DKT39&siteid=27.

5

Coding Storytime for Families

KRISTINE TECHAVANICH
Children's Librarian | Mandel Public Library of West Palm Beach, Florida

PROJECT DESCRIPTION

Coding Storytime for Families reinvents traditional storytime, which focuses on gaining the early literacy skills that young children need before they can begin to learn how to read. Coding Storytime informs caregivers about the growth of the computer science job market, emphasizes the importance of teaching foundational computational thinking skills to children from an early age, and offers practical advice on teaching the skills that children need when they start learning how to code. This storytime uses the same approach of traditional storytimes through presenting picture books and familiar songs that support early literacy to support coding as literacy for the 21st century.

Age Range

- Kids (Ages 3–7)

Type of Library Best Suited For

- Public libraries

Cost Estimate

- $0 (storytime is an integral part of library services to children and coding storytime needs no extra supplies!)

OVERVIEW

As an important digital literacy skill for the 21st century, coding must be accessible for all library users, including the very young child. Coding Storytime, a program for caregivers to attend with young children, provides an opportunity to apply developmentally appropriate practices that support digital literacy and thinking like a future programmer. The program lasts 30 minutes and requires a presenter to read books, lead the audience through fingerplays and songs, empower caregivers with short messages between activities, and prepare an activity for families to do after storytime.

Software/Hardware Needed

No software/hardware is needed for presenting this program. Although it is not required, presenters may prepare a digital presentation using software such as PowerPoint or Google Slides to display during the program.

Materials List

- *Optional:* 5 robots for the flannelboard rhyme; they can be printed out or made from felt pieces
- Carle, Eric. 1969. *The Very Hungry Caterpillar.* Cleveland, OH: World Publishing Company.
- Numeroff, Laura. 1985. *If You Give a Mouse a Cookie.* New York, NY: Harper & Row.

Optional Equipment for End-of-Storytime Activity

- Think & Learn Code-a-pillar by Fisher-Price (MSRP $49.99) provides children aged 3–6 with the opportunity to program the toy's path by attaching segments with commands while refining fine motor skills. Requires 4 AA batteries.
- Code Hopper by MindWare, Inc. (MSRP $24.95) is a game for children 3 and up to follow simple commands on a flowchart such as "touch your nose" or "clap your hands" just like a computer.
- *Optional:* An obstacle course with simple directions for young children can be offered as an activity for families to do together after storytime to reinforce coding concepts through play. Children can pretend to be robots by following commands such as "jump 5 times," "touch your toes," "reach up high for 5 seconds," and "walk in a straight line while beeping." Encourage children to come up with their own commands.

STEP-BY-STEP INSTRUCTIONS

Preparation

Before the program, practice reading aloud the stories and saying the tips for caregivers aloud. You may create a digital presentation of the program to display during the event that includes the song lyrics, action rhyme, and tips for caregivers to follow along. You may also print a brochure with the program content for caregivers to take home. Display books that support coding that attendees can borrow. See the list of picture books in the "Recommended Next Projects" section at the end of this chapter for ideas.

PROJECT INSTRUCTIONS

- *Storytime Introduction.* Defines coding for caregivers.

  Hello, everyone! My name is (*your name*), and I'm glad that you are here at today's Coding Storytime for Families. We'll be talking about coding concepts and seeing how people called "programmers" use computers to solve everyday problems. Computers are all around us, and it's important for us to talk to children about how computer programs work so they can understand the world in which they live today and be prepared for ever expanding technology. Coding is simply creating step-by-step instructions that a computer will understand. Let's begin with our opening song.

- **Opening Song.** Use the song below or your favorite opening song to begin the program.

  Sing to the tune of "Goodnight Ladies."

  Hello friends

  Hello friends

  Hello friends

  It's time to say "Hello!"

- **Message for Caregivers.** Talk about algorithms.

  When computer programmers write a program, they write an **algorithm**, which is a list of steps that computers follow to finish a task. Today's books and activities all follow a very specific order. Talking about numbers as much as you can helps children think about the order of directions. For example, use "one" and "first" or "two" and "second" when talking about the order of things. After reading a book, have your child help retell the story to build his narrative skills. You can even do this with your child as you go about your day! What did you need to do before you arrived at the library today?

- **Book.** *The Very Hungry Caterpillar,* by Eric Carle (World Publishing Company, 1969.)

  Our first book begins on Saturday night and follows a hungry caterpillar through an entire week. What do you do when you're hungry? You eat a meal or a snack when you're feeling hungry. Let's read the book to find out how this little caterpillar solves its hunger problem. (*After sharing the book, talk about the beginning, the middle, and the end of the story.*)

- **Action Song.** Action songs ask children to do a set of motions in a specific order. We're not computers, but action songs are like fun programs that we can do. In this song, we're going to follow the algorithm (the set of directions) of "Head, Shoulders, Knees, and Toes" and touch the parts of your body in the song. First, let's think about it. What's the first and last body part that we touch?

  Head, Shoulders, Knees, and Toes

  Head, shoulders, knees and toes, knees and toes
  Head, shoulders, knees and toes, knees and toes
  And eyes and ears and mouth and nose
  Head, shoulders, knees and toes, knees and toes

- **Message for Caregivers.** Talk about spatial reasoning.

  Some programming languages like Scratch use a building-block visual interface to teach children how to code. The code fits together like LEGO pieces. Children are solving problems using spatial reasoning when they're playing with blocks. Boost your child's spatial intelligence by using rich language like *between, above, below, near, big, tall, little,* and *empty*.

- **Action Song.** In this next song, we'll be performing a movement to support building spatial vocabulary and understanding. Let's stand up for this. First, when we sing "up," you can stand up tall or lift your child up. Then, when we sing "down," you can squat down to the ground or lower your baby down. Then, take a step forward when we sing "forward" and take a step backward when we sing "backward." Finally, spin around when we sing "go round and round." You can find the tune and actions here: https:/kcls.org/content/here-we-go-up-up-up/. Sing to the tune of "Here We Go Looby Loo."

  Here We Go Up, Up, Up

  Here we go up, up, up
  And here we go down, down, down
  Now we go forward, Now we go backward,
  And now we go round and round!

- **Message for Caregivers.** Talk about our technological world.

  Coding is behind the digital technology that surrounds us and helps us solve everyday problems. Let's take a moment to talk about some technology that wouldn't work without programmers, people who write the code. What do elevators do? Elevators save people a lot of time and energy. Along with motors and cables, elevators work by using complex computer algorithms—code that tells the elevator what to do. Let's sing this next song together about this modern marvel.

- **Action Song.** Let's stand up for this next song too. When the song says to go up, you can stand up. When it says to go down, you can get down low. You can find the tune and actions here: https://kcls.org/content/elevator-song/.

  Sing to the tune of "Do Your Ears Hang Low?"

  The Elevator Song

  Oh, the city is great and the city is grand
  There are lots of tall buildings
  On a little piece of land
  We live way up on the fifty-seventh floor
  And this is what we do
  When we go out the door
  Take the elevator up, take the elevator down (3 times)
  Then we spin around

- **Message for Caregivers.** Talk about algorithms.

  Think about what kind of algorithm the elevator follows from the moment you first push the button to the moment you leave the elevator. The elevator has to perform a lot of different actions in a special order. Other everyday machines like washing machines and microwaves have algorithms too. Let's read another book that helps children think sequentially like a programmer.

- **Book.** *If You Give a Mouse a Cookie,* by Laura Numeroff (Harper & Row, 1985)

  This story is circular, which means that the sequence of events leads the reader back to the beginning. In coding terms, you can call this sequence a **loop**. Let's read the story to find out what happens when you give a mouse a cookie.

- **Message for Caregivers.** Talk about conditionals.

  In coding, programmers use conditional statements to change how programs behave depending on certain conditions following the format "If . . .

then . . ." just like in the book! For example, if you press the number 5 on an elevator, then which floor would the elevator go to?

- **Action Song.** Our next song uses conditionals too. Let's sing the song "If You're Happy and You Know It." What actions do we perform after the line "If You're Happy and You Know It"? We clap, stomp our feet, and shout "Hurray!" You can find the tune and actions here: https://kcls.org/content/if-youre-happy-and-you-know-it/.

  If You're Happy and You Know It

  If you're happy and you know it, clap your hands (clap clap)
  If you're happy and you know it, clap your hands (clap clap)
  If you're happy and you know it, then your face will surely show it
  If you're happy and you know it, clap your hands. (clap clap)
  If you're happy and you know it, stomp your feet (stomp stomp)
  If you're happy and you know it, stomp your feet (stomp stomp)
  If you're happy and you know it, then your face will surely show it
  If you're happy and you know it, stomp your feet. (stomp stomp)
  If you're happy and you know it, shout "Hurray!" (hur-ray!)
  If you're happy and you know it, shout "Hurray!" (hur-ray!)
  If you're happy and you know it, then your face will surely show it
  If you're happy and you know it, shout "Hurray!" (hur-ray!)
  If you're happy and you know it, do all three (clap-clap, stomp-stomp, hur-ray!)
  If you're happy and you know it, do all three (clap-clap, stomp-stomp, hur-ray!)
  If you're happy and you know it, then your face will surely show it
  If you're happy and you know it, do all three. (clap-clap, stomp-stomp, hur-ray!)

- **Message for Caregivers.** Talk about emotions.

  Computers continue to become smarter with artificial intelligence. Do robots experience real emotions and feelings like people? No, technology can be programmed to display emotions by people, but they don't actually feel the emotions. Talking to your children about their wide range of feelings such as happiness, fears, anger, and sadness is important so they learn how to express themselves. We're going to sing a song that allows children to act out different emotions.

- **Action Song.** We will do the previous song again with other emotions. *(Optional:* Print out emojis that correspond to the emotions described in the song and then ask the audience to identify them.*)*

  If you're sleepy and you know it, give a yawn . . .

  If you're sad and you know it, wipe your eyes . . .

  If you're mad and you know it, stomp your feet . . .

  If you're excited and you know it, jump up and down . . .

  If you're scared and you know it, hide your face . . .

- **Flannelboard Rhyme.** Robots are invented to help us do many things. Imagine what kind of robots you can build to help you solve your problems. Here are a few robots. Let's count them together! *(Place the 5 robots you made on the flannelboard and share the song. As you are singing, remove a robot and ask your audience how many are left.)*

  Sing to the tune of "Do Your Ears Hang Low?"

  Five Helpful Robots

  Five helpful robots equipped with AI,

  smart machines that we might try.

  Along you came with a problem one day

  and this helpful robot will take it away.

- **Closing Song.** Use the song below or your favorite closing song to end the program.

  Sing to the tune of "Goodnight Ladies."

  Goodbye friends

  Goodbye friends

  Goodbye friends

  It's time to say "Goodbye!"

LEARNING OUTCOMES

Participants will:

- Be introduced to the world of coding through developmentally appropriate activities in the form of books and songs that support early literacy.
- Gain an appreciation of how programmers have influenced our everyday lives through coding.

- Learn about concepts related to coding such as algorithms, loops, conditionals, and artificial intelligence through hearing messages for caregivers.

RECOMMENDED NEXT PROJECTS

Here are a few other sequential picture books, cumulative stories, and books about coding that can be used for your next Family Coding Storytime:

Bernstrom, Daniel. *One Day in the Eucalyptus, Eucalyptus Tree.* 2016. New York City, NY: HarperCollins.

Litwin, Eric. *Pete the Cat: I Love My White Shoes.* 2010. New York City, NY: HarperCollins.

Martin Jr., Bill. *Brown Bear, Brown Bear, What Do You See?* 1967. New York City, NY: Henry Holt and Company.

Mitchell, Susan K. *The Rainforest Grew All Around.* 2007. Mount Pleasant, SC: Sylvan Dell Publishing.

Spiro, Ruth. *Baby Loves Coding.* 2018. Watertown, MA: Charlesbridge.

Rosen, Michael. *We're Going on a Bear Hunt.* 1989. New York, NY: Margaret K. McElderry Books.

Taback, Simms. *There Was an Old Lady Who Swallowed a Fly.* 1997. New York City, NY: Viking Books for Young Readers.

Trapani, Iza. *The Itsy Bitsy Spider.* 1993. Watertown, MA: Charlesbridge.

Wood, Audrey. *The Napping House.* 1984. New York City, NY: Harcourt Children's Books.

This program focuses on the sequential aspect of specific movements, stories, and songs. Coding offers a variety of aspects to explore with young children such as design thinking, problem solving, mathematics, and art. Here are picture books that inspire imagination, creativity, and risk taking—natural fits for a Family Coding Storytime:

Luyken, Corinna. *The Book of Mistakes.* 2017. London, United Kingdom: Penguin.

Pett, Mark. *The Girl Who Never Made Mistakes.* 2011. Naperville, IL: Sourcebooks Jabberwocky.

Portis, Antoinette. *Not a Box.* 2006. New York City, NY: HarperCollins.

Reynolds, Peter H. *The Dot*. 2003. Somerville, MA: Candlewick Press.

Saltzberg, Barney. *Beautiful Oops*. 2010. New York, NY: Workman Publishing.

Santat, Dan. *After the Fall (How Humpty Dumpty Got Back Up Again)*. 2017. New York, NY: Roaring Brook Press.

Spires, Ashley. *The Most Magnificent Thing*. 2014. Toronto, Canada: Kids Can Press.

Yamada, Kobi. *What Do You Do with an Idea?* 2014. Seattle, WA: Compendium.

6

Using Spheros to Retell a Story

SHARON McCUBBINS
School Media Librarian
Cumberland Trace Elementary School Library, Bowling Green, Kentucky

PROJECT DESCRIPTION

Participants will demonstrate an understanding of story events using Sphero robots. By using Spheros to retell a story, participants are empowered to use technology as a way to demonstrate their learning. They become innovative designers by planning out a process in which to retell a story. The goal for participants is not to have complete mastery of all aspects of Sphero technology but rather to develop a basic understanding of how Spheros work and how participants can program the robots to share their knowledge with others. This provides participants with a baseline experience they can use to expand their use of Sphero technology.

Age Range

- Kids (Ages 3–7)
- Tweens (Ages 8–12)

Type of Library Best Suited For

- Public libraries
- School libraries

Cost Estimate

- $50–$1,400 for Sphero robots
- Cost varies based on the type and quantity of Spheros purchased. A Sphero mini costs approximately $50, while the Sphero SPRK+ costs $129. Purchasing a kit of Spheros will cost about $1,400.

- $200 and up for a tablet, iPad, or Chromebook
- A tablet, iPad, or Chromebook is needed for each Sphero in order to program the robot

OVERVIEW

This activity allows participants to explore the STEAM career of a computer engineer. Computer engineers need experience designing, coding, and testing software. They also need to have the ability to work in a team. Using the Sphero program, participants will design how they want the Sphero to function, code the robot to retell the story, test their code, and form small groups to work as a team. If you are using this activity in a school library, your timeline will be 3–4 class periods. If you are using this activity in a public library, you will need to break the activity into 3–4 sessions.

Software/Hardware Needed

- Sphero robots
- Tablets, iPads, or Chrome devices

Materials List

- Drawing paper
- Disposable cup that will fit over the Sphero robot
- Tape
- Crayons, markers, or colored pencils
- Scissors

STEP-BY-STEP INSTRUCTIONS

Preparation

- This lesson can be taught as part of a unit on story elements or as a stand-alone activity on story events. Although not directly teaching about characters or setting, participants should be familiar with both of these elements to be able to identify them in a story.
- Choose a story to share with participants where several story events occur. Most picture books meet this criteria; many folktales, such as *Chicken Little or The Gingerbread Man,* are also great story choices.
- Explore the Sphero drawing program and blocks program. Both of these programs are found within the Sphero app. If you are working with young

children, you should consider using the drawing program. The drawing program allows young children the opportunity to draw their code with their fingers. This works great with non-reading and beginning reading participants. The blocks program requires participants to be able to read basic commands and is more suitable for readers.

- Charge the Sphero robots. Spheros can run about an hour before needing to be recharged.
- Set out paper, scissors, tape, and drawing supplies.

PROJECT INSTRUCTIONS

Sphero Mini-Lesson

- If participants have never used Spheros, you will need to provide them an opportunity to use the robots. If participants are familiar with Spheros, you can skip this lesson.
- Divide participants into groups based on the number of Spheros you have. Teach participants how to aim, adjust speed, and change color. Participants will use the "drive" section of the app.
- Explain to participants that the Sphero can make lots of amazing moves. It can go forward, backward, change color, emit sound, spin, etc. However it can't do any of those things unless we tell it what to do, and we will be doing this by writing instructions for the robot to follow. These instructions have a special name called **code**. When lines of code are used together to tell the robot what to do, this is called a **program**. Participants will be writing their lines of code in the Sphero app.
- Depending on the age level, allow participants to explore the drawing program or the blocks program.
- When using the blocks program for this activity, it is best to focus on the movement blocks. Remember the objective of the lesson is for participants to program the Sphero to retell a story and give them a baseline for understanding how to program a Sphero.

Literature Lesson

- Introduce your chosen story to participants. Do a picture walk through the book. Ask participants to use the illustrations to identify the setting of the story and characters. Encourage participants to share ideas about what is happening in the illustrations. Explain to participants that the word we use to discuss the happenings in a story is called *events*.

- Tell participants that as you read the story, they should listen for the happenings (events) in the story and be ready to share with the class.
- After you read the story, have participants share the story events. Create a list and have participants put the events in order.
- Explain to participants that they will use their Spheros to retell the events in the story.
- Give participants materials to use to make a prop that represents a story event. For example, participants could make a drawing to illustrate the event or they could use materials to represent an important part of the event. The number of events you want them to recall will depend on the age of the students and the number of events in the story.
- After participants have created props to represent the events, they should put them in the correct order.
- Next, have each group draw a picture of the main character in the story. Tape the picture to the disposable cup. The cup will be placed on top of the Sphero and will move around to each event. (See figure 6.1.)

FIGURE 6.1

Student-made characters

Programming Activity

- Now that participants have recreated the events and the main character, it is time to code the program for the Sphero.
- Participants should place the events in order on the floor. The pathway should not be a straight line. You may want participants to create a zigzag or some other pattern that will demonstrate their coding skills and that they know the order of events.
- Once the events are in place, decide on the starting place for the Sphero.
- Next, have participants use either the drawing program or the blocks program to code the Sphero's pathway. (This will take multiple trial and error as they work on their programs.)

- Once participants have created the code for their program, it is time to test it. Have each group run its program while retelling the story.
- If you are in a school setting, this may take 2 class sessions: one to program the Sphero and the second for each group to present its program.

LEARNING OUTCOMES

Participants will:

- Use information gained from the illustrations and words in a print or digital text to demonstrate their understanding of its characters, setting, and events. (CCSS.ELA-Literacy.RL x.7)
- Use technology to seek feedback that informs and improves their practice and demonstrate their learning in a variety of ways. (ISTE Student Standard 1C)
- Recount or describe key ideas or details from a text read aloud or information presented orally or through other media. (CCSS.ELA-Literacy .SL x.2)

RECOMMENDED NEXT PROJECTS

- After participants have learned the movement codes for the robot, teach them about the light and sound commands. Participants can program the robot to stop at each event and speak what happens at that part of the story before moving to the next event.
- You can develop a programming club for participants interested in learning more about Spheros.
- Have participants write their own stories and tell them with the Sphero.

7

Demonstrating Characterization with ScratchJr

SHARON McCUBBINS
School Media Librarian
Cumberland Trace Elementary School Library, Bowling Green, Kentucky

PROJECT DESCRIPTION

Participants will apply programming commands in ScratchJr to illustrate their understanding of the features of a character in a story. Through the use of ScratchJr, participants are empowered to create original works as they communicate to others their analysis of a storybook character. They become computer programmers by writing code for the character's actions. The goal is for participants to develop basic programming skills to create their own backgrounds, design the character, and program the character to act and react in ways supported by the story.

Age Range

- Kids (ages 3–7)
- Tweens (ages 8–12)

Type of Library Best Suited For

- School libraries
- Public libraries

Cost Estimate

- $0 (ScratchJr software is free.)

OVERVIEW

Participants will be fascinated with the many different ways they are able to control and manipulate this program. ScratchJr is a program that can be learned quickly and easily by young learners. Participants will learn how a character moves by using 1-to-1 correspondence with the coding tools in the program. They will experiment with editing the pre-designed characters and settings, or they can create their own settings and characters. Participants can work individually or in partners as they create the program. This lesson works best when taught over the course of several weeks.

Week 1—Scratch Mini-Lesson

Week 2—Literature Lesson

Week 3—Programming Lesson

Week 4—Share Projects

Software/Hardware Needed

- ScatchJr app
- Android, iPad, or Chrome device

STEP-BY-STEP INSTRUCTIONS

Preparation

- Download the ScratchJr app onto the device.
- If participants are using Chrome devices where they have logged into an individual account, they will need to download the ScratchJr app from the Chrome Web Store. Once the app is downloaded, it will be on their account and participants will not need to do that again.
- This lesson can be taught as part of a unit on story elements or as a stand-alone activity on characterization. Although not directly teaching about characters, setting, or events, participants should be familiar with these elements to be able to identify them in a story. This lesson could come after the lesson in Chapter 6: Using Spheros to Retell a Story by Sharon McCubbins because the focus of that lesson is on story events.

PROJECT INSTRUCTIONS

Scratch Mini-Lesson

- If participants have never used ScratchJr, you need to provide them an opportunity to do so. If participants are familiar with ScratchJr, you can skip this lesson.

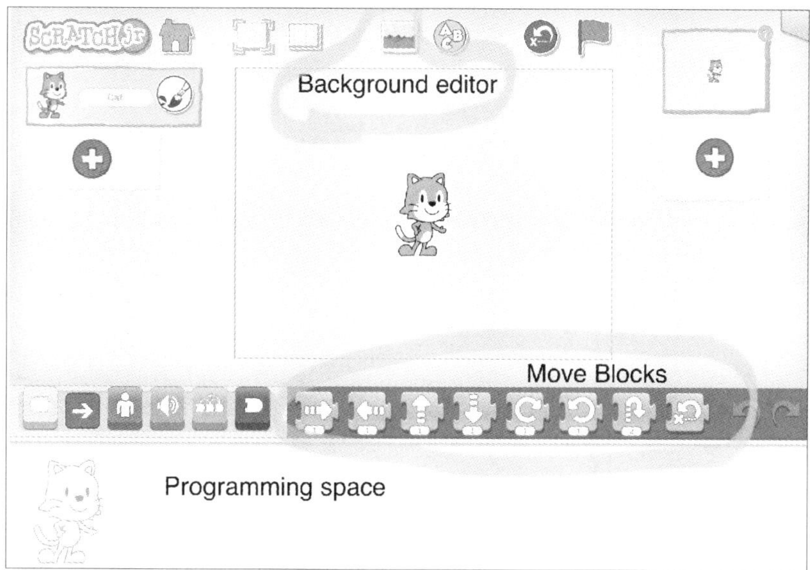

FIGURE 7.1

Scratch programming board

- Open the ScratchJr app (figure 7.1) and demonstrate to participants how to create a new program.
- When participants open the program, the cat is always the default character. Explain to participants that each student will program the cat to walk across the page. Go to the blue move blocks on the bottom of the screen. If participants are younger, demonstrate 1-to-1 correspondence by having them drag a distinct move block down to the programming space for each space they want the cat to move. For older participants, you can have them click the number below the move block and a number pad will appear. This allows participants to program the number of moves instead of dragging a move block down each time.
- Once participants have made the cat walk across the screen, you can show them how to pick a background for their program.
- As participants become more comfortable with the program, allow them time to experiment with the "looks blocks," "sound blocks," and "control blocks."
- Participants can also add another character to program in their scene.

Literature Lesson

- Choose a picture book that features a strong main character. Many storybooks meet this criteria: *Penguinaut!* by Marcie Colleen, *Amazing Grace* by Mary Hoffman, *Stephanie's Ponytail* by Robert Munsch, and *Skippyjon Jones* by Judy Schachner.
- Do a picture walk through the story. Ask participants what they are learning about the main character through the illustrations. Focus on how the character looks, what the character might be doing, and how others are acting toward the character.
- Share the story.
- Revisit participants' answers from the picture walk. Were they correct now that the story has been shared?
- After the story has been shared, in order to get participants to really understand the character, ask follow-up questions such as:
    - Would you want to be friends with this character?
    - Does this character make wise choices? Poor choices?
    - Describe an event in the story that made you think the character made a good choice. Or describe an event in the story that made you think the character made the wrong choice.
    - What is something that you would expect this character to do next? Explain why you think so.
    - After participants have had plenty of opportunity to verbally share their "what next?" ideas, have them write down 1 idea.
    - Give each participant a piece of storybook paper. Have them draw a "what next?" scene for the character in the story. For example, if the story takes place at school, how would the character act at a friend's house? How would the character act on vacation? At her own home? On the playground?
    - In the drawing section of the paper, have participants draw the setting of this new place and include the character in the drawing.
    - Underneath the drawing, have participants explain what is happening in the picture.

Programming Lesson

- Using the drawing that participants have created, they will now turn it into a ScratchJr program.

- Have participants open a new program in ScratchJr. First, participants will choose a background or use the paint editor to design their own background. Participants may also edit a background in the ScratchJr program.
- Next, choose a character. Participants can use the paint editor to design their own character or edit a character in ScratchJr to change the character to look similar to the one in the story. Participants may add more characters if needed.
- Now, participants are ready to program their new story event. Participants should choose the blocks they need to program their new event.
- Once finished, students should share their programs. Participants should be able to explain why the character acted the way it did. Older participants should be able to support their decision based on events that occurred in the story.

LEARNING OUTCOMES

Participants will:

- Use information gained from the illustrations and words in a print or digital text to demonstrate understanding of its characters, setting, or plot. (CCSS.ELA-Literacy.RL.2.7)
- Describe characters in a story (e.g., their traits, motivations, or feelings) and explain how their actions contribute to the sequence of events. (CCSS.ELA-Literacy.RL.3.3)
- Use technology to seek feedback that informs and improves their practice and to demonstrate their learning in a variety of ways. (ISTE Student Standard 1C)
- Create original works or responsibly repurpose or remix digital resources into new creations. (ISTE Student Standard 6B)

RECOMMENDED NEXT PROJECTS

- After teaching about story elements (characters, setting, events, problem, and solution), have participants write their own stories. Once finished with the rough draft, participants can create a storyboard of the story and then program scenes in ScratchJr to share their story.
- For more information about story writing, check out Chapter 13: Tell Me a Story with ScratchJr by Lisa O'Shaughnessy.

- After participants have mastered ScratchJr, this will be the perfect time to demonstrate these skills to parents. For some ideas on this topic, check out Chapter 1: Make Your Own Cartoon with PBS Kids ScratchJr by JoAnna Schofield.
- Once participants have mastered ScratchJr, why not try out Scratch? Several activities in this book can give you some inspiration for projects with students. See Chapter 22: Scratch Coding for Tweens: Creating Cartoons by Karlene Tura Clark and Chapter 32: Scratch Art: Create and Animate Characters Using Scratch by Mary Carrier.

8

Computational Thinking in Storytime

Robots

CLAUDIA HAINES

Youth Services Librarian | Homer (Alaska) Public Library

PROJECT DESCRIPTION

Preschool storytime is a popular library program that supports both young children's growing early literacy skills and parents' roles as their first teachers. But what does early literacy look like in the Digital Age? Integrating computational thinking experiences into storytime, alongside the fundamental early literacy practices, introduces the skills children, and eventually adults, need to find, evaluate, and create information in a growing array of formats. Children are introduced to navigating, investigating, and creating with high-quality media of all kinds, including traditional picture books and robots or other computerized devices.

What is computational thinking (CT)? Generally, CT is a problem-solving process that helps us create possible solutions for complex problems. The solution is presented in a way that humans and computers understand. CT skills include decomposition, pattern recognition, abstraction, algorithm design, and evaluation.[1] For young children, CT activities look different but support the same problem-solving skills. Decomposition, breaking problems down into smaller parts, is used when children sound out words. Pattern recognition, what is similar and what is different, is used to identify letters, shapes, and numbers. Abstraction involves deciding what information is relevant and what is unnecessary to solve the "problem." For example, a preschooler who is learning to write her name decides what letters she needs to include and what shapes she needs to draw to make those letters. Children and adults alike use algorithm design every day. Crafting a plan, with the activities and actions performed in a specific order, are used in recipes, tying shoes, and in computer programs. Telling sequential stories like the *Three Little Pigs* supports the concept of algorithmic design.

This storytime plan uses developmentally appropriate, fun unplugged activities and new media play to support both early literacy and computational thinking in low-pressure experiences. Library staff with minimal or no computer science experience will find the included elements accessible and, in some cases, familiar.

NOTE: This cost estimate assumes that your library has access to a feltboard, iPad or other tablet, monitor, and repurposed materials.

Age Range

- Kids (Ages 3–7)

Type of Library Best Suited For

- Public libraries
- School libraries

Cost Estimate

- $135–$160, including materials that may be on hand or can be repurposed for other activities and programs (based on 50 people, with 25–30 kids)
- $19.95 for 1 set of Roylco's Twist and Spell Exercise Cards
- $49.99 for 1 Fisher-Price Think & Learn Code-a-pillar
- $2.99 for 1 copy of Sago Mini Robot Party app
- $20 for miscellaneous craft supplies for feltboard activity and aluminum can robots
- $20.99 for 1 ALEX Cube Stackers game
- *Optional:* $12–$18 each for Code-a-pillar Expansion Packs

OVERVIEW

This preschool storytime is designed to run for 1 hour and should be staffed with 1 librarian and 1 teen mentor. The first half of the program (approximately 35 minutes), led by the librarian, resembles a traditional storytime and features a robot demo, stories, movement activities, songs, group feltboard play, and "app advisory." The second half of the program (approximately 25 minutes) consists of several activity stations that families can explore informally. The program length could be extended depending on the group size and interest level. The materials and activities listed below accommodated 40–50 people, including approximately 30 children.

Software/Hardware Needed

Necessary Equipment

- Think & Learn Code-a-pillar
- iPad or other tablet
- Sago Mini Robot Party app (iOS/Android)
- "Clap Your Hands" by They Might Be Giants (digital version of the song from the album *No!*)
- Feltboard

Recommended Equipment

- Monitor (if the storytime group is large and the app is used during storytime group activities)
- Think & Learn Code-a-pillar expansion kits (which provide additional coding segments)
- Additional Code-a-pillars (if the group is large)

Materials List

- 1 set of Roylco's Twist and Spell Exercise Cards
- Picture books for sharing, for example: *Pete the Cat, Robo-Pete* by James Dean (Harper Collins, 2015), *If You're a Robot and You Know It* by David Carter (Cartwheel Books, 2015), *Robot Zot* by Jon Scieszka (Simon & Schuster Books for Young Readers, 2009)
- 8–10 aluminum cans (cleaned, sharp edges dulled, and labels removed)
- Craft supplies for robot body parts (may include craft pipe cleaners, large googly eyes, large buttons, wood clothespins, and large nuts and washers)
- 50–70 small magnets (5–7 per each can robot)
- Hot glue gun and hot glue
- Easily identifiable felt shapes, enough for 2 identical robots (suggested: 2 large rectangles, 10 smaller rectangles, 2 hearts, 2 triangles, 4 octagons, 4 diamonds, 4 stars, 4 circles)
- Blue painter's tape
- Crayons or markers
- Optional: additional books about robots for display from a variety of genres and reading levels, including picture books, graphic novels, nonfiction, chapter books.

STEP-BY-STEP INSTRUCTIONS

Preparation

One Day or More Prior to Storytime

- Using hot glue, attach small magnets to the "robot body parts" you choose to include. The magnets allow the craft supplies to stick to the cans in different arrangements, supporting imagination and creativity. And because the magnets stick temporarily, the can robots can be assembled more than once, which minimizes the amount of necessary materials.
- As with all apps for young children, navigate through the entire Sago Mini Robot Party app to identify opportunities for group play (during the demonstration). Anticipate possible challenges that may occur unexpectedly with the app's functionality and content, if any. Draft tips to share with parents and caregivers about using digital media, like apps, with young children to support learning.
- Assemble the ALEX Cube Stackers game pieces and try out the different activities. Review puzzle cards for difficulty and, if desired, select specific cards to include at the storytime station depending on the intended audience.
- Load the Sago Mini Robot Party app onto the tablets being used in the storytime program (in this case, a staff iPad used for the demonstration during storytime and a mounted iPad available anytime).
- Get access to the song "Clap Your Hands" via your preferred music platform (including YouTube via They Might Be Giants official channel, ParticleMen).
- Print out and photocopy a robot-themed coloring sheet for the coloring station.

Day of Storytime

SET UP STATIONS

- Aluminum can robots building (on table)
    - Set out aluminum cans and baskets or tubs of prepared robot body parts. Create an example to spark play. Because of small parts, this station should be located in a space away from babies who might be attending with their siblings.
- ALEX Cube Stackers game (on table)
    - Lay out the pieces and instructions so enticing parts are visible and the station is inviting.

- Sago Mini Robot Party app play (on table or other suitable space)
    - Have headphones plugged into iPad (if desired) and multiple seats available to encourage joint media engagement.*
- Feltboard robot programming (on floor)
    - Move feltboard and felt pieces from group activity during transition to stations.
- Robot coloring sheets (on table)
- Set out coloring sheets and crayons, markers, or other drawing materials.
- Code-a-pillar coding play (on floor)
    - Use painter's tape to create a grid on the floor of the program space. The size of the grid will depend on the size of space. In this program, the grid was in the same space as where stories were shared. Kids sat on top of tape grid.

PROJECT INSTRUCTIONS

STORYTIME PART 1

- Using the Twist and Spell Exercise Cards, play the ABC Body Game, which integrates both early literacy and computational thinking skills into a movement activity. Place 6 letter cards (which spell out the word *robots*) in a small bag and invite a child to select a card (the first her hand touches). As a group, name the letter and then talk about how to make the shape of the letter with your bodies, beginning at the top of the shape. To engage as many kids as possible and to mimic the order of an algorithm, ask questions like:
    - Do we sit down or stand up to make this letter? (Some kids will say we lay down or squat depending on the day's letters.)
    - What do we do first?
    - What are our hands supposed to do?
    - Do you see any shapes you recognize?
    - Are our feet touching?

---

*Joint media engagement (JME) is "spontaneous and designed experiences of people using media together."[2] This kind of engagement supports learning and understanding. Providing JME opportunities, and talking about them, at storytime models for families how to replicate this at home.

Repeat, having different children select a card and then name and act out the letter as a group. Display the cards in the order that spells *robots* and say the word together. The group aspect of this activity models how to support the early literacy skill of letter knowledge. Even children unfamiliar with the individual letters of the alphabet can attempt the physical aspect of this game. Acting out letters helps young children get acquainted with differences and similarities in shapes and letters (pattern recognition), a sequence of actions (algorithmic design) and identifying what movements they need to do (or not do) to form the particular letter (abstraction).

- Introduce robots, using pictures in a book or images found online if you wish. Ask open-ended questions like:
    - What do you know about robots?
    - What do they look like?
    - Do you have a robot at home?
    - What are some differences between robots and children? (Write these on a chalkboard if you would like. This reinforces that text has meaning.)

    Present the Code-a-pillar. Explain that it is a robot and what robots have in common. Then show how the Code-a-pillar works, explain what the different parts are, and discuss what they do. Run a short **program**. Let kids ask questions and tell them that they will have time to program the robot themselves during the second part of storytime. Afterward, put the Code-a-pillar out of reach (or out of sight, if need be).

- Read the book *Pete the Cat, Robo-Pete* by James Dean (Harper Collins, 2015). Talk about how Robo-Pete compares to the robots discussed earlier.
- Next, build a robot as a group on the feltboard. The felt board should be divided into 3 sections using blue painter's tape. If you have used Scratch or another block coding platform, you will recognize the 3 sections as being similar to the "stage," "scripts area," and "blocks palette." Build 1 robot on the far right side beforehand and store the other identical pieces in the thin section of the board on the far left. Arrange the pieces so that matching shapes are close together. As a group, talk about the felt robot's parts and what each might be used for. Start building the new robot out of the other parts with suggestions from the group for where to start, what part to add next, and what shape of felt would represents that part. The idea here is to support shape knowledge but also to practice the process of articulating how to make, do, or build something. Ask kids questions that help them practice using words to identify shape and color names and directional words. Move

the felt piece to the new robot as kids suggest them. (Alternatively, you could use a digital feltboard app to create this activity on a monitor.)

- Read the book *If You're a Robot and You Know It* by David Carter (Cartwheel Books, 2015). The text of this book is similar to the lyrics for the well-known song "If You're Happy and You Know It," so be prepared to read, sing, and dance as you share this book. Explain new words or phrases that will be introduced in the book, like *circuit boards*. Much of the text of the book repeats, in a similar fashion to the song, and kids can pretend they are robots; moving their different robot "parts" in each verse. Introduce the word **loop** and the concept here if appropriate.
- If you have time, read the optional book, *Robot Zot* by Jon Scieszka (Simon & Schuster Books for Young Readers, 2009). This book is silly so be ready to use your animated, loud voices.
- Dance together while listening to "Clap Your Hands" by They Might Be Giants. There are 3 actions in this song that happen in a particular order: 1—clap hands, 2—stomp feet, and 3—jump in the air. Before the dancing begins, place images of each action (5 hands clapping, 5 feet stomping, 4 jumping) on the feltboard or monitor, if using one, to match the number of times the singer says each action. As the song plays and the group is acting out the movements, count down to help kids keep track of progress. If appropriate, explain that the song is divided into beats or sections (measures) and a composer uses symbols (on a musical score) to show musicians and dancers what to do and when changes will happen, much like a programmer does for a computer.
- Describe the stations for the second portion of storytime and invite families to explore them. Encourage grown-ups to play along with their children. If applicable, demonstrate how the Sago Mini Robot Party app works and include a tip about the importance of joint media engagement.

STORYTIME PART 2

Roam from station to station, answering questions and providing conversation prompts as necessary.

- Code-a-pillar coding play
    - Kids program the Code-a-pillar to move toward a target on the blue tape grid using the provided "go" and "stop" discs. Some kids will spend time exploring how the robot works and learning which arrow segment corresponds to the directions left or right, for example. Other kids will

program where the robot should go. Help kids create oral stories about the caterpillar and where it is going; talking about the sequence of events and using directional words. Encourage grown-ups to guide play if appropriate.

- ALEX Cube Stackers game
    - Cube Stackers game is a board game that uses cardboard cubes with colorful robot parts on the different sides to teach basic coding concepts. Kids build robots by twisting and turning the sides based on instructions on the game cards. The game is primarily for kids 5 years and older, including older siblings who come along to storytime. This is an activity that can engage the whole family, especially if grown-ups feel comfortable working through this thoughtful game.
- Aluminum can robot building
    - Young engineers build robots by adding the pre-made, magnetized parts to cleaned-off cans. Model for grown-ups how to talk with kids as they build. Ask open-ended questions about the robot, for example:
        - What is its job?
        - How do the different parts work?
- Robot coloring sheets
    - A simple coloring station is great for kids who like to color, are waiting for space at another station, or need a quieter activity.
- Feltboard robot programming
    - Mimicking this group activity from earlier in the program, children build their own felt robots (figure 8.1) at this station.

FIGURE 8.1

Feltboard robot programming

- Sago Mini Robot Party app on the mounted iPad
    - The Sago Mini Robot Party app is a giggle-inducing activity that involves building digital robots that dance and more. This app is well suited for groups of 2 or 3 because the app is designed with multi-touch, the feature that allows 2 or more fingers to command the screen at once. Kids (or kids and grown-ups) can work, play, and learn together.

LEARNING OUTCOMES

Children will:

- Understand what robots are and how they work.
- Use unplugged and new media tools to learn computational thinking skills.
- Explore coding concepts in play-based activities.

Grown-ups will:

- Be able to see connections between early literacy and computational thinking.
- Learn how to support their child's computational thinking skills with unplugged and new media tools to learn computational thinking skills.
- Understand the value of joint media engagement.

RECOMMENDED NEXT PROJECTS

- For more computational thinking activities, read these chapters: Chapter 9: Pattern Play: Analog Activities to Explore Patterns with Preschoolers and Families by Paula Langsam; Chapter 10: Mazes and Games: How to Integrate Algorithm Design with Analog Preschool and Family Activities by Paula Langsam and Amy Steinbaur; and Chapter 11: Program the Human Robot: Decomposition Activities for Preschoolers and Families by Paula Langsam.
- For more picture books that support computational thinking and computer science, read these chapters: Chapter 19: Great Books for Teaching Coding to Preschoolers by Katie Clausen and Chapter 21: Integrate Picture Books to Teach Computational Thinking Skills by Danielle Arnold.
- Find more programs and resources for preschoolers in the Libraries Ready to Code Collection at www.ala.org/tools/readytocode/.

RESOURCES

BBC BiteSize: "Computational Thinking," https://www.bbc.com/bitesize/topics/z7tp34j/.

Becoming a Media Mentor: A Guide for Working with Children and Families by Claudia Haines, Cen Campbell, and the Association for Library Service to Children (2016).

Coding as a Playground: Programming and Computational Thinking in the Early Childhood Classroom by Marina Umaschi Bers.

Computational Thinking by Jeannette Wing, https://www.cs.cmu.edu/~15110-s13/Wing06-ct.pdf.

"Evaluating Apps and New Media for Young Children: A Rubric." https://nevershushed.files.wordpress.com/2016/09/2016evaluatingappsand newmediafor youngchildrenarubric.pdf.

Supercharged Storytimes: An Early Literacy Planning and Assessment Guide by J. Elizabeth Mills, Kathleen Campana, and Saroj Nadkarni Ghoting (2016).

"Toying with Tech: Early Coding and Computational Thinking in a Museum Setting" http://teccenter.erikson.edu/in-practice/toying-with-tech/.

NOTES

1. BBC BiteSize: Computational Thinking. https://www.bbc.com/bitesize/topics/z7tp34j.
2. Takeuchi, Lori. *The New Coviewing: Designing for Learning Through Joint Media Engagement*. 2011. Joan Ganz Cooney Center. http://joanganzcooneycenter.org/publication/the-new-coviewing-designing-for-learning-through-joint-media-engagement/.

9

Pattern Play

Analog Activities to Explore Patterns with Preschoolers and Families

PAULA LANGSAM

Children's Librarian | DC Public Library, Washington, D.C.

PROJECT DESCRIPTION

Participants will identify similarities and differences using cards with differing shapes, colors, and quantities. This project introduces pattern recognition in a great passive or active program.

Age Range

- Kids (Ages 3–7)
- Tweens (Ages 8–12)

Type of Library Best Suited For

- Public libraries
- School libraries

Cost Estimate

- $0–$20

OVERVIEW

How do you approach a problem or task? Do you break it down into smaller pieces and then figure out which sections can be solved or completed with the same actions? Do you place the smaller tasks in a specific order to complete them and then explain and share information using salient details rather than a full breadth of information? Congratulations, you are using computational thinking!

Computational thinking (CT) is a way to look at and understand problems and how they might be solved. Although there are a number of different facets to CT, decomposition, algorithm design, pattern recognition, and abstraction form the foundation. This activity explores pattern recognition.

Pattern recognition is a way to organize and classify information and activities. By recognizing patterns, actions can be simplified by applying similar actions to similar tasks. The organization of dresser drawers or evening routine are examples of patterns.

This activity consists of a deck of cards with varying shapes, colors, shading, and quantity and 3 ways to use the cards. The activity is best for no more than 4 people per deck. Many decks of cards can be used in 1 activity to support a larger number of participants. If possible, a staff member should be on hand to provide additional assistance.

Software/Hardware Needed

- Instruction card
- Pattern cards

STEP-BY-STEP INSTRUCTIONS

Preparation

- Purchase or create a deck of pattern cards. Note: pattern cards can be made in a number of ways; think about the Memory card game. Cards may contain 1 or groups of shapes such as triangles, squares, rectangles, and circles. Slight differences can be made by shading in some of the shapes. This is a chance to get creative.
- Place the deck of pattern cards on a table. Shuffle the deck of cards to ensure they are mixed up.
- Ensure all participants will be able to reach the cards.
- Place instructions for the type of activity on the table.

Pattern Matching

- Lay out at least 16 cards. These can be placed in any order, but a square grid (4 cards across and 4 cards down) is recommended.
- Participants take turns looking for 3 cards with 1 similarity.
- After finding a collection of cards, have participants tell their tablemates what the cards have in common. Do they share any other characteristic?
- Remove those cards from the face-up grid.
- Add cards to the grid to fill in the blanks.

- Challenge participants to look for a collection of cards that share 2 or 3 similarities.

Pattern Memory Game

- Lay out at least 16 cards. These can be placed in any order, but a square grid (4 cards across and 4 cards down) is recommended. Place the cards face down.
- Have participants talk with their tablemates to decide the matching criteria. For example, same shape *or* same color.
- Take turns looking for matches.
- Lay out additional cards when matches are collected.
- Challenge participants to select cards with 2 matching criteria. For example, same quantity *and* same shading.

Continuing Patterns

- Lay out a large number of cards. Make sure a variety of colors, shapes, quantities, and shadings are shown.
- One person chooses at least 3 cards to begin a pattern.
- Tablemates try to identify the pattern and continue it with 3 additional cards.
- Discuss the original pattern and if it stayed the same with the additional cards. Was a different pattern identified in the original pattern?
- Take turns creating and stumping each other with intricate pattern series.

LEARNING OUTCOMES

Participants will:

- Explore 2 to 3 different ways to classify objects.
- Gain confidence looking for and identifying commonalities in different shapes and objects.
- Learn vocabulary for how to talk about patterns.

RECOMMENDED NEXT PROJECTS

- Chapter 21: Integrate Picture Books to Teach Computational Thinking Skills by Danielle Arnold
- Chapter 8: Computational Thinking in Storytime: Robots by Claudia Haines
- Chapter 1: Make Your Own Cartoon with PBS Kids ScratchJr by JoAnna Schofield

10

Mazes and Games

How to Integrate Algorithm Design with Analog Preschool and Family Activities

PAULA LANGSAM and AMY STEINBAUER

Children's Librarians | DC Public Library, Washington, D.C.

PROJECT DESCRIPTION

Using a grid layout to create a maze or series of tasks that must be completed in a specific order, participants use specific instructions (or commands) to complete the maze or task. This activity is a great way to introduce basic coding command structure and debugging (i.e., fixing mistakes or errors in the completion of tasks or command lines).

Age Range

- Kids (Ages 3–7)
- Tweens (Ages 8–12)

Type of Library Best Suited For

- Public libraries
- School libraries

Cost Estimate

- \$0–\$50

OVERVIEW

As discussed in the previous chapter, computational thinking (CT) is a way to look at and understand problems and how they might be solved. Although there are a number of different facets to CT, this activity explores algorithm design.

Algorithm design refers to an ordered number of steps needed to complete a task. Steps are needed to be followed in a precise order to get the desired results. An example of this might be the order of operations for a mathematical computation or following the recipe to make a cake. In both of those examples, participants must follow the exact steps in an exact order or they will not have the desired results. In the activity below, it is helpful to remember that specifics are required—going forward and changing directions are 2 different commands.

This activity consists of asking participants to move along a grid system using directional ("command") cards to complete specific tasks. It can be repeated multiple times with varying tasks and increased difficulty either in 1 program or over a series of programs. The command cards are the ordered steps to complete a task. In addition, this activity may be a way to introduce programming concepts before moving to a digital environment.

Different versions of this activity can be used as a 15–30-minute passive program or a 30–60-minute interactive program. If a tabletop version is used, no more than 4 participants should be at each board. If using a floor version, groups of participants can form teams to participate. Ideally, there is at least 1 adult per board and 1 staff member for every 2 boards.

Software/Hardware Needed

Tabletop Version Materials

- Printed paper with squares at least 1"×1". The number of squares (i.e., size of the grid) can be determined by the size of paper.
- Action or command cards: forward, left turn, and right turn arrow cards. These should be the same size as the squares on the grid. You will need enough forward arrow cards to move the full perimeter of the board. You will need enough left and right turn arrow cards for the longer side of the board. Include specialty cards for specific actions participants may need (i.e., pick up or put down object, open or close door, etc.).
- Figurines to move around the grid. Whatever object is used should have a face/front to denote "forward."
- Cardboard, yarn, LEGOS, and other craft material or toys to create obstacles or a maze participants will navigate.
- Labels for the start and finish points.
- Additional blank paper the same size as the action/command cards. When participants have advanced enough to introduce **loops** and **conditional statements** (If/Then phrases), these cards can be used.

Floor-Size Version Materials

- Tape or mats to create a grid on the floor or ground.
- Action or command cards: forward, left turn, and right turn arrow cards. These should be the same size as the squares on the grid. You will need enough forward arrow cards to move the full perimeter of the board. You will need enough left and right turn arrow cards for the longer side of the board. Include specialty cards for specific actions participants may need (i.e., pick up or put down object, open or close door, etc.).
- Labels for the start and finish points.
- Figurines to move around the grid. Whatever object is used should have a face/front to denote "forward." On this larger scale, you may choose to have participants move around the grid so figurines would not be needed.
- Cardboard, yarn, LEGOS, and other craft material or toys to create obstacles or a maze participants will navigate.
- Additional blank paper the same size as the action/command cards. When participants have advanced enough to introduce **loops** and **conditional statements** (If/Then phrases), these cards can be used.

STEP-BY-STEP INSTRUCTIONS

Preparation

- Choose to play this activity as the tabletop or floor version. Make your decision based on the room size and shape and age of participants.
- Decide on the final goal of the activity as well as any sub-goals. For example, do you want participants to collect a certain number or type of objects before reaching the end, find the fastest route, use the least number of turns, etc.?
- Collect materials needed (see materials sections above).
- Print instructions to be placed by each grid.
- Lay out material in the activity area to ensure there is enough space to easily move around and all participants can access material. Maze-building material should be put to one side for participants to create the space themselves. Action/command cards should be put to another side for easy access.
- Label the start and finish points.

PROJECT INSTRUCTIONS

- Welcome participants into the space. Give a light introduction to activity and computational thinking.
- Participants may need to be broken up into groups. If possible, there should be no more than 4 participants at each tabletop grid and 1 staff member for every 2 boards.
- Have participants lay out obstacles or build a maze with material provided.
- Decide if participants will work cooperatively or competitively and instruct them to take turns creating and navigating the gridded space.
- Place figurines at the starting point.

Beginning Ordered Instructions (For Younger Participants and Those New to Ordered Tasks)

Each figurine will move around the space using the arrow action/command cards.

- To move, place the arrow on the square pointing the direction of the movement. The figurine can only move in the direction that it is facing. This is important to remember during turns—where is the front facing?
- When moving left or right, first place the turn card *under the figurine* to change the direction the figurine is facing. Then place a forward arrow card.
- Continue through the grid until the finish. Watch for obstacles!
- Each person takes turns moving toward the finish.
- Repeat this version until all participants have had an opportunity to use the action/command cards and can easily navigate the space. Participants may choose to change the grid layout after each completion.

Moving Off the Grid (or Board)

When participants are comfortable using the action/command cards, try adding a level of difficulty to the activity.

- Create an Action/Command Center in front of each participant.
- When moving around the grid, have participants place the action/command cards in a row in the Action/Command Center.
- Like the beginning step, place 1 action/command card and then

move the figurine. Participants are building a line of actions/commands (much like a code) while moving through the space.

- Repeat this scaffolded version until everyone is comfortable with the space between the action/command cards and moving around the board.

Simple Automation

Computers can take multiple lines of code at a time to complete a task. It's time to try a similar functionality in a paper environment.

- Keeping the figurine at the starting point, lay out all the action/command cards in the Action/Command Center in the order needed to reach the finish. This is the command code to complete the task.
- Move the figurine through the space following the command code.
- If the figurine cannot reach the finish (i.e., the code is wrong), return the figurine to the starting point and change (i.e., debug) the code.
- Repeat this simple automation version until all participants can successfully create a command code and are comfortable debugging.

Adding Extras

Use loops and conditional codes to make shorter command codes.

- Write "X," "IF," and "THEN" on some of the blank action/command cards.
- Hand additional blank cards to participants for them to fill in.
- Ask participants to use the "X" + "[number written]" to create action loops. For example, rather than placing 4 forward arrows in the command center, place 1 forward arrow, then "X," then "4" to indicate the figurine should move forward 4 times.
- Conditional "IF/THEN" cards can be used in a similar manner: "IF" + "[no obstruction]" + "THEN" + "[action card]" or "IF" + "[obstruction]" + "THEN" + "[action card]".

LEARNING OUTCOMES

Participants will:

- Learn the basics of algorithm design and how it relates to computational thinking.

- Practice following the specific commands to form their own algorithm design.
- Gain confidence and independence making decisions and solving problems.

RECOMMENDED NEXT PROJECTS

- Chapter 2: Before You Plug In, Analog Games to Play with Young Children: Story Mapping by Stacy Hurt
- Chapter 3: Before You Plug In, Analog Games to Play with Young Children: The Human Robot by Stacy Hurt
- Chapter 8: Computational Thinking in Storytime: Robots by Claudia Haines
- Chapter 21: Integrate Picture Books to Teach Computational Thinking Skills by Danielle Arnold
- Chapter 12: IF You Can Imagine It, THEN You Can Code It: Mini-Stories with Dash Robotics by Alessandra Affinito

11

Program the Human Robot

Decomposition Activities for Preschoolers and Families

PAULA LANGSAM

Children's Librarian | DC Public Library, Washington, D.C.

PROJECT DESCRIPTION

Your robot friend needs help! Teach the robot (i.e., library staff member, adult participant, or other youth participant) how to lace and tie shoes. This program introduces how to break a large task into smaller pieces.

Age Range

- Kids (Ages 3–7)
- Tweens (Ages 8–12)

Type of Library Best Suited For

- Public libraries
- School libraries

Cost Estimate

- $0–$20

OVERVIEW

As discussed in Chapter 9, computational thinking involves ways to look at and understand problems and how they might be solved. Although there are a number of different facets to computational thinking, this activity explores decomposition.

Decomposition refers to breaking larger, complex tasks into components, but it does not specify an order to complete the smaller tasks. For example, preparing a meal, getting ready for bed, or planning a trip. Preparing a meal can be broken down into the preparation of each dish but not the order that each dish would need to be made. Getting ready for bed may involve brushing teeth, putting on pajamas, and setting an alarm for the morning, but the completion of the tasks is not reliant on their order. Planning a trip requires many different decisions—where to go and for how long, how to travel there, and what you may do while there—but these tasks may need to be completed in concert, but not a specific order.

This activity consists of participants teaching an adult (or each other) how to lace and tie shoes. The overall structure of the program could be used for a number of different tasks: spreading peanut butter on bread, dressing dolls/stuffed animals/figurines, or brushing teeth, for example. Any one of these activities would be a great program and exploration of computational thinking. Kids always love being able to tell adults what to do! It's even better when the adults (or other "robots") follow instructions to the letter, highlighting assumptions about processes.

There is no limit to the number of participants, but everyone should have their own shoe lacing card and shoelace. Participants will be working in pairs or triplets. This program works best when there is 1 staff member or adult for every 4 participants.

Software/Hardware Needed

- Lacing card in the shape of a shoe. If possible, print these on cardstock and laminate them. The eyelets should be hole-punched out.
- Shoelaces, ribbon, or yarn. If using ribbon or yarn, tape the ends to simulate the aglet. This will make it easier for participants to move the material through the holes.
- *Optional:* Robot masks.

STEP-BY-STEP INSTRUCTIONS

Preparation

- Organize seating arrangements so participants can easily pair off. If there are a limited number of adults (i.e., "robots"), consider having groups of 3 with 2 youth and 1 adult.
- Place 1 lacing card and 1 shoelace by each seat.
- Have an additional area to welcome everyone and introduce the activity. If additional space is not available, chairs and material can be organized after the introduction.

PROJECT INSTRUCTIONS

- Welcome participants to the program.
- Gather everyone together to introduce the activity.
- Introduce the activity: "Today, some of us are going to be transformed into robots. As robots, there is very little we know how to do, and we really want to learn how to lace and tie shoes. We're going to see if we can teach our robot friends how to tie shoes."
- Break up participants into pairs or small groups.
- Send the person, i.e., teacher, to the seating sections to familiarize themselves with the material.
- Provide additional instructions to the robots. They should follow the instructions precisely and not make any assumptions about how to hold the shoes, where to start lacing, how far to pull the shoelace, etc. Encourage them to put on the robot mask and talk in a robot voice. Remind them that the robots have never encountered shoes or laces before, so they need basic instructions and information.
- Send the robots to their human teachers.
- Begin the process of learning how to lace and tie shoes.
- As library staff walks around the room to observe the program, offer encouragement and suggestions with specific and descriptive language. This is important to help the teachers remember how basic their instructions must be—this is a new and unknown concept for the robots, and the library staff can help serve as reminders!
- When the shoes are laced and tied, ask participants to switch roles and try a different lacing method or pattern.

LEARNING OUTCOMES

Participants will:

- Learn how to break down tasks into smaller components following the concept of decomposition.
- Practice giving and following specific instructions.
- Practice using descriptive and specific language to describe actions and material.
- Gain confidence and independence making decisions and problem solving.

RECOMMENDED NEXT PROJECTS

- Chapter 8: Computational Thinking in Storytime: Robots by Claudia Haines
- Chapter 13: Tell Me a Story with ScratchJr by Lisa O'Shaughnessy
- Chapter 10: Mazes and Games: How to Integrate Algorithm Design with Analog Preschool and Family Activities by Paula Langsam and Amy Steinbauer
- Chapter 21: Integrate Picture Books to Teach Computational Thinking Skills by Danielle Arnold

12

IF You Can Imagine It, THEN You Can Code It

Mini-Stories with Dash Robotics

ALESSANDRA AFFINITO

Library Information Assistant, Children's Department

New York Public Library, Chatham Square Branch

PROJECT DESCRIPTION

Kids will develop their own interactive mini-story for the programmable Dash robot to navigate and use code to help him react to his environment. They will learn the universal coding concepts of loops and conditional If/Then statements as they warm up their minds and bodies with a Red Light, Green Light game before moving on to their Dash stories. Although Dash is an especially easy-to-use and fun tool, the concepts in this project can easily be explored using other tools like Sphero or even the online Scratch programming environment if you don't have Dash robots.

Age Range

- Kids (Ages 3–7): This project is geared toward the youngest age range in this collection, aiming to spark an interest in new tools and skills that can be built upon later.

Type of Library Best Suited For

- Public libraries
- School libraries

Cost Estimate

- $150–$800 (As low as $150 with 1 Dash robot or as high as $800 with a multi-pack of Dash robots and Challenge Cards.)
- The concepts of loops and conditionals introduced in this project can be applied for $0 with online programs like Scratch.

OVERVIEW

In this project, participants will learn more about the coding principles of **loops** and **conditional statements** by constructing a mini-story for Dash the programmable robot to interact with. **Loops** are how commands are repeated in programs without having to re-input information over and over. **Conditional statements**, also known as **if/then** or **if/else** statements, allow programs to navigate changing situations. If you think about it, we use these principles all the time, especially conditional statements. Consider the weather: **if** it's raining outside, **then** you bring an umbrella. **If** it's sunny, **then** you leave your umbrella at home. Voila, you've constructed a conditional statement! Kids who can navigate these concepts within the framework of computer programming will be able to apply them to virtually any coding language out there.

For this project, kids will be helping Dash navigate his way through a problem of their choice and programming how he reacts to that situation. They will learn how to use the Blockly app to code a program that uses loops and conditional statements and will be introduced to the other functionalities of this fun little robot. This challenge will help participants hone their problem-solving skills and develop computational thinking skills in a creative, open-ended way. We chose Dash the robot to teach these concepts because of its opportunities for customization and ease of use for a younger age range. Dash is a physical robot that can be coded to do actions in real time, showing kids a tangible representation of the code they're creating. Also, the coding app Blockly that is used in tandem with Dash employs color-coded tools that are easy for young children, even pre-readers or transitional readers, to manipulate successfully.

Software/Hardware Needed

- Dash robot and Blockly app
- Tablet or device with bluetooth capabilities
- Paper and pencils
- Miscellaneous craft materials for constructing Dash's environment or obstacles for him to encounter

- Empty boxes
- Withdrawn books
- Masking tape or painter's tape to put on the ground

STEP-BY-STEP INSTRUCTIONS

Preparation

In your prep time for this activity, you'll need to brush up on some coding concepts, get familiar with the Blockly software, and prepare your robots and materials for the day.

- Charge your Dash Robot(s) using the mini-USB cable.
- Charge your tablet and make sure that the Blockly app is installed and connected via bluetooth to Dash.
- Set out materials for creating Dash's environment.
  - This can be anything from storytime puppets to leftover craft materials.
- Familiarize yourself with the Blockly interface. Here are 2 recommended approaches:
  - One option is to take some time to go through the puzzles built into the Blockly app. There are 13 levels, but completing the first 3 to 4 should give you everything you need for this project:
    - **Driving School Puzzle:** Teaches about the blocks in the **Drive** section that make Dash move forward, backward, and turn.
    - **Dash the Snowman Puzzle:** Introduces the **Repeat** block, different **Start** options, and some of the available **Animations.**
    - **Interrupting Robot Puzzle:** Introduces the **Wait for** block which allows you to activate different sensors.
    - **Dash on Planet X:** Continues teaching about the different sensors and speech capabilities of Dash with the **Wait for** and **Say** blocks.
    - NOTE: this project often replaces the **Wait for** block with the slightly more advanced, **If/Else** blocks, but both employ conditionals.)
  - Another option is to experiment solo with the different block categories by building your own mini-programs. These can just be various strings of code that help you see how each block plays out in real time.

There are several different categories color-coded into the block system. For our program, we'll be using elements of **Start, Drive, Look, Light, Sound, Animations,** and **Control:**

- Light green **Start** blocks are the beginning to every code, but for our project, we can just use the default **When Start** block that appears every time you start a program.
- Teal **Drive** blocks allow Dash to move forward and backward, turn left or right and to a voice, and rotate his wheels.
- Light blue **Look** blocks allow Dash to look in all directions or toward a voice.
- Dark purple **Light** blocks can change the color and pattern of Dash's head and eye lights.
- Orange **Sound** blocks allow Dash to say different preprogrammed noises or a sound that you record.
- Light purple **Animation** blocks allow Dash to activate some of his preprogrammed actions that include sound and movement. (Note: ignore the **Answer Dot** and **Play Dot** blocks unless you have a Dot robot!)
- Finally, the most important blocks for this program are those in the yellow **Control** section. (See figure 12.1.) They allow you to repeat certain lines of code using the loop blocks (**Repeat ___ times** and **Repeat forever**). They also allow you to have Dash react to his environment using the **If/Else** blocks and the **Wait for** blocks.
- You can customize variables within yellow blocks by clicking on the paler yellow boxes. For example, clicking Obstacle in Front within the **If/Then** block will let you select another triggering input, like "Hear Voice."

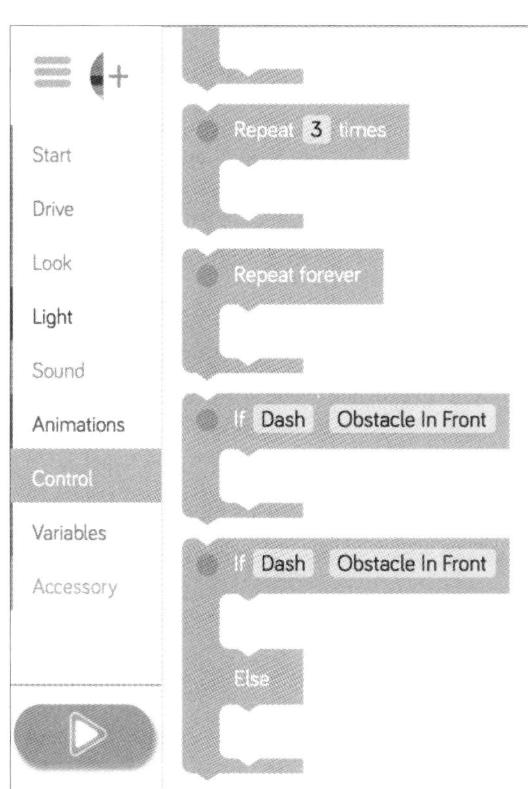

FIGURE 12.1

Blockly control section

- It might feel overwhelming to have all these different blocks, but most of them are self-explanatory and all are easy to edit using drag and drop. Have fun seeing what Dash can do so you have exciting things to show your group!

PROJECT INSTRUCTIONS

Engage

In our opening activity, we're going to spark interest by playing the familiar game Red Light, Green Light game. It gets everybody up and moving and just happens to employ both the concepts of **loops** and **conditional statements**.

- Before playing, talk with your group about the rules of the game:
    - **If** the leader says "Green Light," **then** you can walk toward him (conditional statement).
    - **If** the leader says "Red Light," **then** you have to freeze (conditional statement).
    - The leader **repeats** these commands until someone reaches the finish line and becomes the new leader (loop).
- After a few rounds, discuss with participants how these concepts are also used in coding to help devices "react" to different situations. See if kids can think of a program where a conditional statement might be useful.
    - Some questions to facilitation conversation:
    - How do you react to different situations? For example, what do you do if you hear a loud noise?
        - What are some "robots" or other technology you already use?
        - If you had a robot, how would you want it to help in your everyday life?
        - Example: A program that patrols my room so my little sister can't come in! **If** my sister tries to sneak through my door, **then** my robot sounds an alarm.

Explore

For the main part of this program, you and your group will plan a step-by-step scenario where Dash uses his sensors to react to his environment. After seeing an example, kids will plan their own story on paper using conditional formatting and then put it into action using Blockly coding.

- First, the facilitator will help kids decide what kind of situation they want Dash to encounter. A good place to start is for you to model a program you constructed that demonstrates the conditional and loop structure. Here are a few examples:

  - Dash is being too loud in the library, and when it hears the librarian say "SHHHH," he says "Uh-oh" and his lights turn red.
  - There's a scary monster behind Dash, and when Dash sees him, it says "Help!" and runs away.
  - Dash is playing freeze dance. He starts dancing, but when you clap your hands, he has to freeze or he loses the game.

- Once you've modeled your program, list out on chart paper the different inputs that Dash can react to—sound, touch, and getting close to an object—so your group has an idea of their options. You can also show off the available craft/miscellaneous materials you prepped.
- To help encourage active engagement with the project, it helps to have your group construct a narrative out of the situation as opposed to focusing exclusively on the code.
- Next, have everyone write their **conditional statements** on a piece of paper using simple language. For kids who aren't writing yet, they can pair up with an older child or a caregiver, or you can write for them. The important part is to lay out a step-by-step plan *before* attempting to code it. Use the keywords **if** and **then**. Then have them decide how many times they want their code to repeat and what kind of **loop** they will need.
  - Example: **If** Dash hears the librarian say "SHHHH," **then** he says "Uh-oh" and his lights turn red. **If** Dash does not hear the librarian say "SHHHH," then he can make whatever noise he wants. He does this **3 times**.
  - Then, it's time to move the code on to the Blockly interface. Examine each of the different types of blocks and what they do. Most importantly, we'll be examining the If blocks, If/Else blocks, and the loop blocks in the yellow Control section. The other types of blocks are used to add the "flair" to our narrative.
  - Depending on the group's familiarity with Blockly, it might be helpful or necessary to go through some of the beginner tutorials to get acquainted with the basics of the interface. They will also introduce all the fun pre-programmed actions that Dash can perform.
- Put your code in action!
  - Depending on the size of your group relative to how many Dash robots you have, kids can take turns using the interface or while they wait, they can use paper to write out the exact code blocks they will need.

- If your group is feeling comfortable with the basic **If** block, try adding in the **If/Else** block. This block is another step in the conditional statement and means that Dash has the option of doing several things depending on the situation. When the conditional is satisfied, they do the **if** action. Otherwise, they do the **else** action.
- Sometimes, code will go wrong or not work as you expected. That's okay! Computer programmers have to "debug" their work all the time. Use each hiccup as a way to ask your group questions, and encourage them to experiment with different solutions.

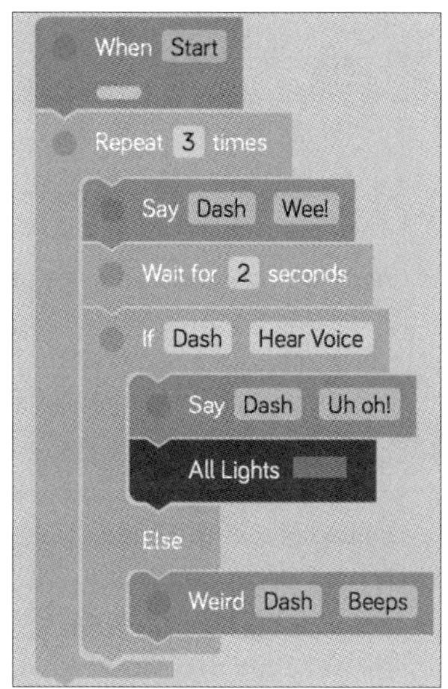

FIGURE 12.2
Example solution

- Figure 12.2 shows what a finished program could look like, one using just the **If** block, and the other using the **If/Else** block. (Note: add the **Wait 2 Seconds** block after the initial action so that kids have time to shush him before he moves on to the next code block.)

Empower

In the final section of the program, we want to inspire kids to take the concepts they've learned and expand upon them through experimentation and free play.

- Once your group has successfully gotten their conditional statement working, kids can choose to continue solving Blockly puzzles or formulate their own code. This is the chance for them to explore features that interested them and work without an explicit goal in mind.
- Some questions to ask: What happens if you program more than 1 conditional statement? What are some of the other ways Dash can interact with his surroundings? What are some things that we needed to change about our code to make it work better?
- If you have a larger group, have everyone work together to construct a maze of obstacles and see if you can take turns "coding" your way out.

- As kids and parents head out, consider pointing them toward a few resources they can use to keep coding at home, including:
    - Websites such as Code.org and scratch.mit.edu.
    - Books such as *Coding Games in Scratch* by Jon Woodcock and *A Beginner's Guide to Coding* by Marc Scott.

LEARNING OUTCOMES

Participants will:

- Learn to effectively utilize the concepts of **loops** and **conditional statements** generally as well as in the context of Dash's Blockly coding language.
- Be able to see connections between coding in a computer and real-life experiences.
- Be able to understand the ways that technology can be used to solve problems or actualize ideas.
- Use technology and coding to communicate effectively and express themselves creatively.
- Improve their computational thinking skills by identifying and breaking down a complex problem in a way that allows computers to be used to solve them.

RECOMMENDED NEXT PROJECTS

- If your group enjoyed the challenge portion of the activity, consider purchasing the Dash and Dot Challenge Cards, which expand on the concepts explored in this project.
- Scratch uses yellow Control blocks in a similar setup to Blockly and can be used in tandem with this project or as a way to extend the lesson onto a different platform.

13

Tell Me a Story with ScratchJr

LISA O'SHAUGHNESSY

Children's Librarian | East Orange (New Jersey) Public Library

PROJECT DESCRIPTION

Everyone has a story to tell—even the youngest of children. Imaginative play and simple story telling are ingrained in childhood play from a very young age and promote early literacy skills. From puppets to action figures and now digital animations, children love having the opportunity to create and share their stories. ScratchJr provides a unique opportunity to teach children simple block coding skills allowing them to animate their stories and bring them to life.

Age Range

- Kids (Ages 3–7)
- Tweens (Ages 8–12)

Type of Library Best Suited For

- Public libraries
- School libraries

Cost Estimate

- $0–$4,000
- The cost depends on your access to desktop, laptops, or tablet devices. If you have a set of tablets, the ScratchJr software can be downloaded for free from the Google Play or Apple App store. If you have a set of desktop computers or laptops, an android emulator such as Bluestacks 3 can be used to download the ScratchJr app from the Google Play or Apple App store. Tablets can range from $50 to $1,000 apiece.

In the Tell Me a Story project, children will be introduced to the ScratchJr interface, learn about the different blocks and what they do, how to combine the actions into a sequence, and how to utilize sound. Students will then divide their story into 3 scenes (beginning, middle, and end), pick a setting, pick characters, and create dialogue and actions. These simple steps will enhance their digital learning skills and result in an exciting interactive animation.

OVERVIEW

During Tell Me a Story, students will create a 3-scene digital story. Each story must include a beginning, a middle, and an end. Their stories should also include 2 or more characters, a background, 1 action per scene, dialogue between characters, and 2 or more sounds. The actions listed above will not only help students create a more engaging story but will also give students a chance to test all the tools available within the ScratchJr interface.

The entire program will take about 1.5–2 hours, including introduction, teaching the ScratchJr interface, and providing time for story building and sharing stories at the end of class. I recommend keeping your group small. No more than 10–12 students. It is possible to teach this class on your own. However, I would recommend having 1 or 2 volunteer assistants, if possible. Sometimes, younger and pre-literate learners need a bit more support with questions and help navigating the interface.

Software/Hardware Needed

- 10–12 tablets, desktop computers, or laptops.
- If you plan to run your program on desktop/laptop computers (MAC or Windows), you will need to download a free Android or iOS emulator. I recommend Bluestacks 3 (https://www.bluestacks.com).
- ScratchJr app, which is available at the Google Play or Apple App store.
    - ScratchJr runs on both iPads and Android tablets. It will run on any iPad 2 or later, including all iPad minis with iOS 7.0 or later installed. Note: newer versions of ScratchJr will only run on iOS 8+. It also runs on any Android tablet, 7"or larger, that is running Android 4.2 (Jelly Bean MR1) or higher. It does not need web access to run. For more information, see https://www.scratchjr.org/about/faq./
- Cardstock to print out ScratchJr cards.

STEP-BY-STEP INSTRUCTIONS

Preparation (60 minutes)

- Print ScratchJr cards available at https://www.scratchjr.org/teach/curricula/.
- If using a tablet, download ScratchJr from the Google Play or Apple App store and test the interface on each tablet.
- Charge tablet before class.
- If you are using a desktop computer or laptop, download Bluestacks 3 android or iOS emulator at https://www.bluestacks.com.
- Install Bluestacks 3 on each device.
- Install ScratchJr app on each device.
- Open each app and test the interface to ensure proper functionality.

Project Introduction (20 minutes)

- Welcome students and give a quick overview of what they are going to accomplish that day.
- Call students up to the front of the room and show them the different ScratchJr cards. Run a short Simon Says, or in this case "Scratch Says," by holding up each card and asking students to act out the corresponding action.
- Show students the home screen and how to create a new project.
- Go over the interface (figure 13.1) and what each object on the screen does. For example, how to add a character, how to pick a setting, where the script area is, and how to drag code blocks onto the corresponding script area.
- Give students 10 minutes to try out the interface and create a simple project.

FIGURE 13.1

Screenshot of ScratchJr sample story

The Project (40–60 minutes)

- Call students up into a story circle.
- Tell students a simple story.
- Show students an example of a 3-scene story you have made.
- Go over what you want students to do:
    - Create a 3-scene story with a beginning, a middle, and an end.
    - Each story must have 2 or more characters.
    - Each story must have a background.
    - Each scene must have at least 1 action. Go over what the actions are (move to left, move up, hop, etc.).
    - Each story must have 2 or more sounds.
    - Each page must have dialogue.
    - Show students the page change block and what it does.
- Send students back to their seats to begin their stories.
- Walk around to help with questions.

Story Share (15–20 minutes)

- After all stories are completed, invite students back to the story circle.
- Ask students to tell you 1 thing they liked about this experience.
- Tell everyone you are now going to have a story share.
- Depending on your setup: Option 1, pull everyone's project up on a projected screen and share each; Options 2, walk around to each student's station and demonstrate each story.

LEARNING OUTCOMES

Participants will:

- Be introduced to the ScratchJr interface.
- Gain a basic knowledge of block coding and sequencing.
- Improve literacy skills through a digital storytelling activity.

RECOMMENDED NEXT PROJECTS

- There is a wealth of supportive material, a digital community, and a variety of suggested projects available at https://www.scratchjr.org.
- Refer to other ScratchJr projects in this book.
- Once students have mastered the ScratchJr program, introducing them to Scratch (https://scratch.mit.edu) would be the natural next step. There are also a variety of resources on the Scratch website and a scratch community called ScratchEd (http://scratched.gse.harvard.edu).

14

Storytime Coding

MARISSA GUIDARA

District Library Youth Services Consultant | Reading (Pennsylvania) Public Library

PROJECT DESCRIPTION

Are you nervous or overwhelmed at the prospect of introducing coding to little ones? There are many activities and computational thinking elements you can easily add to your regular storytimes that will help kids get ready to code. By adding a few twists on typical activities, you can combine classic storytime elements with computational thinking and coding skills to set your kid up for success.

Age Range

- Kids (Ages 3–7)

Type of Library Best Suited For

- Public libraries

Cost Estimate

- $0–$?
- Start off by working with what you have, whether it's introducing a tech toy or including an unplugged computational thinking activity. You can always add more later when you're more confident and know how you'd like to expand your efforts.

OVERVIEW

Storytime is a very familiar avenue for most youth services librarians, so framing coding within this recognizable program pattern—with songs, stories, crafts, and activities—will help librarians feel more at ease and take ownership over the program.

With the popularity of tech and coding, there are tons of great storybooks featuring robots. Using this as a gateway, librarians can offer a series of storytimes focused on coding and computational thinking, or just slip these elements into regularly scheduled themes and lesson plans.

To tech or not to tech? Coding often relies on apps, tech toys, and robots. While these are flashy, there are also unplugged activities that offer similar opportunities for computational thinking and coding learning. Try a mix and match of both.

Software/Hardware Needed

- Storytime books
- Songs
- Craft or activity
- Coding games or toys (optional)

STEP-BY-STEP INSTRUCTIONS

Preparation

- Each of us have a preferred method for storytimes, so please stick with the ways you are most comfortable with when incorporating coding into your plans.
- Prepare any crafts beforehand.
- Charge tech toys as needed.

PROJECT INSTRUCTIONS

With the popularity of tech and coding, there are lots of great storybooks featuring robots. Using this as a gateway, librarians could offer a series of storytimes centered around or featuring robot characters with an ending activity involving a coding robot or a computational thinking activity.

Robot books themselves don't necessarily teach coding, but they are often funny and thoughtful picture books that inspire children to think about what exactly a robot or a computer is and how we communicate with and control them. For this example, consider:

Robo-Sauce by Adam Rubin—A science sauce inadvertently turns everything, even the book, into a robot

Hello Ruby: Adventures in Coding by Linda Liukas—Ruby communicates with the world the same way programmers communicate to computers via coding.

Three Little Aliens and the Big Bad Bot by Margaret McNamara—A riff on an old classic, 3 robots have to build homes to protect their homes from a big, bad bot.

Robots, Robots, Everywhere by Sue Fliess—A menagerie of robots to compare and contrast.

Rex Wrecks It by Ben Clanton—a T-rex wreaks havoc on a group of friends, including a brainy robot, who are trying to build with blocks.

Sing

You may be familiar with the idea of taking a classic kids' tune and retooling the words a bit to match your storytime theme or lesson plan. Songs like the "Hokey Pokey" can easily be turned into the "Robot Pokey" with gears, wheels, and laser beam eyes put "in" and "out" to the tune. The classic "If You're Happy and You Know It" can easily morph into "If You're a Robot and You Know It" with beeps, spins, and even the classic 1980's robot dance.

Activities Featuring Coding Toys

Storytime is a great place to introduce coding toys such as Code-a-pillars and Bee-Bots. Yes, they help teach coding, but these items are called tech toys for a reason—at the heart of it all, they're *toys*. Treat them like toys and incorporate them into your activities the same way you would for any other storytime.

As an example, consider these activities as an extension for the book *The Three Little Robots and the Big, Bad Bot,* a take on the classic Three Little Pigs fairy tale:

- Engineering a house of blocks or LEGOS for the Bee-Bot (How big does the house have to be so that the robot can drive inside?)
- A design challenge for the robot toy (Let's build the biggest house we can and have our big, bad bot knock it down.)
- Problem solving (How can the little bots get past the big, bad bot?)

Do you need coding tools and robot toys to teach computational thinking and coding skills? Not necessarily. Many experts believe that computational thinking skills can be found in activities outside of technology. Try these coding and computational thinking-based activities that involve no tech at all:

- WYSIWYG game—WYSIWYG is a type of computer editing program that stands for "what you see is what you get." This simple action game plays on this notion. Played like a real-life version of the 1980's electronic game Simon, librarians take on the role of "coder" and act out a series of movements, claps, etc., and little ones act out the same by following the "code." They'll later learn that this is what they are doing with the coding robots themselves.
- Let's Go Code! game—This floor game can be purchased (or a similar game can be created) and provides a directional learning experience and algorithm design practice without the use of a robot. The board is large enough for kids to actually walk on as "coders" direct each other to certain spots on the board.
- Is the Let's Go Code game still too complicated? Try a simple maze worksheet. Kids will practice similar problem-solving and directional skills.
- Robot crafts with a nod to design thinking—Having children make a robot craft seems like a no-brainer for a coding storytime. But adding a few questions before kids start creating will help elevate a simple craft into a design thinking project. Tell the children that they need to design a robot that will help clean up the library after storytime. Give the children some prompts to consider:
    - How will the robot put the books away?
    - How will it clean the storytime carpet?
    - How will the robot say goodbye?
- Asking these simple questions turns a simple a craft into a design thinking experience by asking children to solve the problems you're asking for help with. Have kids share their designs with each other.

LEARNING OUTCOMES

Participants will:

- Gain a familiarity with coding tools and toys.
- Practice problem-solving skills.
- Demonstrate design thinking.

RECOMMENDED NEXT PROJECT

- Chapter 16: Bee-Bot Bowling by Marissa Guidara

15

TechTacular

MARISSA GUIDARA

District Library Youth Services Consultant | Reading (Pennsylvania) Public Library

PROJECT DESCRIPTION

Coding may be a hot topic, but don't take it for granted that everyone knows what it means or entails. Some parents and kids may even shy away from programs that are advertised as coding because they are unsure what it really means or don't think they're computer savvy enough for the class. A TechTacular is the perfect way to introduce your families to coding programs and tech toys, like the Cubetto (figure 15.1), and get families talking and excited

FIGURE 15.1

Discovering the Cubetto for the first time

about your innovative programming and their benefits. So what is it? It's a party; a fun fair where library stations will highlight coding activities and tech toys so families can explore these activities together using inquiry-based learning methods.

Age Range

- Kids (Ages 3–7)
- Tweens (Ages 8–12)

Type of Library Best Suited For

- Public libraries
- School libraries

Cost Estimate

- $0–$1,000
- Use what you have. This is a perfect way to introduce and highlight coding toys and materials you already own and a great way to figure out what to purchase next.

OVERVIEW

Library stations will highlight coding toys and activities that families will explore and play with in an inquiry-based learning experience. Volunteers or staff members at each station can help guide the experience by asking questions, answering questions, and highlighting your future programs. After a child participates in every station, she can earn a special TechTacular-themed sticker or badge as a prize.

Each station is based on exploration and inquiry-based learning rather than instruction. Children and parents will naturally have questions about how coding works, and station staff will ask questions to further their curiosity. Together, they will learn by doing, trying things out, and even (gasp!) failing. There is no need to get anything right or perfect at a TechTacular. This is merely an introduction to what everything is and what library programs may be like for participants.

A TechTacular is also a great time to reach out to community partners (other libraries, schools, and tech organizations) to see if they'll offer their time or expertise at these stations or even let you borrow their coding gadgets for the stations.

This can be set up as a big one-time event, either a drop-in style activity where families can stop by between certain hours or as a program that starts and ends at a certain time as you guide families through activities. Communicating and explaining the benefits of these activities is key, as is collecting feedback and interest levels, so it's recommended that you have a staff member or volunteer at most stations. Therefore, the scope and size of this event can be flexible to fit your needs. If you have 3 people helping, then keep it limited to 3 stations and perhaps some passive or independent crafts or a LEGO building station. If you have a dozen people helping, then expand it to involve more hands-on coding activities.

Software/Hardware Needed

- Whatever you have! Bust out all of your coding and tech gadgets at once. This is a great place to show off Code-a-pillars, Dash and Dot robots, Spheros, Bee-Bots, and other tech toys.
- If you're low on tech supplies, reach out to your community—other libraries, schools, tech students, etc.—and ask them to come on board with their supply of tech toys.
- Supplement your activities with STEAM-based stations, such as Keva or LEGO blocks, coding crafts like binary bracelets, or robot-design crafts.
- TechTacular ticket
- Stickers or badges as a giveaway

STEP-BY-STEP INSTRUCTIONS

Preparation

- Each station should be run by a volunteer or staff member. Some of these items may be new to them, too. Let them familiarize themselves with the gadget or activity at their station. They don't have to be experts. Learning alongside kids and parents is great, but they should be able to troubleshoot if problems or questions arise. They should also be informed if there are future programs you'd like them to talk up to the families while they're playing.
- Discussion prompts for station staff.
- Charge any devices that will be used so they're ready to go.
- TechTacular ticket. This can be a plain note card or a specially designed paper with your logo on it. This will be used by families to collect stickers at each station, indicating that they've participated in each activity.
- Create special TechTacular badges or purchase stickers as a farewell gift.

PROJECT INSTRUCTIONS

- Welcome families as they enter and give each child a TechTacular ticket. The ticket can be a simple note card or specially designed slip of paper and will encourage children to talk to the station staff members as they'll have to ask for a sticker or a stamp for their ticket as they visit each station.

- Each station staff member will be given discussion prompts to help lead families in inquiry-based learning. These prompts should invite children to explore the activity rather than simply teach children how to use the toy. For instance, a leader of a station featuring a Cubetto might explain to a family, "This is our Cubetto. Why don't you pick out 3 pieces for it and we'll see what it does? . . . What if we want the Cubetto to turn right? Which piece do you think would make him do that?" As children and parents explore, they'll work out the directions for themselves. The discussion prompts model questions for parents to ask and guide their play without being intrusive to their discoveries.
- Meanwhile, the leader can also explain to parents what is happening while their children play and that these types of skills are being brought into library programs. "Your child is learning directional skills with this toy. By placing these pieces together on the Cubetto, your child is creating an algorithm. He's actually practicing the same coding skills he will need one day to create a website!"
- After each activity, the station leader will add a sticker or stamp to the TechTacular ticket to indicate that the family has visited that station.
- Once families visit all stations, they can hand in their ticket to a special station or to the host who greeted them for a sticker or badge. You might even consider using this ticket as a raffle ticket to give away a small coding toy or coding book.

In addition to spreading the word about your coding and computational thinking efforts, a TechTacular can also be used to:

- Highlight future projects or storytimes that will feature these coding and computational thinking with posters and flyers. ("Did you like playing with Bee-Bot? See him again next week at storytime!")
- *Collect feedback:* Have children vote on their favorite toy or station before picking up their sticker or badge. This is a great way for librarians to collect feedback and gauge interest levels to determine future programming or needs.
- *Get other library departments involved:* With all this talk of tech, this is a great time to get adult services librarians to talk up your library's e-resources, computer classes, and streaming services. Set them up at their own station so they can sign up adults for ecards, show off their e-book collection, or teach adults how to log in to streaming services.
- *Publicize:* Just as many parents and kids might not know what coding is or how you are offering it in your programs, your community might not know

either. This is a great story for your local news to pick up. Reach out via a press release or e-mail and try to get a news story run featuring the smiling faces of kids who are practicing coding.

- *Grants:* If you're having difficulty raising funds to purchase desired coding tools or tech, use feedback and participation numbers from this event as proof of interest in coding for your next grant application.
- *School visits:* A TechTacular also works great when a class visits the library. Students can visit stations in groups and rotate through each. Teachers and students often think about a field trip to their public library in terms of books and library cards. Highlighting your coding activities through a TechTacular will enlighten them to the type of programming you're offering and open their eyes to library resources beyond the traditional.

LEARNING OUTCOMES

Participants will:

- Gain a familiarity with coding and tech tools.
- Practice inquiry-based learning and curiosity.
- Learn about library e-resources and programs.
- Practice social and communication skills.
- Demonstrate problem-solving skills.

RECOMMENDED NEXT PROJECTS

- This could easily be adapted to work for all age groups—coding is still new for many teens and adults, too.
- Use feedback to determine your next steps. If kids enjoyed a certain toy or activity, be sure to incorporate that into more programming and advertise it on your flyers. You can also use feedback to determine which toys or activities to invest your budget in for the future.

16

Bee-Bot Bowling

MARISSA GUIDARA

District Library Youth Services Consultant | Reading (Pennsylvania) Public Library

PROJECT DESCRIPTION

Ready to "bowl" over the kiddos with this fun activity? In this project, kids will go Bee-Bot Bowling, learning how to code their Bee-Bot to knock down plastic bowling pins in a special robo bowling alley. Kids will learn directional skills and algorithm design as they create instructions for their Bee-Bot to follow. The new coding skills kids will learn are sneakily hidden within the familiar activity of bowling so they'll feel comfortable at the activity even if they've never seen a Bee-Bot before.

Age Range

- Kids (Ages 3–7)
- Tweens (Ages 8–12)

Type of Library Best Suited For

- Public libraries
- School libraries

Cost Estimate

- $100
- A single Bee-Bot costs $90 and is perfect for small groups that can take turns. Classroom bundles of six Bee-Bots cost about $500.
- A plastic bowling set costs about $10; multiple sets might be needed for large groups or classrooms.
- You may want to spend a few dollars of your budget for paper and craft supplies to build a robo bowling alley.

OVERVIEW

The first thing you may notice when playing with a Bee-Bot coding robot for the first time is that there isn't a screen to code on. That's because a Bee-Bot is "tangible tech," meaning it does not use a computer or app to code; it's screen-free. Instead, the robot features a series of buttons that are put into a sequence (in coding terms, this is an **algorithm**). A child presses "go," and *voila!*—the robot completes the sequence in the code.

Bee-Bots and other similar tangible tech toys are a great way to introduce coding if you or parents are concerned about screen time. Such robots pull children away from their tablets and iPads and reframe coding into a form of physical "play." Children will sit on the floor playing with the tech toy with a group of friends, all the while secretly learning the basics of coding.

In this activity, children will incorporate coding elements into the familiar, fun activity of bowling. This is perfect for almost any size group, as kids in large groups can take their cue from real bowling and practice sharing and taking turns. It's also an easy activity that requires few staff members. Once rules and instructions are established, game play mimics the already familiar game of bowling so kids will already have some idea of how to play without the aid of adults.

Software/Hardware Needed

- 1 or more Bee-Bots
- Plastic bowling pins
- Specially made robo "bowling alley" (optional)
- Paper or whiteboard (optional)

STEP-BY-STEP INSTRUCTIONS

Preparation

- Creating a grid to use as a robo "bowling alley" (figure 16.1) helps children understand how far the Bee-Bot will travel. Each Bee-Bot goes forward 15 cm (5.9"), moves backward 15 cm (5.9") and turns right and left 90 degrees. Each bowling alley can be made by measuring out these lengths and creating a grid for the Bee-Bot to travel on. The overall size of the alley is completely up to you and the size of your group. This grid helps children visualize the route their Bee-Bot will have to take to reach a bowling pin and will help them strategize as they create their algorithms. Get fancy if you wish and decorate your grid/bowling alley with robot-inspired motifs.

- Bee-Bots should be charged before your activity. Each Bee-Bot comes with a USB cord, and a bundle may be purchased with a "hive" charger that allows you to charge six Bee-Bots at once.

FIGURE 16.1

Encourage kids to take the time to strategize and make a plan before entering their algorithms into the Bee-Bot

PROJECT INSTRUCTIONS

- Set up your space before children and families arrive. Place bowling alley(s) on the floor or on a table.
- Introduce children to the Bee-Bot and explain its buttons. Before moving on to the bowling game, let them try out the Bee-Bot and get a feel for how it works. A common assumption with Bee-Bots and other coding toys is that when a child directs it to go left or right, the Bee-Bot will turn and then move forward. The Bee-Bot will only turn 90 degrees and await further instruction to move forward in that direction. Further, a cancel button needs to be pressed to start a new sequence. These helpful hints are best to share before the bowling game starts.
- When kids are ready, go bowling! Place several pins on the bowling alley. Start out easy, placing the pins so the Bee-Bot must go in a straight line to knock them down. Each child can have her own space on the alley or can take turns just as in real bowling.
- Encourage kids to help out one another and offer each other guidance. If the Bee-Bot doesn't make it to its intended pin, ask children what must be added to the directions to make it work.
- Algorithm design: Once children get the hang of the controls for the Bee-Bot, place the pins in more complex arrangements. This forces children to strategize. They'll have to look at the game board and plan their movements ahead before entering the sequence of directions into the Bee-Bot. This sequence of directions they are creating is actually an **algorithm**.
- Ask children to write down the algorithm on a piece of paper or whiteboard as they strategize. Jotting it down can help them visualize the necessary sequence as well as emphasize the meaning of an algorithm.

- Add further levels of complexity to Bee-Bot bowling as kids get the hang of it by:
    - Placing obstacles on the bowling alley, marking squares on the grid as squares that must be avoided.
    - Dividing the children up into teams and asking each to set up pins and challenges for their opponents to traverse.
    - Are your kids feeling competitive? Have them keep score. Whoever can knock down the most pins wins the game and becomes the Bee-Bot Bowling champion.

If you have a group of regulars who have played the game, you could even leave the Bee-Bot and the robo bowling alley out for a self-directed program. Its simple design is perfect for an after-school program for kids or tweens to try on their own, and the Bee-Bot's sounds can be silenced so it won't interfere with other library visitors.

LEARNING OUTCOMES

Participants will:

- Design algorithms.
- Practice directional language and concepts.
- Become familiar with tangible tech devices
- Demonstrate computational thinking and problem-solving skills.
- Practice kindergarten readiness skills like sharing, taking turns, and following directions.

RECOMMENDED NEXT PROJECTS

- This project could be altered to fit almost any robot coding device, such as Spheros, Dash and Dot robots, and Cubettos. In fact, it could be used as a scaffolded program where children first start off by using tangible tech and then move toward block coding app-controlled robots.
- Replace the robo bowling alley with a maze (perhaps even of the children's own design) and kids can use their newly acquired algorithm design skills to direct their Bee-Bots through a more complex environment.

17

Preschool Coding
How to Teach Coding to Children

KATIE CLAUSEN
Coordinator of Early Literacy Services | Gail Borden Public Library, Elgin, Illinois

PROJECT DESCRIPTION

What is coding in its simplest form, and how do you teach it to preschoolers? **Coding,** also called programming, is simply telling a computer what you'd like it to do. A **computer program** is a list of step-by-step instructions that tell a computer what to do. This activity will take you through a lesson plan introducing children as young as 3 to the foundation for beginning coding. First, you will teach and practice the concept of sequencing (or patterning). You will demonstrate that **sequencing** is simply an arrangement of items in an order. Then, you will use a device of your choosing to teach children how to code the device to move the direction you would like it to.

Age Range

- Kids (Ages 3–7)

Type of Library Best Suited For

- Public libraries
- School libraries

Cost Estimate

- $25–$80 per robot. For larger groups (over 15 kids), I recommend purchasing at least 2 of the robots of choice.
- $5–$19.99 for sequencing materials. I like Lakeshore Learning's Patterning Family Engagement Pack (sequencing owls) and also use candy (M&Ms or Skittles) to make patterns (then kids can eat them after!).

OVERVIEW

Computers are not humans, right? If I told you to "Go do your laundry," you would understand instinctively that this means there are many steps involved: grabbing your hamper of dirty clothes, putting them in the washing machine, measuring the soap, adding the soap, shutting the machine, and pressing the start button. However, a computer does not have the same innate knowledge; a computer needs step-by-step instructions to perform the task you want.

Using a coding device of choice (Code-a-pillar, Bee-Bot, or Robot Mouse), participants will be guided step by step through a hands-on activity that lays the foundation for beginning concepts of coding. Through experimentation and discovery-based play, participants will build a code with 1 of 3 goals: have a Code-a-pillar reach a green leaf, have a Bee-Bot reach a honeycomb, or have a Robot Mouse reach a piece of cheese.

Software/Hardware Needed

- Think & Learn Code-a-pillar by Fischer-Price ($25–$49.99): This robot features easy-to-connect segments (USB) that preschoolers can arrange and rearrange to "tell" the toy how to move: forward, left, right, wiggle, or dance. This is the easiest of the 3 robots.
- Bee-Bot ($79.95): This device uses directional buttons (forward, back, left, and right) that participants enter at one time. Then, press the green GO! button and Bee-Bot is sent on its way.
- Code & G Robot Mouse by Learning Resources ($29.99): If you purchase the entire activity set, you receive maze grids, maze walls, tunnels, and coding cards. You can purchase just the robot and make your own mazes or tunnels out of things like cardboard. This robot is the most complicated of the 3 choices because it features two speeds along with colorful buttons to match coding cards. This is best for the older range, 5–7 year olds.
- Arrow Cards: Small cards can be purchased with the Robot Mouse Activity Kit. For a program or classroom, I prefer larger arrows so everyone can see from a distance. My larger arrows can be downloaded at:
    - Arrow Card 1—https://www.dropbox.com/s/9jkn23840f99ycy/Arrow%20Coding%20Cards%2001.jpg?dl=0 or https://bit.ly/2yT3g7J
    - Arrow Card 2—https://www.dropbox.com/s/09h6usv1kyt389q/Arrow%20Coding%20Cards%2002.jpg?dl=0 or https://bit.ly/2AmtUbm
    - Arrow Card 3—https://www.dropbox.com/s/fx06b265y3jr4uc/Arrow%20Coding%20Cards%2003.jpg?dl=0 or https://bit.ly/2J9sV0V

- Arrow Card 4—https://www.dropbox.com/s/5y5xnyp2jfnba11/Arrow%20Coding%20Cards%2004.jpg?dl=0 or https://bit.ly/2EAdyA0
- Sequencing or patterning tools, such as pom poms, blocks, Skittles, or M&Ms.
- Miscellaneous craft materials for constructing the Code-a-pillars green leaf, the Bee-Bot's honeycomb, and the Robot Mouse's cheese.

STEP-BY-STEP INSTRUCTIONS

Preparation

- To make green food materials for Code-a-pillar: I used green metallic foil paper, green raffia ribbon, and fake floral leaves.
- To make Bee-Bot's honeycomb: I purchased a Styrofoam ball and then wound around yellow yarn and tissue paper to make the beehive. For the bees: I used yellow pom poms wrapped with black pipe cleaners.
- For Robot's cheese, purchase play food.

PROJECT INSTRUCTIONS

- Introduce the term *coding* (telling a computer what you would like it to do) and explain how it is very similar to sequencing and patterning.
- Practice sequencing and patterning with non-tech tools such as pompoms or Skittles. Introduce these sequences as "lists," and tell children that a code is simply a list that a computer can understand. (Example: "Let's do an AB pattern! This means alternating between 2 colors: red, blue, red, blue, red, blue . . ." (Tip: Practicing patterns helps prepare children for understanding number concepts and mathematical operations used in school. Patterns allow them to see relationships between things and put things in order.)
- Next, bring out the coding cards. Show the different arrows, and use directional words such as *forward, backward, to the left,* and *to the right*. Explain that the arrows you choose will be the directions the robot goes. These arrows build the code.
- Bring out the robot. Allow children to familiarize themselves with the coding device, and give time to explore and play with it. Testing it through trial and error is called discovery-based play or inquiry-based learning. Kids learn best through their own questions and curiosity.

- Next, have 1 child be the "programmer" and 1 child be the "computer." Have the programmer put the arrows in a specific order, and then have the computer walk in the exact sequence the programmer coded.
- Repeat this code with the robot (figure 17.1). Code your robot to do the exact same path that the child assigned to be the computer went and see if it matches. It will!

FIGURE 17.1

Bee-Bot reads the code embedded by pressing the directional buttons and finally the green "go!" button and is about to reach its beehive

- Now, put your robot on one side of the room and its object of desire (green leaf, cheese, or honeycomb) somewhere else in the room (start small—even just a few feet away). Ask children: How do we help the caterpillar get to what it wants?
- Children can work individually, in groups, or in a large group to brainstorm a path for the robot to get to its desired item. You can do this free and open on the ground, or you can create a grid with duct tape on the ground. For example, put the object of desire in the corner of the room. What pattern would work for the robot to reach it? Does it need to go diagonally? How can children make it go diagonally?
- If children are not getting their robot to the object, ask open-ended questions such as:
  - What do you think you need to adjust for the robot to get to the object?
  - Which part of the code (or sequence) is not working?

- Let's trace the path together. Where should we change the direction (or code) to get the robot to its destination? Do we need to change more than 1 direction?

What I like about this activity is that kids must *experiment* with what paths work best. There is no right path or correct way to it—there are many!

LEARNING OUTCOMES

Participants will:

- Understand and articulate what coding is and what a computer program is.
- Formulate a code on the Code-a-pillar, Bee-Bot, or Robot Mouse that successfully follows a path to their end goal.
- Exercise higher-order skills, such as critical thinking, problem solving, sequencing, and programming fundamentals—all of which prepare them for school.

RECOMMENDED NEXT PROJECTS

- Mazes and barriers: Once you get the hang of how the devices work, you can build your own maze or have children build their own maze using LEGOS or DUPLOS, cardboard, foam core, or even colored duct tape on the floor. Then, have kids try to get the robot through the maze using the correct code. Learning Resources also has kits for building with the Robot Mouse.
- Have a "Tiny Tech" program: If you can purchase more than 1 device, have a program where patrons can come in for open play with the robots. Try having different stations set up, and they all do not need a robot! Some could be patterning stations, some could be screen-free coding, and some could be other emerging technology.
- Circulate your robot: Although there is always the risk your robot could get damaged, children and families will love the opportunity to check out the coding device from the circulating collection for at-home exploratory play.

18

Screen-Free Coding for Preschoolers

KATIE CLAUSEN

Coordinator of Early Literacy Services | Gail Borden Public Library, Elgin, Illinois

PROJECT DESCRIPTION

Think you need fancy gadgets and expensive robots to teach coding? Does the concept of teaching coding to preschoolers sound intimidating? Fear not—these projects will give you some practical, interactive, and screen-free activities to teach basic coding principles. A series of group activities and a craft are easy enough for someone without any computer science background to run this coding program successfully!

Age Range

- Kids (Ages 3–7)

Type of Library Best Suited For

- Public libraries
- School libraries

Cost Estimate

- $25 for beads, pipe cleaners, or elastic string

OVERVIEW

Leading 3 group activities (Break It Down!, If/Then Group Game, Binary Coding Bracelets), you will understand a variety of ways to teach coding to preschoolers without technology. You will teach 3 coding concepts:

Break It Down: A computer needs to know what you want, step by step. To tell the computer what to do, you need to break an activity down into steps.

If/Then Statement: This is the most basic coding statement. It tells your program to execute code *only if* a particular situation occurs. For example, IF the weather is nice, THEN we will go to the park. IF you eat lots of candy, THEN you will get a toothache. Essentially, If/Then is cause and-effect.

Binary Coding: Computers do not understand language the way we do. Computers read code in a system of 0s and 1s and translate it to a language called ASCII. A specific string of code determines what numbers, letters, and symbols the computer understands. The reason it is called "binary" code is because there are only 2 options for coding: 0s and 1s.

You can do each of these activities separately, or you can do them sequentially as 1 program. I like to use an "If/Then statement in a regular storytime as a substitute for a flannelboard rhyme or group song.

Software/Hardware Needed

- White board, chalk board, or easel with flip chart *(Break It Down)*
- Writing utensil for board—dry erase marker, chalk, or regular marker
- ASCII Binary Coding Sheet (*Binary Bracelets*) [downloadable at ASCII Binary Alphabet: https://www.dropbox.com/s/z05slud81ioy6zj/9215%20ASCII%20Binary%20Alphabet.pdf?dl=0 or https://bit.ly/2CzZdB0]
- Practice Sheet (*Binary Bracelets*) [downloadable at Binary code worksheet: https://www.dropbox.com/s/6dfepq9zhs5u14w/Binary%20code%20worksheet.pub?dl=0 or https://bit.ly/2yrVan5]
- Pipe cleaners or elastic cording for jewelry (*Binary Bracelets*)
- Beads—at least 2 color options (*Binary Bracelets*)

STEP-BY-STEP INSTRUCTIONS

Preparation

- Download and print the ASCII Binary Alphabet Sheet.
- Download and print the Practice Sheet.
- Prepare 2 (or 3, if you want a third color for spaces between letters) different colors of beads. Make sure they are sorted.
- Cut elastic string or pipe cleaners the proper size to fit a child's wrist.

PROJECT INSTRUCTIONS

Break It Down!

- Begin with open-ended questions about daily activities, such as brushing your teeth, going to the park, and eating dinner. How do you go to the park? What do you need to do first to go to the park?
- Give children a chance to respond, and draw simple pictures of what they say on the board or paper. For example, if children say "We drive," draw a car. Perhaps they say, "We get our coats!" or "We bring snacks!" Draw these pictures on the board.
- Ask children if the pictures are in the correct order. Do we drive first, then bring our snacks? No. Put the pictures in order together by drawing a sequence on a line, or you can draw a grid and put 1 picture in each box.
- Break it down even further. What do you need to do to put on your coat? You must take it off the hook, put 1 arm through the hole, and then put the other arm through the other hole. Then, zip up the coat and put on the hood. You can break it down even further by indicating how you take the coat from its hook (lift up arm, grab the coat, close your hand, etc.). As you can see, *you can break down everything you do into a smaller and more specific sequence.* This is **coding**.
- If you would rather not draw, you can also print out pictures of preplanned activities and break them down into their proper sequence.
- Want to extend the activity? You can talk about a programming bug or the importance of **debugging**. A bug is simply a mistake in a program. Debugging means you look for and find mistakes in your program. What if things are out of order (for example, you put on your shoes first and then your socks!). This is a bug! What if you are missing an instruction (for example, you forget your boots and accidently wear only your socks to the park and it's a rainy day!). This is a bug! You must take a look at the sequence, find the bug, and fix the order so the code is correct. The best way to prevent bugs is to go step by step very carefully. However, everyone makes mistakes, and that's why finding the bugs is important.

If/Then Group Game

- Introduce the concept of the If/Then statement. Tell kids it is very similar to a true/false question. Is something true? If that answer is yes, it can prompt an action.

- You (the librarian) will be the "programmer." This means you are giving the instructions, or commands. Everyone else is the "computers," and they must follow the commands. You will be giving them the "code."
- You, the programmer, stand in front of the computers and give them a command. If I ____ (fill in the blank), then you _____ (fill in the blank). Essentially, it is a more technical version of Simon Says. There are easy and more difficult ways to do this.
    - Easy: The computers mimic the programmers.

Here are ideas to get the programmer started:

- "If I spin in a circle, then you spin in a circle."
- "If I act like an elephant, then you act like an elephant."
- "If I jump up and down, then you jump and down."

More Difficult

To make the "code" more complicated, make your "Then" action different than your "If" action. This means the computers do something different than the programmer.

Here are ideas to get the programmer started:

- "If I reach for the sky, then you touch your toes."
- "If I pat my head, then you rub your belly."
- "If a jump up and down, then you make yourself into a ball on the ground."

Most Difficult

Introduce the If/Then/Else statements. "Else" simply means, "If I don't do it, then . . . ." This level is mainly for kindergarten and up.

Here are ideas to get the programmer started:

- **Programmer commands:** "If I jump up and down, then you do jumping jacks. Else you sit down crisscross applesauce." If the programmer jumps, then everyone does jumping jacks. If the programmer stands there and does nothing, everyone should sit down crisscross applesauce.
- **Programmer commands:** "If act like an elephant, then you act like a monkey. Else you act like a snake." If the programmer stands there and does nothing, everyone should act like a snake.
- **Programmer commands:** "If I scratch my back, then you scratch your back. Else you scratch your friend's back." If the programmer stands there and does nothing, everyone should be scratching each other's back.

Binary Coding Bracelets

During this activity, you will write your initials or your name using the ASCII binary code that computers read to make a piece of jewelry (either a bracelet or necklace, depending on the length of the name). Younger kids do best with just initials.* Older kids can handle their names.

*NOTE: Preschoolers may not know what initials are. You can explain that everyone has a first name and a last name, and the initials are the first letter of our first name followed by the first letter of our last name. We use initials sometimes as a shortened version of our name. Be aware that not all cultures use a first name/last name structure; in that case, have participants choose any letters they would like to identify themselves.

- Give each child a copy of the ASCII Binary Alphabet Sheet as well as a blank piece of paper or a paper with squares for them to fill out their code.
- Choose 1 color of bead to represent 1 and another color bead to represent 0.

  Example: 1 = purple and 0 = yellow.

- Have children write their initials vertically on a sheet of paper 2 times—once for the binary code (0s and 1s) and once for the colors.

  Example: the initials DR (figure 18.1).

- Next, preschoolers will "spell" their initials in binary code using the ASCII Binary Alphabet (using 1s and 0s).

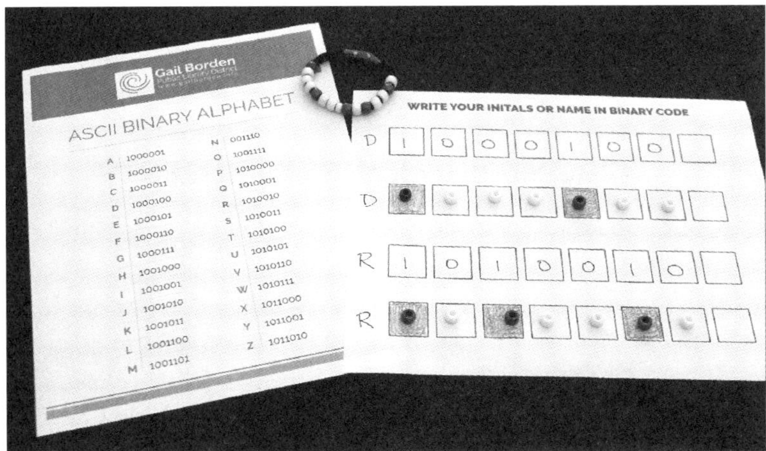

FIGURE 18.1

This example of the binary code project shows the initials D and R, as well as the binary code sequence and the corresponding color sequence. The bracelet is the final product

- Next, preschoolers will color their sequence according to the colors they chose for 0s and 1s. We used crayons to color the boxes so preschoolers can place matching beads on top to "see the sequence."

Example, for the initials DR, I write out the binary code sequence for D, then write out the binary code sequence for R. Then, I color the squares below to see the bead sequence.

- Finally, preschoolers will make their bracelet or necklace following the exact sequence of colored beads that corresponds with their binary code sequence. We used purple for 1s, yellow for 0s, and a small white bead for a space between the initials.

LEARNING OUTCOMES

Participants will:

- Learn and practice the following foundational coding concepts: If/Then statement, debugging, and binary code.
- Participate collaboratively in coding activities and successfully demonstrate their ability to build and follow a code or program.
- Understand that computers do not understand our language. Instead, they read a language called binary code, which uses 0s and 1s in various sequences.
- Work individually to encode letters into binary code using their own name or initials.

RECOMMENDED NEXT PROJECTS

- **If/Then:** preschoolers can become the "programmers" and make up their own If/Then statements.
- **If/Then:** Make it a competition! If a child does not follow the commands correctly, she is eliminated. The last child standing wins.
- **Binary Code:** Extend this so children can create any word or sequence they want. This sequence or code could be a special friendship bracelet with a message. For a socio-emotional component, kids can choose a special word that reminds them of home when feeling alone or school. They could also code special days like a birthday using numbers instead of letters.

19

Great Books for Teaching Coding to Preschoolers

KATIE CLAUSEN

Coordinator of Early Literacy Services | Gail Borden Public Library, Elgin, Illinois

PROJECT DESCRIPTION

This list of resources features books that explore coding principles for the library's youngest users—even babies! Along with each book is a short description highlighting specific content, as well as ideas of how to use the book in a program or collection.

Age Range

- Kids (Ages 3–7)

Type of Library Best Suited For

- Public libraries
- School libraries

Cost Estimate

- Average cost of a board book: $7.99
- Average cost of picture book: $16.99
- Cost of professional development book, *Coding as a Playground Programming and Computational Thinking in the Early Childhood Classroom* by Marina Umaschi Bers: $34.95, paperback

OVERVIEW

In the Digital Age, practically everything around us uses coding to function. Cars, cell phones, gaming systems, water heaters, washing machines—even traffic lights! Because our daily life relies on these systems, our daily life relies on codes.

Even our littlest library users can begin to understand the basic concepts of programming. Teaching young children to code does not mean teaching them a particular computer programming language. Rather, it means giving preschoolers experiences where they can *make* rather than observe. Technology does not have to be synonymous with passivity; we can make it playful by encouraging 21st Century Skills such as imagination, constructive decision making, creative problem solving, collaborating, and critical thinking. All of these skills are necessary to write a program.

As digital natives, preschoolers already have an aptitude for coding; we can extend that intuition with hands-on practice so their brains naturally think like computer programmers. Every child will not become a computer programmer or web developer. However, children can be active creators, not passive consumers. The earlier we teach children digital literacy skills like programming, the better prepared they will be for more complicated creating and problem solving later in their lives.

As a children's librarian, I am a firm advocate for early literacy. I dedicate a huge portion of my work to enhancing children's language and literacy skills and encouraging a love of reading. However, too much of the time, language and literacy are our *only* focuses. Reading and writing are foundational skills, but other 21st Century Skills are also valuable for children's future success in our digital world.

Coding can sound intimidating. I was an English major, not a computer scientist! However, coding is not in opposition to language and literacy. Rather, logical and sequencing skills can actually *enhance* reading, science, and math skills. In fact, the foundation of reading is organization and order. Letters are set in an order to form a word; words are set in an order to form a sentence. Additionally, coding builds core socio-emotional skills such as perseverance, conflict resolution, and distress tolerance. It is not always easy to find a solution to a problem, but finding where the "bug" is and being creative and resilient while practicing solution construction builds grit and innovative reasoning.

The list of books in this chapter will help you and your library patrons understand the fundamentals of coding and engage the littlest minds with beginning programming.

Software/Hardware Needed

You can purchase these books through your library's vendor or any number of websites.

LIST OF RESOURCES

Board Books (Best for Ages 0–3)

Baby Code! [series] by Sandra Horning; art by Melissa Crowton. New York: Penguin Workshop, an imprint of Penguin Random House, LLC, 2018.

- Baby Code!: Art
- Baby Code!: Music
- Baby Code!: Play

Babies learn through engaged play, especially by using their bodies to learn about the world around them. In this series, each double page spread contains: baby doing a play, music, or art activity on the verso (left page) and technology doing a similar activity on the recto (right page). For example, 1 spread features a baby on the left page, with the text, "Baby uses words to tell Doggie what to do. 'Sit, Doggie, Sit!'" On the right page, "Code uses letters and numbers to tell computers what to do!" This combination of non-tech and tech shows that coding is all around us—even in basic experiences in a baby's world.

Follow the Trail [series] by Dawn Sirett; design and illustrations by Rachael Parfitt Hunt and Charlotte Milner. New York: mediaName Book, DK Publishing, 2018.

- Follow the Trail: Trucks
- Follow the Trail: Wild Animals
- Follow the Trail: Farm
- Follow the Trail: Baby Animals
- Follow the Trail: Baby Dinosaurs
- Follow the Trail: At the Zoo
- Follow the Trail: Bugs

This series is perfect for hands-on learning about sequencing. Before babies can understand coding, they need to practice simple tasks that hone their hand-eye coordination and fine motor skills. In this board book series, babies trace textured, glittery, and bright trails to help animals find their homes, help dump trucks find their construction sites, or connect animals to the products they give us. The variety of lines—zigzags, curves, and loops—invite readers to use directional language to introduce coding, such as *forward, backward, turn,* and *stop.*

Baby Loves Coding! by Ruth Spiro; illustrated by Irene Chan. Watertown, MA: mediaName Book, Charlesbridge, 2018.

How does Baby fix her train? She must first find the caboose, then walk the correct path to reach the toy box. How many steps does she need to go? What direction? Baby must think step by step. Although the vocabulary is a tad elevated, this creative board book lays the foundation for thinking like a programmer. Additionally, it is colorful, dynamic, and features a character of color. This book would work well in a baby storytime to introduce beginning coding concepts.

Picture Books (Best for Ages 3–6)

How to Code a Sandcastle by Josh Funk; illustrated by Sara Palacios; foreword by Reshma Saujani, founder of Girls Who Code. New York: mediaName Book, Viking, 2018.

Pearl and her robot Pascal are on a quest to build an indestructible sandcastle! Through endearing illustrations and lively storytelling, this book explains how Pearl breaks down each problem into smaller problems and tells Pascal in a language he understands. Funk gives definitions for coding vocabulary (code, sequence, loop if-then-else), and demonstrates that it takes trial and error to learn coding. For example, when Pearl tells Pascal that he must build the castle on land, he starts building on the parking lot instead of the beach. Whoops! Pearl needs to be more specific and break down the code even more. This interactive picture book is endorsed by computer science nonprofit *Girls Who Code*. It is a great choice for a preschool storytime focused on coding or STEAM.

Margaret and the Moon: How Margaret Hamilton Saved the First Lunar Landing by Dean Robbins; illustrated by Lucy Knisley. New York: mediaName Book, Alfred A. Knopf, 2017.

Did you know that a woman named Margaret Hamilton helped the National Aeronautics and Space Administration (NASA) put a man on the moon? A problem solver at heart, Margaret loved studying math to solve the world's problems. After attending the Massachusetts Institute of Technology, she became director of software programming for NASA and wrote original code that allowed a spacecraft's computer to solve any problems it might encounter. This picture book is short enough for storytime, and the illustrations—reminiscent of a graphic novel—make it appealing to a wide audience.

Grace Hopper: Queen of Computer Code by Laurie Wallmark; illustrated by Katy Wu. New York: mediaName Book, Sterling Children's Books. 2017.

This picture book biography follows the story of Grace Hopper from her childhood through her education and career as a computer programmer. Through creativity, ingenuity, and problem solving, Grace shows readers that hard work and determination are the keys to changing the world. Although too long for a traditional storytime, this book works well for a 1-to-1 read or a STEM-based program. The end pages include a detailed timeline of Grace's life and accomplishments.

Nonfiction Books (Best for Ages 4–7)

Hello Ruby [series] by Linda Liukas. New York: Feiwel and Friends, 2015.

- Hello Ruby: Adventures in Coding
- Hello Ruby: Journey Inside the Computer

Part stories, part activity books, these titles explore coding concepts through the eyes of Ruby, a "small girl with a huge imagination." Divided into short chapters, these books are ideal for kids who want a bit more challenge with their coding skills. Ruby is a problem solver; when her dad leaves her a postcard with a surprise game to find 5 gems, Ruby makes a plan with a map, a path, and step-by-step instructions. These books illustrate that coding is not only about numbers; it is about thinking outside the box. This series would be great for a teacher unit or longer sit-down read, but it is not an ideal choice for storytime because of its length.

Kids Get Coding [series] by Heather Lyons; illustrations by Alex Westgate and Dan Crisp. Minneapolis, MN: Lerner Publications, 2018.

- Kids Get Coding: Coding to Create and Communicate
- Kids Get Coding: Learn to Program
- Kids Get Coding: A World of Programming

Playful and appealing, this series introduces coding concepts and suggests activities to solidify a child's knowledge. The title *Learn to Program* gets into nitty-gritty coding vocabulary and details, but it does so in a clear, concise, easy-to-understand way. This series is designed for very beginning programmers who want to know coding vocabulary and different programming languages, but this book does not explain the *how* yet.

My First Coding Book: Packed with Flaps and Lots More to Help You Code without a Computer! by Kiki Prottsman; illustrated by Molly Lattin. New York: DK Publishing, 2017.

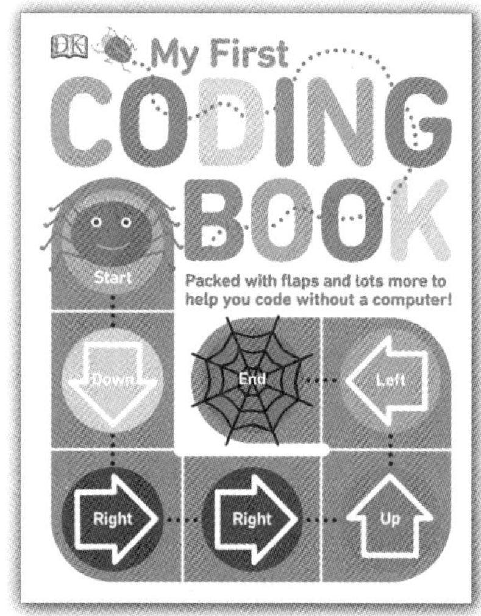

FIGURE 19.1

My First Coding Book

This book (figure 19.1) contains rich coding vocabulary, practical examples, and program ideas. It is my personal favorite because of its hands-on, lift-the-flap activities, non-jargon explanations, and bright, colorful illustrations. For example, on one double-page spread, readers can experiment with directional tabs to build a code that helps an "explorer" navigate through a maze without hitting a dangerous swamp, a terrifying lion, and a venomous snake. To check accuracy, readers lift a flap that gives the correct sequence. This book is sturdy, appealing, and a great beginning guide for those who are not familiar with coding.

PROFESSIONAL DEVELOPMENT MATERIAL FOR LIBRARY PROFESSIONALS

Coding as a Playground: Programming and Computational Thinking in the Early Childhood Classroom by Marina Umaschi Bers. New York: Routledge, 2018.

This resource is the first professional book to explore coding principles and programming for children ages 0–6. Marina Umaschi Bers, professor at the Eliot-Pearson Department of Child Study and Human Development and the Department of Computer Science at Tufts University, explains the theory and importance of digital and coding literacy, along with ideas of how to teach coding in the classroom and library. Broken into easy-to-follow chapters, this book is a great book to begin a coding program for preschool and younger children and to understand that coding develops 21st Century Skills.

LEARNING OUTCOMES

Participants will:

- Gain knowledge of a wide variety of books and materials to assist them with coding programs and projects, including board books, picture books, and nonfiction materials.
- Be inspired to utilize books for hand-on activities in their libraries.
- Decipher what coding books and projects work well for beginning coders.
- Understand coding skills are not just for computer specialists, but are a part of a holistic education that encompasses a diverse set of 21st Century Skills.

RECOMMENDED NEXT PROJECTS

- Make your own bibliography of recommended books and resources on coding for preschoolers. In addition to books, you can recommend well-reviewed apps, blogs, and articles.
- Develop circulating kits using books and materials for preschoolers and their parents. Choose a cute and inspired name, like “Tiny Tech Toes” or “Kiddie Coding Kits.” Pair a coding book with a robot, or a coding book with a list of screen-free coding activities and instructions.

20

Coding Stations in a K-3 School Library

DANIELLE ARNOLD

School Library Media Specialist | Belmar (New Jersey) Elementary School

PROJECT DESCRIPTION

Learning stations have been a part of classrooms for years. Educators value the opportunity to differentiate instruction in a small setting, while most students enjoy the ability to move from station to station and engage in a variety of activities during a period of time. In this activity, you will learn how to incorporate coding stations into your library environment. The stations can be modified by leveling the activities or simply by adding or deleting stations to ensure participants' needs are met.

The stations included focus on children in kindergarten through third grade but can be modified to be easier or more challenging if needed. Children will have a blast making binary bracelets, acting as a robot, and being able to code on a device.

Age Range

- Kids (Ages 3–7)

Type of Library Best Suited For

- Public libraries
- School libraries

Cost Estimate

- $25 and higher
- Costs will depend on the stations selected and the number of supplies needed for each.

OVERVIEW

Coding stations require a lot of planning, including determining how long the program will take place, how many staff and volunteers are available to assist with the program, and identifying the number of participants your library can accommodate. The number of supplies available will ultimately determine how many participants and stations your program will have. It is recommended that group sizes stay to approximately 4 participants and have at least 1 staff member or volunteer to teach the mini-lesson and assist participants.

Additionally, it is imperative when planning to implement stations that classroom management is established early on and participants are aware of the rules and their expectations. When planning, ask and answer these questions to ensure that the routines are established:

- How will I group students?
- How much time is needed at each station?
- How will students know where to go next?
- What will students do when they get to each station?
- What do students do if they finish the task early?
- How should a student ask for help?
- What does cleanup look like?

Software/Hardware Needed

Station 1: Binary/Pattern Bracelets

- Colored plastic beads
- String/chenille stems (pipe cleaners)
- Binary Bracelets Worksheet from Code.org
- Crayons

Station 2: Robot Turtles

- Think Fun Robot Turtles board game

Station 3: Robot Races

- Alex Toys Future Coders Robot Races

Station 4: Cube Stackers

- Alex Toys Future Coders Cube Stackers

Station 5: ScratchJr

- Devices with ScratchJr app

Station 6: Ozobots

- Ozobot robots and cards
- Black, blue, green, and red markers
- Paper

STEP-BY-STEP INSTRUCTIONS

Preparation

- Answer all of the questions that are listed in the "Overview."
- Set up the space to best accommodate each station.
- Set up each station with the materials and supplies needed.

PROJECT INSTRUCTIONS

Station 1: Binary/Pattern Bracelets—recommended for any group size

- Show Code.org video if time permits.
- Introduce key term, **binary**, a way of representing new information using only 2 options (Code.org).
- Model an example for students—find the first letter of your name.
- Choose 2 colors (one to represent 0 and one to represent 1).
- Complete the binary bracelet code on the worksheet.
- Once completed, have students create a bracelet using the beads copying their paper bracelet.
- Younger participants may make a bracelet using a pattern rather than binary code.

Station 2: Robot Turtles by Think Fun—recommended 1 game per 4 participants

- Demonstrate how to use Robot Turtles.
- Set up the board game according to the provided instructions.
- Model how to play the board game.
- Participants will take turns creating an algorithm using the arrow cards to make their turtle move from the start to their colored gem.
- Participants are allowed to use 1 card per turn.

- The game continues until all participants reach their gem. Emphasize that there is not a first, second, third, or last place.
- Inform students that if they make a mistake with their code, they can hit their "bug" button and shout "bug!" to fix their mistake.
- To make the game more challenging, you can add obstacle cards for participants to avoid.

Station 3: Robot Races by Alex Toys Future Coders—recommended 1 game per 4 participants

- Demonstrate how to use Robot Races (figure 20.1).
- Assign the roles to participants. One participant will be a robot, the second will be the computer program, the third will be the game board designer, and the fourth will be the timer.
- The game includes 20 level cards. Have the designer use the level cards to set up the track or have the designer create his own track for the robot to follow.
- The game includes 30 directional arrows. Have the programmer use the directional arrows for the robot to follow. Encourage the programmer to also verbalize the directions. Example: Take 1 step forward, turn left 90 degrees, etc.
- While the robot is navigating through the track, have the timer time the robot.
- Repeat with other participants to see if they can beat the record time.

Station 4: Cube Stackers by Alex Toys Future Coders—recommended 1 game per 2 participants

- Demonstrate how to use Cube Stackers.
- Using the provided puzzle cards, participants will follow the sequence to build animal bots with cardboard cubes.
- Participants will check their finished bot against the answer key. If something is different, participants will find the "bug" and try again.

Station 5: ScratchJr—recommended up to 2 participants per device

- Demonstrate how to use ScratchJr. Show participants how to change their character and background, add movement and voice, etc.
- Participants will log in to ScratchJr to create their own story.
- Have participants create a new program or continue from a previously saved program.
- Select a character and a background (setting) for your story.

- Using the different programming blocks, participants will drop and drag to create a script for the character to follow.
- Ensure participants include a Start code block to make their script run.
- Encourage participants to add multiple pages, backgrounds, and characters to their story.

Station 6: Ozobots—recommended up to 4 participants per Ozobot

- Explain to participants that they will be using colors to code a robot.
- Demonstrate how to use Ozobots.
- Ask students what speed they want the Ozobot to drive. Read the choices from the Ozobot Color Code Reference Chart. Ask a participant to answer the question.
- Explain how the lines must be drawn. Use the Ozobot Color Code Tips Sheet.
- Demonstrate a correct line and an incorrect line.
- Using the correct line, use the Ozobot Color Code Reference Chart to draw the speed the participant responded.
- Demonstrate more examples if needed.
- Provide participants with supplies.
- Encourage participants to use the provided cards to create their own color codes.

LEARNING OUTCOMES

Participants will:

Station 1: Binary/Pattern Bracelets—The Binary Bracelet Lesson Plan from Code.org is available at https://code.org/curriculum/course2/14/Teacher/.

- Encode letters into binary.
- Decode binary back to letters.
- Relate the idea of storing initials on a bracelet to storing information in a computer.

Station 2: Robot Turtles by Think Fun

- Use commands and understand their outcomes.
- Combine commands to form a line of code.
- Encounter bugs and then examine code and edit accordingly.

Station 3: Robot Races by Alex Toys Future Coders

- Break big problems into smaller ones.
- Understand the importance of providing detailed instructions.
- Check line of code for bugs and edit as needed.

Station 4: Cube Stackers by Alex Toys Future Coders

- Break big problems into smaller ones.
- Follow a sequence to create a bot.
- Check line of code for bugs and edit as needed.

Station 5: ScratchJr

- Design a story, including a setting and characters.
- Create and sequence instructions.
- Move blocks into the scripting area to create a line of code.

Station 6: Ozobots

- Learn how to operate an Ozobot.
- Create lines for the Ozobot to follow.
- Create a color code for Ozobots to follow.

RECOMMENDED NEXT PROJECTS

- Each station can be modified to be more or less challenging. It is recommended that participants continue with these stations until they've completed and mastered the lesson or activity.
- Once ready to create a new station, try:
    - Chapter 16: Bee-Bot Bowling by Marissa Guidara
    - Chapter 10: Mazes and Games: How to Integrate Algorithm Design with Analog Preschool and Family Activities by Paula Langsam and Amy Steinbauer

21

Integrate Picture Books to Teach Computational Thinking Skills

DANIELLE ARNOLD

School Library Media Specialist | Belmar (New Jersey) Elementary School

PROJECT DESCRIPTION

In this project, you will learn computer science and computational thinking skills while reading your favorite picture book! Children will be engaged from the story read aloud through the movement activity, which focuses on teaching the child how to **sequence**. Participants will see the importance of breaking a large problem into smaller, more manageable steps. During the movement activity, participants will see firsthand how to write an **algorithm**, what it's like to be a **programmer**, and how to fix a **bug**.

Age Range

- Kids (Ages 3–7)
- Tweens (Ages 8–12): This project is geared toward ages 5–7, but it can be modified for older kids by selecting an age-appropriate book.

Type of Library Best Suited For

- Public libraries
- School libraries

Cost Estimate

- $0–$150

OVERVIEW

In this project, participants will be exposed to computer science and computational thinking (CS/CT) skills through literacy. When integrating picture books into computer science, one of the most important strategies you can do is transition your common language to include computer science concepts. For example, instead of instructing students to summarize the story, now ask them to sequence the story. When defining concepts, provide a clear definition, examples, and ask students for understanding. Regularly using CS and CT vocabulary in your instruction reinforces coding concepts in a nondirective approach, and the learners will begin to use these concepts in their common language as well.

In the example provided, *The Very Hungry Caterpillar* by Eric Carle was used with kindergarten-age students, but this project can be modified for any age group by selecting a book with high interest and that is age appropriate for your audience. The project can be completed in under an hour, depending on the length of the story and the number of activities you wish to complete afterward. If your library has enough staff or volunteers, it would be recommended to read the story in a whole group setting and then break off into smaller groups of 4–6 students to complete the activities.

Software/Hardware Needed

This project can be modified to be plugged or unplugged.

- Unplugged equipment
  - *The Very Hungry Caterpillar* by Eric Carle
  - Cutouts of the events in the story using 8" × 11" paper
  - A large grid on the floor using either tape, a purchased mat, or carpet
  - Printouts of grids and events in the story for participants
  - Scissors for participants
  - Glue for participants
  - Crayons (optional)
  - Whiteboard (optional)
  - Whiteboard markers and eraser (optional)
- Plugged equipment
  - *The Very Hungry Caterpillar* by Eric Carle
  - Cutouts of the events in the story using 8" × 11" paper

- A large grid on the floor using either tape, a purchased mat, or carpet
- Devices with ScratchJr installed

STEP-BY-STEP INSTRUCTIONS

Preparation

- Create cutouts of each of the foods in the story, a caterpillar, and a butterfly.
- Create cutouts of directional arrows.
- Create a large grid on the floor either using tape or a purchased mat.
- Create a smaller grid and illustrations of events in the story. Make copies for participants.
- Gather glue, scissors, and crayons for participants.

PROJECT INSTRUCTIONS

- Prior to reading, inform students they will need to remember the sequence of events throughout the story. Define the term **sequence**: a particular order in which related events, movements, or things follow each other (dictionary .com) or provide a similar definition.
- Read aloud the story, *The Very Hungry Caterpillar* by Eric Carle.
- Following the story, place the butterfly (start code) and caterpillar (end code) on the grid. Place them in opposite areas to create a maze for students.
- Then, call on volunteers to identify the foods that were eaten in the story. Each time students correctly identify a food, have them place 1 of the cutouts on a random square on the map. This step does not need to be completed in chronological order to the story.
- Next, tell students they are going to create an **algorithm**: a list of steps to finish a task (Code.org) or similar definition. The task will be to get the caterpillar to eat the foods in the correct sequence of the story, ending at the butterfly.
- Select 1 student to be the **computer** and the rest of the class will be **programmers**.
- Programmers will take turns using the directional arrows to navigate the computer through the story. Encourage students to say their directions as well (for example, "turn right" or "turn right 90 degrees" for older students).

- Record the algorithm on the board or have a student write the algorithm on the board.
- If students make a mistake in their code, let them shout, "**bug**!": an error in a program that prevents the program from running as expected (Code.org).
- Together, students will find the bug and make changes.
- When the task is completed, have students repeat by moving the cutouts on the grid and assigning new roles.

LEARNING OUTCOMES

Participants will:

- Retell a story using computer science and computational thinking skills.
- Be introduced to vocabulary terms: **sequence, algorithm, programmer, computer,** and **bug**.
- Break larger problems into small ones.
- Work together in a collaborative setting to create an algorithm.

RECOMMENDED NEXT PROJECTS

- Participants can complete this activity on paper independently or with a partner.
- Participants create a similar activity using Scratch/ScratchJr.

PART II

PROGRAMS FOR TWEENS

(AGES 8-12)

22

Scratch Coding for Tweens

Creating Cartoons

KARLENE TURA CLARK

Coordinator of Circulation Services and Student Employment

Chester Fritz Library, University of North Dakota, Grand Forks

PROJECT DESCRIPTION

Scratch is a free coding program developed by the Lifelong Kindergarten Group at the Massachusetts Institute of Technology Media Lab in 2007 to help students ages 8–16 with no computer or coding experience begin to explore the ability to make games and cartoons in an easy and safe environment. It addresses multiple subject areas, including language arts, science, math, computer science, and the arts through graphical blocks that represent commands. It also encourages digital citizenship as they learn to work, act, and model in ethical connectivity while helping them become computational thinkers, creative communicators, and empowered learners. Many schools are already utilizing Scratch as part of computer classes, but students may create within the library and seek help with it.

This *Dinosaurs at the Movies* project creates a cartoon where the "sprites" interact, speak, and move.

As an instructor, a "classroom" can be requested to help manage student projects within a single class or across multiple "classrooms" at https://scratch.mit.edu/educators#teacher-accounts/. Instructors use their own e-mail for all student accounts in the group, allowing them to get all accounts ready before the first session.

Age Range

- Tweens (Ages 8–12)
- Young adults (Ages 13–18)

Adults Type of Library Best Suited For

- Public libraries
- Academic libraries

School Libraries Cost Estimate

- $0
- Libraries already have the necessary equipment, as listed under "Software/Hardware Needed." The only cost is librarian time in preparation and teaching.

OVERVIEW

Dinosaurs at the Movies is a cartoon that teaches the commands that allow "sprites" to move, speak, and interact with each other. Learners are shown how to create backdrops and change the appearance of their sprites.

Software/Hardware Needed

- Computer speakers
- Network connection (The author has found that the Chrome Internet browser works the best.)
- Method of projecting the instructor project during the lesson
- Current version of Adobe Flash Player

STEP-BY-STEP INSTRUCTIONS

Preparation

- Set up accounts ahead of time.
- Create a classroom account, if desired.

Engage

- Have students log in.
- Give them 10minutes to play a few example cartoons. For example:
    - https://www.youtube.com/watch?v=TJ-KwrTDDI4/ (basic animation)
    - https://scratch.mit.edu/projects/850247/#player/ (Yoda vs. the Door)
    - https://scratch.mit.edu/projects/119277479/ (Ghost in the Library)

Create

- The instructor demonstrates on a screen, letting students follow along with the steps to create a foundational project: a short cartoon.
- Start by clicking Create in the upper left corner of the screen, next to the Scratch logo. The coding screen (currently empty) will appear on the right, with coding blocks in the center and their first sprite, Scratch Cat, in the center of the left window.
- At the bottom, delete the cat.
- To choose a new one, click the little figure next to New Sprite. Some of them will have only 1 image and some will have multiple costumes. For this project, choose Dinoaur1.
    - Click the Costumes tab at the center top. You'll see he has 7 costumes. Let's use him!
- He's going to need a backdrop. At the bottom left, click Stage and notice the blue box around it—this means it is the active item.
    - New backdrops can be added at the top center or under the Stage.
    - Just under the word *new* is an image of mountains, a pen, a folder, and a camera. For now, use the mountain portrait to choose a backdrop from the library.
    - Choose "the movies inside."
- Drag the dinosaur down to the lower left corner. His sprite box should now be outlined in blue again so we can work with him.
- Click the Scripts tab again.
    - To make anything happen, we need an Event (brown) to get things started. Specifically, choose "when green flag clicked."
    - Motion (blue) allows movement, sets locations, and determines graph coordinates. To make the dinosaur always start where he was moved to, now choose the block "go to x: O y: O." The numbers in the coordinates will be different for each person, depending on where the dinosaur is resting.
    - Drag the block over to the right pane and attach it under the Flag.
    - Move down to Looks (purple) and choose "say Hello! For 2 secs." Change the "hello" to "Should we go to the movie?"
- Because this is to be a cartoon, he needs someone to say this to. Let's make another Dinoaur1 sprite. (Repeat the fourth step above to find another dinosaur.)

  - Click the "i" in the top left corner of his box. Change his name to something like Movie Fan.
  - Size and direction—Costumes
    - Because he shouldn't be rude, go back to Costumes and, on the right side panel, flip him around so he faces the other guy.
    - Above the red stop symbol, there's an inkblot, a scissor, and options to enlarge or shrink. Let's make him a little smaller. Click the arrows and then click the sprite until he's the size you like.
- Switch back to the Scripts tab.
  - Just like the first dinosaur, we need the "when green flag clicked" block and that same blue motion block.
  - He needs to answer the first dinosaur with something like "hurray." Get the same purple block and type in an answer.
- Now, try pressing the green flag at the top, next to the stop button. You'll see that they both talk at the same time. In order for them to speak to each other, they need to Broadcast to each other.
  - This is under the orange Events blocks.
  - Dinoaur1 needs "broadcast message1" and Movie Fan needs "When I receive message1." Notice that this starts another set of blocks. That's okay!
  - To make Dinoaur1 react to the answer, we'll need another "broadcast message1" block, only this time on Movie Fan.
    - But you can't have 2 message1s, so in the dropdown of the block, choose "new message."
    - Type in something that relates to what is being responded to. In this case, "hurray."
    - Back on Dinoaur1, add "When I receive message1" and choose the correct response in the dropdown.
- Now, cartoons need movement. Let's make Movie Fan dance! This will happen by doing costume changes on the sprite.
  - Back under purple Looks, add 3 Next Costume blocks, which will make him do an original dance.
  - Don't forget you can review the look under the Costumes tab.
- Try playing the cartoon by pressing the green flag again. What a short dance!
- To slow it down
  - Go to yellow Control and place a "wait 1 secs" block under each of the purple costumes.

    - This will still be too short, so place a yellow "repeat 10" block around those yellow and purple blocks just added. Change the 10 to 3.
- Now music needs to be added.
    - Starting with Dinoaur1, go to the Sounds tab and click the speaker to choose a sound from the library. Choose "dance celebrate."
    - Go back under the Scripts tab and find the light purple Sound block. Choose "play sound dance celebrate."
- But now the song is longer than the dances! To make Movie Fan dance longer
    - You can choose Control (yellow) options of either "forever" or "repeat 10."
        - For this project, choose "repeat 10" and place it only around the costume changes for him.
    - Under the repeat block, add "switch costume to dinosaur1-g" and use the dropdown to change it to costume a.
- Dinoaur1 needs to have a reaction to this silly Movie Fan. For him
    - Choose a purple Look "switch costume to dinosaur1-g" block to place under the "play sound" block.
    - Use the dropdown to pick the look you want. Don't forget you can review what each looks like under the Costumes tab.
- Try playing the cartoon by pressing the green flag again. Notice that they don't go back to the original costume? Let's fix that!
    - For each dinosaur, add a Look "switch costume to dinosaur1-a" under the first coding block of "when green flag clicked" "go to x:O y:O." You'll have to try moving the block on Dinoaur1 to find the right spot for it!
- Congratulations! You've just created your first 15-second cartoon. The challenge now is to add another 15 seconds. We're going to discuss how to do that in a minute. First, I want everyone to share their projects (and add them to the classroom, if relevant).
    - The share button is up in the top right corner.
    - Next, in the top left corner, you need to give your cartoon an original name.

See the complete code in action—Dinosaur Dancing created by the author: https://scratch.mit.edu/projects/236796387/.

Playtime

For tweens, the lesson should take about 40 minutes. By this point, they are ready to start playing and try doing it for themselves. They need to be given

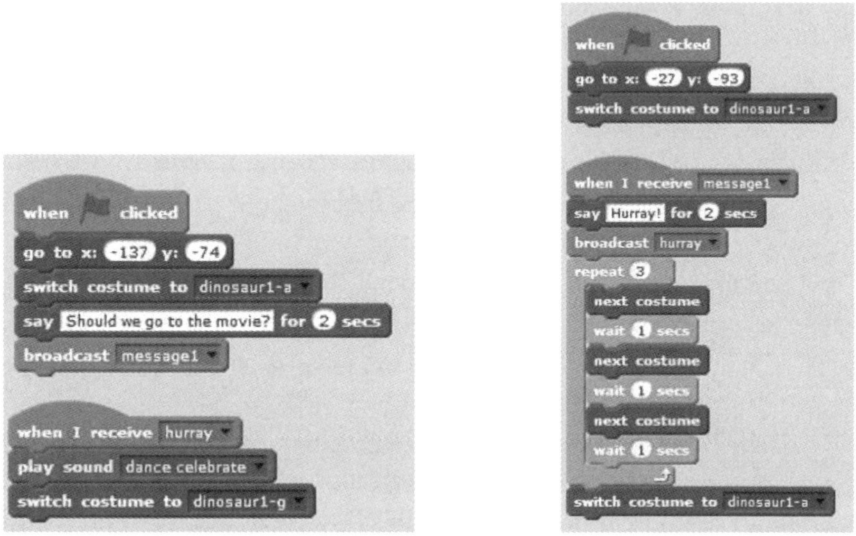

```
when [flag] clicked
go to x: -137 y: -74
switch costume to dinosaur1-a
say Should we go to the movie? for 2 secs
broadcast message1

when I receive hurray
play sound dance celebrate
switch costume to dinosaur1-g
```

Dinoaur 1

```
when [flag] clicked
go to x: -27 y: -93
switch costume to dinosaur1-a

when I receive message1
say Hurray! for 2 secs
broadcast hurray
repeat 3
    next costume
    wait 1 secs
    next costume
    wait 1 secs
    next costume
    wait 1 secs
switch costume to dinosaur1-a
```

Movie Fan

FIGURE 22.1

What the coding should look like at this point

time to play and explore. If another session is set up, give them permission to take their usernames and passwords home; encourage them to create a brand-new cartoon. Encourage them to explore their classmates' projects, look at other Scratch cartoons, and view the numerous YouTube videos created by others.

Additional Blocks to Discuss with Tweens

There are many ways to get the dinosaurs to move beyond the simple dance. By clicking on the different purple blocks, tweens can see exactly what each one does. Do they want the dinosaurs to walk? Under Motion, they can play with "move 10 steps" or "glide 1 secs to x:O y:O." The number of steps and the number of seconds determines how fast the sprite moves on the screen. Encourage them to play with the timing.

Do they want the dinosaurs to speak more? Ask if they remember how to make it happen (broadcasting). Perhaps they want the dinosaur to change color. To put the dinosaur back to "normal" at the beginning of each time, they will need to know to choose "set color effect to 0" under all other blocks attached to "when green flag clicked."

Assessment

Although a few tweens are apprehensive when first faced with Scratch, a recent group of 11 tweens that were taught by the author found that only 1 tween chose not to continue a 6-session module involving 3 different projects. The others were all very excited on the last day of class when they were told they could invite a grown-up along to show them what they learned. They were each asked to come to the front and demonstrate how each project (cartoon, maze, or point collecting) worked, as well as share 1 thing they had learned, were surprised by, or loved about the coding blocks.

LEARNING OUTCOMES

Participants will:

- Create a cartoon project that introduces the basic building blocks of the Scratch coding program, focusing on
  - Events (how to make things happen)
  - Looks
  - Motion
  - Costume
  - Sound
- Demonstrate mastery by
  - Having a cartoon that runs for a minimum of 30 seconds
  - Has a backdrop
  - At least 2 sprites (the figures on the screen) that speak, move, interact with each other, and have a variation (costume) change.

RECOMMENDED NEXT PROJECTS

- The foundational scripts needed for beginners in Scratch are Motion, Looks, Sound, Events, and Control. With just half of the scripts, young coders can do a wide variety of projects.
- Many quickly adapt to the coding structure and challenge themselves to more and more advanced projects, leading into the other scripts:
  - The Pen script teaches them how to draw lines by using "pen up" and "pen down," as well as how to change color and line size.

    - They can add these to the dinosaurs if they discover it, or it could be a second lesson where projects such as a maze, or an Etch-a-Sketch style game could be created.
  - Sensing, Operators, and Data are slightly more challenging and work best for tweens after a few other projects are created, each building and reinforcing previous blocks and coding.
    - A favorite encountered by the author is "enemies" tweens inserted into maze games, where the sprite is blocked, stopped, or reset by encountering another sprite.

REFERENCES

Brennan, K., Balch, C., & Chung, M. (2014). Creative Computing. *Harvard Graduate School of Education.* http://scratched.gse.harvard.edu/guide/files/CreativeComputing20141015.pdf.

ISTE. (2018). ISTE standards for students. *International Society for Technology in Education.* http://www.iste.org/standards/for-students/.

Scratch. (2007). https://scratch.mit.edu.

23

Bring Your LEGOs to Life with LEGO Education WeDo

JOANNA SCHOFIELD

Branch Services Librarian-Generalist | Cuyahoga County (Ohio) Public Library

PROJECT DESCRIPTION

Young children and tweens are known for being fans of LEGO. They build towers, Star Wars space ships, and every Minecraft set available. But imagine if their creations could come to life? That's possible using LEGO Education WeDo robotics kits (figure 23.1). These kits combine traditional LEGO blocks with robotic elements, such as sensors and motors. In these programs, students will build chomping alligators, twirling birds, or roaring lions. This program was conducted with LEGO Education WeDo 1.0. LEGO currently supports LEGO Education 2.0, which likely has different builds. In the near future, LEGO Education 3.0 will be available.

Age Range

- Tweens (8–12)
- Young adults (13–18)

Type of Library Best Suited For

- Public libraries
- School libraries

Cost Estimate

- $200
- Each LEGO Education WeDo 2.0 set costs $189.95. This set includes all of the LEGOs, software, and lesson plans needed for a group of 2.

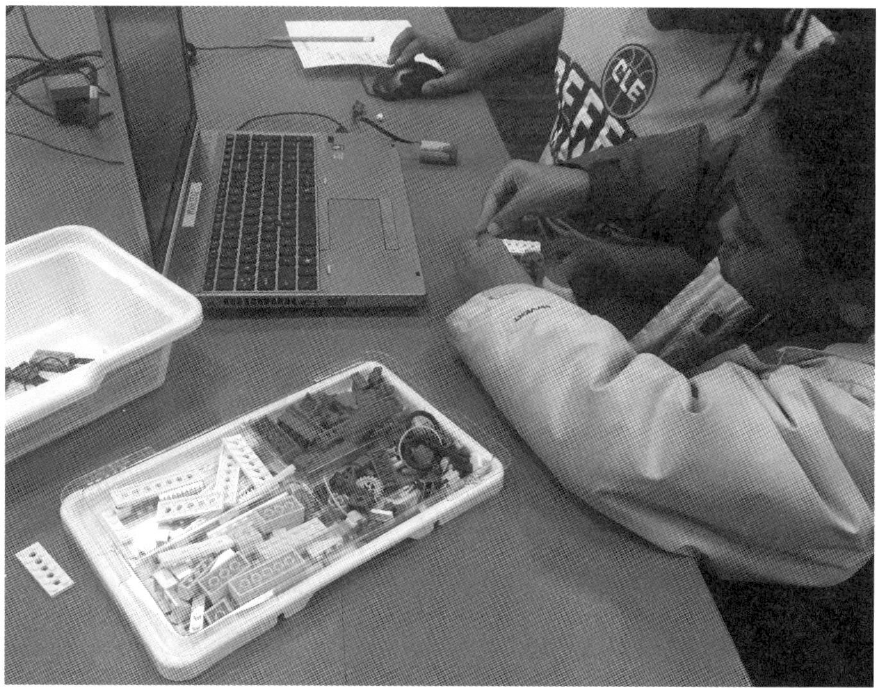

FIGURE 23.1

LEGO Education WeDo robotics kits

OVERVIEW

LEGO Education WeDo is an engaging robotics set for the earliest of explorers. When accompanied by an adult, children as young as 3 can build the creations in the building guide and program them using the LEGO Education WeDo software. In this program, participants select 1 of the 3 animals to build (Hungry Alligator, Roaring Lion, or Flying Bird). They begin by building their LEGO kits according to the instructions. After the groups build their animal creations, they are shown an example of the code on the computer and then follow the steps to program their creature to perform a certain task. For example, the Hungry Alligator opens and shuts his jaw, while the Roaring Lion leans up to roar and then settles back down when finished.

For this program, you ideally want 2 children to 1 LEGO Education WeDo set. When matching children into groups, try to keep the group members around the same age so that the older student does not monopolize the kit. The appropriate time for this program is 1–1.5 hours.

Software/Hardware Needed

- Projector attached to a computer that can run the LEGO Education WeDo software
- Each pair requires:
  - LEGO Education WeDo set, including LEGO bricks, motors, and sensors
  - Copy of the building instructions
  - Computer with LEGO Education WeDo software downloaded

Materials List

- Inquiry handouts (Sample shown in figure 23.2, at the end of the chapter.)
- Writing utensils
- Camera

STEP-BY-STEP INSTRUCTIONS

Preparation

- Check all of the kits against the inventory to make sure each kit has all the pieces.
- Design an inquiry handout to support children further exploring the gears, motors, or other pieces of their design.
- Set up every table with 2 chairs, 1 robotics kit, 2 copies of the handout, 1 computer, and a few writing utensils.
- Build your own lion, bird, and alligator so you are familiar with the building instructions and can answer questions from children as they progress through the process.

Tips for Working with the Robots with Kids

- In the beginning, walk through what each box contains, what motors and sensors look like, and give a brief overview of the LEGO Education WeDo software on the computer with the projector. Talk about what each icon means and show students how to navigate to the specific building instructions for each animal.
- Instruct students not to mix and match parts from other robotics kits. This will help tremendously with cleanup.

During the Program

- Observe students selecting their animal and working through the building phase. There may be frequent questions about where a brick goes or how the rubber bands work. If you are lucky enough to have volunteers at your program, this is a great time to assign volunteers to sets of groups to help facilitate the building phase.
- Once the building phase is complete, assist students with coding their design. The software is not intuitive and will most likely require a little assistance.
- Encourage each group to work through the modification handout to manipulate their designs in different ways and observe how small changes can alter results. A big thank you to Maria Trivisonno, children's supervisor at the Warrensville Heights, Ohio, Branch Library of the Cuyahoga County Public Library, for her modification handout (figure 23.2).
- Once the animal does its intended move, encourage students to play around with the code to have their animal do different things. There are sounds they can program, or they can remodel their animal to something new.
- Use your camera to take lots of pictures of students building and coding their designs to showcase at your library.

PULLEY CONFIGURATION SPEED		DIRECTION
Both gears are the same size		
One gear is small and one gear is large		
The gears are the same size, but the belt is crossed		

FIGURE 23.2

Modification handout

LEARNING OUTCOMES

Participants will:

- Learn how to follow directions to build a LEGO animal.
- Gain experience working with LEGO Education WeDo software.
- Develop strategies for working together in small groups.
- Gain a better understanding of motors, gears, rubber bands, and sensors.

RECOMMENDED NEXT PROJECTS

- Once students have mastered the animal creations, there are numerous other builds they can complete with the LEGO Education WeDo software and instructions (for example, titling airplanes or soccer players that kick a paper ball).
- Students can also continue to use LEGO Education WeDo robotics paired with Scratch.
- After students have gained mastery in building with LEGO Education WeDo, they can progress to working with LEGO MINDSTORMS robots.
- Students can also further explore coding using Codecademy, Scratch, or ScratchJr, or other coding tools like the Ozobot.

24

Program a Mad Libs Game with Python

CONNOR McNAMARA

IT Assistant | Clarkston (Michigan) Independence District Library

PROJECT DESCRIPTION

Get your game on! Teach patrons how to create a simple text-based game using Python, one of the computer science industry's most popular programming languages. Patrons of all skill levels will get an introduction to Python while being able to leverage their creative side by writing silly stories and having players fill in the blanks. Teach the fundamentals of programming, including variables and the print and input functions, all in a program that can be completed in less than 2 hours.

Age Range

- Tweens (Ages 8–12)
- Young adults (Ages 13–18)
- Adults

Type of Library Best Suited For

- Public libraries
- School libraries

Cost Estimate

- $0 provided you have some computers you can leverage for the project, ideally at a 1:1 computer-to-patron ratio

OVERVIEW

The Mad Libs game is the first in a series of Python projects designed to build on one another (the other 2 being the Number Guessing Game and the SUPER Number Guessing Game in chapter 25 and chapter 26, respectively). The instructions below lay out the specific code needed to make the project function, but they also include detailed descriptions of why, with the hopes that the skills learned here can be translated to other projects, guided or otherwise.

It's important to note that simply following the steps and writing the code are only 1 piece of the puzzle; understanding how those pieces function is the more valuable aspect of these projects and should be conveyed as the project is being facilitated.

Depending on the number of patrons attending, the average age, and experience, this project could take anywhere from 45 minutes to 1.5 hours. Even though it is designed as a starting point for the other 2 projects, it can be done as a one-off program if desired.

One librarian or staff member should be designated as the facilitator/instructor, leading the group through the project, while explaining the concepts along the way. Additional staff members (1 to 3) should be on standby to assist with any questions. It isn't necessary for any of these staff members to be proficient in Python or any programming language. The concepts that will be facilitated are all contained in this chapter.

Software/Hardware Needed

Required

- Thonny—A free Python IDE available at https://thonny.org
- Computers (preferably 1 for each patron)
  - Any computer will work. Thonny runs on all major operating systems and requires very little computational power for the basic programs patrons will be creating.
- Projector with screen (for the facilitator) or some other means of showing your computer screen to the group

Optional

- Flash drives for each patron (for saving their work and taking it with them)
- Paper and pens (for story planning; this can also be done on the computer)

STEP-BY-STEP INSTRUCTIONS

Preparation

- Ensure that Thonny is installed and running on all computers.
- Make sure all participating staff members read this chapter and complete the example project at least once.

PROJECT INSTRUCTIONS

Getting Started

- Have patrons open up Thonny (if it isn't already opened) and take them on a tour.
  - Thonny is an IDE, or integrated development environment, which is designed to make programming easier. Patrons could write code in any plain text editor, but IDEs make writing, running, and testing code much easier. The IDE is one of a programmer's most frequent and trusted tools.
  - Point out the split window design. The top two-thirds of the window is where patrons will be writing their code, while the bottom section is where they will see that code's output. This bottom section is called the Python shell, and its integration into Thonny is one of the main advantages of using it over a more traditional text editor like Notepad.
- Review what the project goals are. At its core, the Mad Libs game is made up of 3 parts:
  - Printing text to the screen so players can read the silly story
  - Taking in user input from players so they can change the story
  - Integrating players' input back into the original story

Their First Program

- The first goal is learning how to print text to the screen. Patrons can do this using Python's **print function**. On the big screen, type the following in the top of the Thonny window, while patrons follow along:

  print("Hello World!")

- Just like that, patrons have created their very first Python program! They can run the program by clicking the green "Play" button at the top of the Thonny window or by pressing the F5 key on their keyboard. Before they can see the fruits of their labor, however, the program will need to be saved.

    - Each time a Python program is run, it is saved first. Be sure patrons keep this in mind if they're making big changes to their project that they may want to undo.
    - Point out that Python is a case-sensitive language, which means that *Print* and *print* are not the same. Trying to run this program with a capital "P" would result in an error. This applies to all the code in this section and Python as a whole.
- After clicking Run, patrons will see "Hello World!" (sans quotes) appear in the Python shell.
- They can add multiple print functions to their program to print multiple lines of text. Try having patrons print their name on the next line after Hello World!:

```
print("Hello World!")
print("Connor")
```

- Notice how the code runs procedurally. That is, Hello World appears first in the shell because it is at the top of the program. If patrons wanted *Connor* to appear before *Hello World*, they would put that print function above the Hello World function.
    - Procedure is the first of the 3 pillars of programming. All procedure code runs from the top of the page to the bottom of the page.
    - These pillars form the basis for all computer programs.

Creating the Silly Story

- Now that patrons have gotten their feet wet with printing text to the screen, have them work on the creative aspect of the project. Have each patron create his own silly story, replacing key words in the story with blank spaces, to be filled in by the player (the person who will be playing the game).
- Once they've written out the story, either on paper, or on the computer, have participants enter it into Thonny as a collection of print statements. In place of the words that will be replaced by the player, put the word *type* in triangle brackets (adjective, noun, verb, etc.).
    - Here is an example story for the facilitator or patrons to use (if necessary):

```
print("This is the start of my <adjective> coding adventure!")
print("I've been so <adjective> to learn that my <noun> had to tell me
    to stop <present-tense verb> around the house!")
print("With my new coding skills, I plan to become a <career>, that
    way I can tell all the <plural noun> everything about coding!")
```

print("My name is <name> and I'm on my way to becoming an expert coder!")

- If patrons run this program now, they will see their entire silly story printed out, including the placeholder words. This is cool, but it isn't exactly what the game calls for. Their game needs some level of interactivity or else it isn't much of a game! That's where the second part of the project comes in: user input.

Getting Input

- Taking in text can be done in much the same way that patrons output text. The **print function** is used to output text, and, likewise, the **input function** can be used to ask the user to, well, input something!
- Type the following on the big screen, and have patrons follow along:

input("Enter an adjective: ")

- This line of code tells Python to prompt the player to enter in some text. Like the print function, the text placed in quotes (inside the parentheses) is printed to the screen. This time, however, it is used as a prompt so the player knows what to type.
- If patrons run this program, they'll notice that it stops when it reaches this line, with a flashing cursor being displayed next to their prompt. Typing something and then pressing enter will allow the program to continue.

```
Enter an adjective:Soggy
Enter an adjective: Soggy
```

FIGURE 24.1

An example of an input statement without and with a trailing space

  - Notice the extra space between the colon and the closing quote. This is intentional. Python, as with all programming languages, is very explicit. So while a space between the end of the prompt and the beginning of the user's input is expected, Python will not add one for us by default (figure 24.1).

- So, patrons can take in their player's input, but now there is another problem: As soon as the player hits enter, poof! The answer is gone. It hasn't been saved anywhere. Think of it like writing a paper on the computer and closing it without hitting save; you've entered in the information but didn't tell the computer where to store it.
- In programming, **variables** are used to store data.
  - Variables are the cornerstone of any programming language.

  - Patrons can think of variables, on a basic level, as a sort of magic box. Data gets put into the box, and then, later, the box can be opened up so that data can be taken back out and used.
- Using variables in Python is easy—all patrons need to do is come up with a name for them. Variable names must:
  - Start with a letter or underscore.
  - Contain only letters, numbers, or underscores.
  - Have no spaces.
- Have patrons modify their input statement from earlier to save what the player types to a variable:

```
adj1 = input("Enter an adjective: ")
```

- Here, a variable was created called adj1, and the information inside that variable will be whatever the player types when asked to enter an adjective.
  - Point out how the variable name lines up with what one would expect the variable to store. Just because a variable can be called whatever doesn't mean it should be given a random name. Variable names should be concise enough to be easy to remember and type but descriptive enough so their value can be ascertained at a glance.
- Have patrons verify that their input statements are working by printing the value of their variable.

```
print(adj1)
```

  - Mention how, when printing a variable, quotation marks aren't used. When Python sees a word outside of quotes, it assumes that word is special and it should know what to do with it. Because the patron already told Python what "adj1" means, when she defined the variable, Python knows to just print whatever the value of that variable is. If the patron tries to put "adj1" in quotes, however, Python would treat it literally and print "adj1" to the screen.
- Armed with the knowledge of variables and input functions, patrons can complete the second part of their game: getting the user to enter words. Before their print functions, have patrons place input functions to get all the words they will need for their story.
  - For our example project, the code would look like this:

```
name = input("Enter your name: ")
adj1 = input("Enter an adjective: ")
adj2 = input("Enter another adjective: ")
noun1 = input("Enter a noun: ")
```

```
verb1 = input("Enter a present tense verb: ")
career = input("Enter a career: ")
noun2 = input("Enter a plural noun: ")
```

- Remember, Python code runs from top to bottom, so players will be asked for their name, then an adjective, followed by another adjective, and so on.

Tying It All Together

- Now that patrons have learned how to print text to the screen, and how to take in user input, their last step is to put the 2 together.
  - Patrons know that they can print whatever they want by using the print function and putting the text they want displayed in quotes.
  - Patrons also know that they can print the value of variables by placing them inside the print function without quotes.
- What if they want to do both? For example, what if they want to write a sentence and replace one of the words with one that the player chooses?
  - To achieve this, patrons will need to use a concatenation character. Concatenation is just a big fancy word for "putting 2 things together."
  - Examine one of the sentences from the example story, with a variable concatenated to it:

    ```
    print("This is the start of my", adj1,"coding adventure!")
    ```

  - Notice how the comma appears outside of the quotation marks before and after the variable. This tells Python that we want the value of our variable "adj1" to be placed at this spot in the sentence.
- Just like all problems one can solve with programming, this problem has multiple solutions. Instead of commas, it is possible to use the plus sign, like this:

    ```
    print("This is the start of my " + adj1 +" coding adventure!")
    ```

  - The difference here is that the comma adds in spaces automatically (and would do data conversion if necessary—more on that in the Number Guessing Game), while the plus does not. Because this game only requires concatenating to provide output, the comma is much more effective in this scenario.
- With that, patrons can finish their game. Have them add variables to all of their print statements as placeholders for our player's chosen words:

```
print("This is the start of my", adj1,"coding adventure!")
print("I've been so" , adj2 , "to learn that my", noun1, "had to tell me
    to stop", verb1, "around the house!")
print("With my new coding skills, I plan to become a",career,", that
    way I can tell all the", noun2, "everything about coding!")
print("My name is" ,name, "and I'm on my way to becoming an expert
    coder!")
```

- Now, if patrons run their game, they will be prompted for a set of words at the beginning, via their input functions. Then, those words will be saved to variables and plugged into their silly story. For reference, here is the completed code for the project:

```
name = input("Enter your name: ")
adj1 = input("Enter an adjective: ")
adj2 = input("Enter another adjective: ")
noun1 = input("Enter a noun: ")
verb1 = input("Enter a present tense verb: ")
career = input("Enter a career: ")
noun2 = input("Enter a plural noun: ")
print("This is the start of my", adj1,"coding adventure!")
print("I've been so" , adj2 , "to learn that my", noun1, "had to tell me
    to stop", verb1, "around the house!")
print("With my new coding skills, I plan to become a",career,", that
    way I can tell all the", noun2, "everything about coding!")
print("My name is" ,name, "and I'm on my way to becoming an expert
    coder!")
```

  - Mention that the order you get the variables in doesn't dictate what order you use them in. In this example, for instance, the game asks for the player's name first but doesn't actually use that information until the end of the story. Once a variable has been defined (assigned a value) it can be used anywhere as many times as necessary.

- Patrons can now use the remaining time to modify their games, adding additional print functions and input functions, to expand the story. Now is also a good time to have patrons play each other's games. Our completed game is shown in figure 24.2.

```
Shell
>>> %Run SillyStoryGenerator.py

  Enter your name: Connor
  Enter an adjective: fuzzy
  Enter another adjective: soggy
  Enter a noun: library
  Enter a present tense verb: leaping
  Enter a career: librarian
  Enter a plural noun: cats
  This is the start of my fuzzy coding adventure!
  I've been so soggy to learn that my library had to tell me to stop leaping around the house!
  With my new coding skills, I plan to become a librarian , that way I can tell all the cats everything about coding!
  My name is Connor and I'm on my way to becoming an expert coder!
>>> |
```

FIGURE 24.2

A sample of our completed game

LEARNING OUTCOMES

Participants will:

- Learn how to output text to the screen via Python print functions.
- Get an introduction to procedure-based code, 1 of the 3 core pillars of programming.
- Learn how to ask players for input and understand how to save that information.
- Learn how to combine variables and static text into print functions to create a dynamic program.

RECOMMENDED NEXT PROJECTS

- Chapter 25: Program a Number Guessing Game with Python by Connor McNamara
- Chapter 26: Program a SUPER Number Guessing Game with Python by Connor McNamara

25

Program a Number Guessing Game with Python

CONNOR McNAMARA

IT Assistant | Clarkston (Michigan) Independence District Library

PROJECT DESCRIPTION

Continue creating games with Python! Building on the concepts from the Mad Libs game, patrons will learn how to generate random numbers, and let players try to guess what they are! Show patrons how to build a smarter game with decision code in the form of "if" statements, and get an introduction to data types--all in one simple project that can be completed in under an hour, for patrons of any skill level.

Age Range

- Tweens (Ages 8–12)
- Young adults (Ages 13–18)
- Adults

Type of Library Best Suited For

- Public libraries
- School libraries

Cost Estimate

- $0 (provided you have some computers you can leverage for the project, ideally at a 1:1 computer-to-patron ratio)

OVERVIEW

This Number Guessing Game is the first of 2 games found in this book. This project stands on its own but is then iterated upon in chapter 26: Program a

SUPER Number Guessing Game with Python. In addition, the instructions assume that patrons have already completed the Mad Libs project (in chapter 24) and are familiar with the concepts discussed there. Although it isn't strictly necessary that patrons have completed that project before doing this one, many of the skills learned there are used here.

The instructions below lay out the specific code needed to make the project function, but they also include detailed descriptions of why, with the hopes that the skills learned here can be translated to other projects, guided or otherwise.

It is important to note that simply following the steps and writing the code are only 1 piece of the puzzle; understanding how those pieces function is the more valuable aspect of these projects and should be conveyed as the project is being facilitated.

Depending on the number of patrons attending, the average age, and experience, this project could take anywhere from 30 minutes to 1 hour. Even though it is designed as the middle of a 3-part series, it can be done as a one-off program with modifications. (Namely, teaching the concepts introduced in the Mad Libs project as well as the new ones. Note that this will inflate the time prediction.)

One librarian or staff member should be designated as the facilitator/instructor, leading the group through the project, while explaining the concepts along the way. Additional staff members (1 to 3) should be on standby to assist with any questions. It isn't necessary for any of these staff members to be proficient in Python or any programming language. The concepts that will be facilitated are all contained in this chapter and the previous Mad Libs chapter.

Software/Hardware Needed

Required

- Thonny—A free Python IDE available at https://thonny.org
- Computers (preferably 1 for each patron)
    - Any computer will work. Thonny runs on all major operating systems and requires very little computational power for the basic programs patrons will be creating.
- Projector with screen (for the facilitator) or some other means of showing your computer screen to the group

Optional

- Flash drive for patrons to save their work

STEP-BY-STEP INSTRUCTIONS

Preparation

- Ensure that Thonny is installed and running on all computers.
- Make sure all participating staff members read this chapter and complete the example project at least once.

PROJECT INSTRUCTIONS

Getting Started

- Before patrons begin another exciting coding adventure, review the goals for this project. Like with the Mad Libs game, this game can be broken into three key parts:
  - Generate a random number within a certain range
  - Let players guess a number of their own
  - Compare the 2 numbers to see if the player wins or loses
- Along the way, patrons will also have to tackle the concept of data types, which will be explored later in this project.

Getting the Random Number

- The first problem patrons will need to solve is how to pick a number for the player to try and guess. It wouldn't be much fun if this number was the same each time, and as the programmer, the patron won't be around to change it every time the game is run.
- Python has a built-in module called random, which can generate random numbers.
  - What is a module? One important thing to understand about programmers is that they don't like reinventing the wheel, so to speak. If code has already been written to solve a particular problem, there's no reason to waste time creating another version.
  - Modules help with this. Modules are a collection of functions, or prewritten code, which can be leveraged in different programs. For example, the random module contains functions for generating random numbers from a variety of different algorithms, useful for a Number Guessing Game.

  - Some modules may be very specific, and contain very few functions, while others can be vast and varied, with many functions useful for solving a wide range of problems.
  - Colloquially, larger modules are sometimes referred to as libraries. The term *library* doesn't have a formal definition in Python, but the concept is analogous to the brick-and-mortar library patrons are probably learning in right now: a repository of information and resources patrons can leverage in day-to-day life, or, in this case, Python programs!
- The random module comes with Python, but it isn't included in new programs by default. This is because not every program will need to use the code contained in the random module.
- To make use of all the functions in the random module, have patrons add this at the top of their game:

  import random

- Now that the game has access to the code in the random module, generating a random number is easy. Have patrons type the following code below the import random line.

  number = random.randint(1, 10)

  - This code creates a variable called number, which stores the value of a random number between 1 and 10.
  - Point out the syntax for the random number generation (figure 25.1). First, from left to right, patrons specify that they want to pull code from the random module. Next, they specify that they want to use the randint function, which generates a random integer. Finally, this function allows us to specify different parameters in the parentheses. In this case, we can specify the range we want our random number to be generated in.
  - randint is a function, just like print and input, but it is coming from the random module.

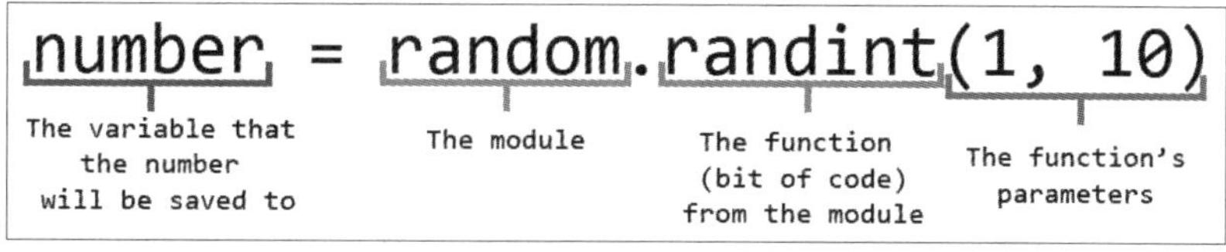

FIGURE 25.1

A visual breakdown of the random number generation code

- Have patrons verify that their random number generator is working as intended by printing the number (figure 25.2) and running the program a few times to see the different results. Have them place this code after their random number generation.

  print(number)

  - Remember that "number" is the name of the variable that stores this random number. If the patron used a different variable name, put that in the parentheses instead.

```
Shell
>>> %Run NumberGuessingGame_pt1.py
  5
>>> %Run NumberGuessingGame_pt1.py
  6
>>> %Run NumberGuessingGame_pt1.py
  9
>>> %Run NumberGuessingGame_pt1.py
  5
>>> %Run NumberGuessingGame_pt1.py
  3
>>>
```

FIGURE 25.2

A sample output of the random number generation

- After they've verified that the random number generator is working properly, have patrons erase the print statement; they wouldn't want to give away the number before the player gets a chance to guess!

Building the Game

- Now that the game has a random number to work with, it's time to let the player take his best guess at what it is. Remind patrons that they can accomplish this with the input function:

  playerGuess = input("Guess a number between one and ten ")

- Now, the game has a random number selected by the computer, and it has the player's guess as to what that number is. The final step is to compare the 2 and see if the player was right.
- Patrons can do this using an **if statement.** If statements are how programmers build smarter programs; if statements allow those programs to make decisions. They do this by asking a simple true/false question. For example, "is the player's guess the same as the randomly generated number?" If the answer is yes, the game will run one set of code, whereas if the answer is false, the game will run another set of code.

- In Python, if statements look like this:

```
if (playerGuess == number):
print("You Guessed Correctly!")
else:
print("You Guessed Incorrectly!")
```

- In English, this would read: If the variable playerGuess is equal to the variable number, then print "You Guessed Correctly!" Otherwise, print "You Guessed Incorrectly!"
- Up until now, all the code patrons have written has been procedural code, that is, every line runs from top to bottom.
    - This marks their first foray in decision code, the second pillar of programming. Executing (the running of the code) still starts at the top, but depending on the answer to the question, either the code directly under the **if statement** will run (printing "You Guessed Correctly!") or the code below the **else statement** will run (printing "You Guessed Incorrectly!")
    - It isn't possible for both pieces of code to run—it will always be one or the other.
- Point out how 2 equal signs are used for comparison. This is how Python differentiates between setting a variable and checking a variable.
    - One equal sign is used to set a variable equal to a new value, like patrons did earlier when they generated the random number or took the player's input.
    - Two equal signs are used if patrons want to check and see if a variable is equal to something else. For example, this game requires patrons to check and see if the variable playerGuess is equal to the variable number.
    - Remember: one set, two check.
- Also remind patrons to pay attention to the indentation. This is important as it is how Python knows when to run certain pieces of code. Any code indented under the if statement will run if the statement (our true/false question) is true, while any code indented under the else statement will run if the statement is false.
    - Even though this game has only 1 line for each of these paths, it is possible for multiple lines of code to exist under 1 section of an if statement.
- Finally, if patrons are getting errors, be sure that they're not forgetting colons. It is very easy to forget the trailing colons, but leaving them out will prevent the code from running!

Dealing with Data Types

- At first glance, it seems that the game should be done now. All the pieces are there, a random number is generated, players are asked to guess, and then the game checks to see if they're right. However, if patrons play their game, they'll notice that they never actually win.
- To "debug" the game, have patrons print the number after it is generated but before the input function asking them to guess. That way, they will be able to confirm that they aren't just getting very unlucky.

```
...
number = random.randint(1, 10)
print(number)
playerGuess = input("Guess a number between one and ten ")
...
```

- This is because the random number is an **integer** while the number the player types in is a **string**.
    - Integers and strings are **data types**, and they tell a programming language what type of data it is dealing with.
    - Patrons are probably familiar with integers from math class; an integer is just any whole number. That's why the randint function never generates any decimal numbers—because it only generates integers, and integers are always whole numbers!
    - **String** is probably a new term, though. In programming, strings are simply a string of characters. Typically, this refers to letters or words, but strings can be numbers as well.
    - The input function always saves whatever the user inputs as a string.
- So when Python evaluates the if statement, it asks: "Is 5 the string equal to 5 the integer?" And the answer is no. Even though the player guessed 5, and the random number was 5, they weren't of the same data type, so the program doesn't work as expected.
- All hope is not lost, however. Python makes it easy to convert strings to integers! Have patrons make this modification to their if statements:

```
if (int(playerGuess) == number):
        print("You Guessed Correctly!")
else:
        print("You Guessed Incorrectly!")
```

- **int()** is another function, just like print, input, and randint. This function takes whatever data is put inside the parentheses and tries to convert it to an integer. Provided the player enters a number, this handy function will convert that number from a string into an integer.
    - If players don't enter a number, say they type in a letter, the game would crash because it isn't possible to convert a letter to an integer. For now, assume that players are going to enter numbers only.
    - Note that this is an in-place conversion only; the value of the playerGuess variable isn't actually changing.
- With that quick change, the game is complete! Be sure to instruct patrons to remove the print function that prints the random number if it was added back in for testing purposes.
- Have patrons play each other's completed games.
- For completeness, here is the finished code for the Number Guessing Game Part 1:

```
import random
number = random.randint(1, 10)

playerGuess = input("Guess a number between one and ten ")

if (int(playerGuess) == number):

        print("You Guessed Correctly!")
else:
        print("You Guessed Incorrectly!")
```

LEARNING OUTCOMES

Participants will:

- Learn about Python modules and how to import them.
- Learn how to generate random numbers in Python.
- Learn about decision code with if statements, the second pillar of programming.
- Get an introduction to data types, learning about integers and strings.
- Learn how to convert a string to an integer in Python.

RECOMMENDED NEXT PROJECTS

- Chapter 26: Program a SUPER Number Guessing Game with Python by Connor McNamara

26

Program a SUPER Number Guessing Game with Python

CONNOR McNAMARA
IT Assistant | Clarkston (Michigan) Independence District Library

PROJECT DESCRIPTION

With the first Number Guessing Game (in Chapter 25) completed, it's time to ramp up the complexity. You'll start by showing patrons how to modify the code of the original Number Guessing Game to include multiple attempts at guessing the number; this will introduce the idea of loops, and with them the third and final pillar of programming: repetition. Next, you'll detail how to modify the game to give the player hints as to what the number is. Finally, you'll give patrons some additional practice with data conversion to give their game a satisfying conclusion.

Age Range

- Tweens (Ages 8–12)
- Young adults (Ages 13–18)
- Adults

Type of Library Best Suited For

- Public libraries
- School libraries

Cost Estimate

- $0 (provided you have some computers you can leverage for the project, ideally at a 1:1 computer-to-patron ratio)

OVERVIEW

The SUPER Number Guessing Game is an iteration of the first Number Guessing Game, found in chapter 25. It is meant to be the conclusion to a 3-part series of Python workshops designed to teach the basics of programming in general and Python specifically. The first project in the series (the Mad Libs game in chapter 24) is not required, but its concepts are. The first Number Guessing Game is required, as this project picks up right where that one left off.

The instructions below lay out the specific code needed to make the project function but they also include detailed descriptions of why, with the hopes that the skills learned here can be translated to other projects, guided or otherwise.

As with the previous chapter, it is important to note that simply following the steps and writing the code are only one piece of the puzzle; understanding how those pieces function is the more valuable aspect of these projects and should be conveyed as the project is being facilitated.

Depending on the number of patrons attending, the average age, and experience, this project could take anywhere from 30 minutes to 1 hour. One librarian or staff member should be designated as the facilitator/instructor, leading the group through the project, while explaining the concepts along the way. Additional staff members (1 to 3) should be on standby to assist with any questions. It isn't necessary for any of these staff members to be proficient in Python or any programming language. The concepts that will be facilitated are all contained in this chapter and the previous 2 chapters.

Software/Hardware Needed

Required

- Thonny—A free Python IDE available at https://thonny.org
- A completed Number Guessing Game Part 1 project
- Computers (preferably 1 for each patron)
    - Any computer will work. Thonny runs on all major operating systems and requires very little computational power for the basic programs patrons will be creating.
- Projector with screen (for the facilitator) or some other means of showing your computer screen to the group

Optional

- Flash drive to save patrons' work on

STEP-BY-STEP INSTRUCTIONS

Preparation

- Ensure that Thonny is installed and running on all computers.
- Make sure all participating staff members read this chapter and complete the example project at least once.

PROJECT INSTRUCTIONS

Getting Started

- Instruct patrons to create a new Thonny project by clicking File>New in the Thonny window.
- Because the SUPER Number Guessing Game builds directly on to the first Number Guessing Game, copy all the code from the original Number Guessing Game into this new project and have patrons do the same.
    - For reference, here is the code for that project again:

```
import random
number = random.randint(1, 10)
playerGuess = input("Guess a number between one and ten ")
if (int(playerGuess) == number):
print("You Guessed Correctly!")
else:
print("You Guessed Incorrectly!")
```

- Get patrons to save the new project somewhere they'll remember with the name SUPER Number Guessing Game.

  With the project set up, review the new features patrons will be including in the SUPER Number Guessing Game (SNGG).

    - Allow players multiple guesses. In the original Number Guessing Game, the player gets one guess to get the number right. In the SNGG, the project is going to expand to give the player many guesses.
    - Give the player hints. If the player's first guess is too low or too high, the new game will let him know to guide him toward a correct answer.
    - Add a friendly conclusion. In the original Number Guessing Game, if the player guessed incorrectly, she was never told what the number actually was. Patrons will fix this in the SNGG by including a "Game Over" line that tells the player what the random number was.

Giving Multiple Tries

- Currently, the player only gets one try at guessing the number correctly because the code all runs procedurally (from top to bottom) and there is only one line of code that allows the player to guess.
- To allow the player another chance at getting the number right, patrons will need to repeat the code they have written.
    - They could copy and paste the code as many times as needed, but this would get very messy very quickly. What if they wanted to give the player 20 different guesses? 100?
    - What if players get the answer correct? They're still going to have to sit through all the lines of code they've copied.
- Thankfully, there is a better way: **Loops!** Loops are the backbone of repetition code that, as the name implies, repeat sections of written code. This is the third and final pillar that all programming is built on (the other 2 being procedure, learned in Creating the Silly Story in chapter 24, and decision, learned in Number Guess Game Part 1 in chapter 25).
- For this task, patrons will be using **while loops,** which are a lot like if statements, where they ask a true/false question.
    - If the answer is true, the code under the while loop runs. If the answer is false, the code under the while loop is skipped.
    - The difference is that when the code under the while loop is finished running, Python returns to the original question and asks it again. If the answer is still true, the code runs all over again!
- While loops rely on a **loop control variable** to tell them if they should keep repeating or not. This variable forms the base of the true/false question.
    - For this example, demonstrate how to give the player 3 guesses. That means patrons will need to repeat the section of code where they ask the player to guess a number, and the following if statement, 3 times.
    - Instruct them to create a loop control variable, call it guess, and set it equal to 0. Create this variable just after the number variable.

      ```
      guess = 0
      ```

    - Now, they'll need to create a while loop. Just before the input function, where the player is asked to make a guess, have the patron enter this code:

      ```
      while guess < 3:
      ```

    - Just like an if statement, Python only knows code belongs to a loop if it is indented under that loop. Because all the code left in the game has to repeat 3 times, have patrons indent all the rest of the code in the game under the new while loop.

- Their game should now look like this:

```
import random
number = random.randint(1, 10)
guess = 0
while guess < 3:
    playerGuess = input("Guess a number between one and ten ")
    if (int(playerGuess) == number):
            print("You Guessed Correctly!")
    else:
            print("You Guessed Incorrectly!")
```

- The loop control variable is guess because this variable tells the loop when to continue.
  - As long as guess is less than 3, the code under the loop will continue to run.
- Patrons might notice a problem with this new game already. Guess is set equal to 0 at the beginning of the game, but it is never changed! Therefore, guess can never be greater than 3, and the loop will never end!
  - This is called an **infinite loop,** and it often happens when the loop control variable is not modified (or modified incorrectly) inside the loop.
  - To get the loop to stop, patrons need to add 1 to the value of guess each time the player gets a wrong answer.
  - To do this, have patrons set the value of guess equal to itself plus 1, after telling the player they guessed incorrectly.

```
else:
        print("You Guessed Incorrectly!")
        guess = guess + 1
```

  - Alternatively, they can use this shorthand format that accomplishes the same thing with less typing:

```
else:
        print("You Guessed Incorrectly!")
        guess += 1
```

- Now, each time through the loop, if the player gets the wrong answer, the game adds 1 to the total count of the player's guesses. If that number hits 3, the loop ends and the game is over.

- But what if players get the right answer? After they guess correctly, the game is over. Currently, however, players will be asked to guess until they run out of guesses, regardless of whether they're right or not.
    - This problem could be fixed by simply setting the guess variable to 3 on a successful guess, but there is a better way.
    - The **break** statement tells Python to exit the loop and continue with the game.
    - By adding a break statement after telling the player he guessed correctly, the loop can end, and the player can revel in his hard-earned victory instead of being forced to guess again.

    ```
    if (int(playerGuess) == number):
            print("You Guessed Correctly!")
            break
    ```
- Have patrons swap and play each other's games. They should now all have 3 guesses to get the number correct instead of just one. Neat!

Helpful Hints

- Now that patrons are giving their players more than one guess, it would be helpful to guide those players in the right direction of the correct number if they get the answer wrong.
- Right now, the logic for determining if the player guessed the correct number or not is very binary.
    - The guess is equal to the number, and therefore they win.
    - Or it isn't, and they lose.
- Patrons need a way to get more granularity. If the initial if statement is good, they will always want to know if the player guessed correctly. Instead of a catch-all else statement, however, it would be nice to ask a follow-up question:
    - Is the number the player guessed lower than the correct number?
    - If not, is it higher than the correct number?
- This can be accomplished by using **elif statements**.
    - Elif is shorthand for else if, and it allows programmers to ask a follow-up question if the initial if statement question ends up being false.
    - So, for instance, the player guesses a number incorrectly, but instead of just telling her she's wrong, the elif statement triggers and asks if the number was higher than what she should've guessed.

Have patrons modify their current if statement to look like this:

```
if (int(playerGuess) == number):
        print("You Guessed Correctly!")
        break
    elif (int(playerGuess) > number):
        print("Your Guess was Too High!")
        guess += 1
    elif (int(playerGuess) < number):
        print("Your Guess was Too Low!")
        guess += 1
```

  - Essentially, this is just creating a new if statement within the existing if statement. The main difference is that these elif statements only run if the initial if statement is false. This makes sense, as the playerGuess variable cannot both equal the mystery number and be greater than it at the same time.
  - By using elif statements, instead of multiple if statements, the game saves the computer time. Because only one of these can be true, Python won't bother to check all of them, which it would do if they were separate if statements.
- Point out how the example adds another guess += 1 line to the new elif statement. Remember, all paths in the while loop need to increment the loop control variable (or contain a break statement) otherwise the game will get stuck in an infinite loop.
- Also mention that there is no else statement. It is possible to include an else statement at the end of all the elif statements, but in this case all possible paths are accounted for.
- Again, have patrons swap places and play each other's games. Now, in addition to having 3 guesses, the game will also give the players a hint if they guess incorrectly. Nifty!

A Satisfying Conclusion

- The last thing missing from the game is a conclusion. If the player is unable to guess the correct number, the game never tells him what the number was. It is the patron's responsibility to provide players with closure!
- The conclusion should only run after the player has either guessed the number correctly or exhausted all of her guesses. Therefore, the conclusion

shouldn't be nested within the while loop, otherwise it would repeat every time the player made a guess.

- After the while loop, have patrons add in a print function that says "Game Over!" Remember: This shouldn't be indented at all, otherwise Python will consider it to be inside the while loop, no matter how much white space is left.

```
while guess < 3:
        playerGuess = input("Guess a number between one and ten ")

        if (int(playerGuess) == number):
                print("You Guessed Correctly!")
                break
        elif (int(playerGuess) > number):
                print("Your Guess was Too High!")
                guess += 1
        elif (int(playerGuess) < number):
                print("Your Guess was Too Low!")
                guess += 1
print("Game Over!")
```

- Now, patrons will need to tell the player what the number was; add a second print function with this information.
    - Recall during the Creating Silly Story project, you taught 2 different ways to concatenate (read: stick together) variables and strings. Demonstrate the plus sign method first:

    ```
    print("The number was " + number)
    ```

    - Run the game and, uh-oh, that didn't work as intended (figure 26.1).

```
Game Over!
Traceback (most recent call last):
  File "T:\Connor's Files\Project Files\5
    print("The number was " + number)
TypeError: must be str, not int
```

FIGURE 26.1

An error received when trying to print a string and an integer to the screen in the same print function

- Reading the error message, patrons will see: "TypeError: must be str, not int." That sounds like data types!
  - Even though Python allows for passing an integer into the print function on its own and have it print to the screen without issue, trying to combine a string (the text "the number was ") and an integer together causes issues.
  - Just like when patrons compared the player's guess to the randomly generated number in part 1, the key here is to convert the number variable into a string.
  - This can be done in much the same way they converted the string value into an integer. Have patrons modify the final print statement to look like this instead:

```
print("The number was " + str(number))
```

- Again, this is an in-place conversion. The value of number is still an integer; the code is only converting it to a string for this one function.
- Now demonstrate the other method of concatenation, the comma:

```
print("The number was," number)
```

- Based on the last example, patrons might expect another error, but this code works without issue.
  - The clever Python creators knew that programmers often print text to the screen of various different datatypes and that typing in conversions can be a pain.
  - The comma aims to make concatenation for printing much easier by doing the data conversion and adding spaces automatically.
- Have patrons swap places and play their neighbor's game one last time. Now, they have a Number Guessing Game that generates a random number, lets players take a guess, and gives them clues if they get the answer wrong. Once the game is over, patrons have written the code to print a "Game Over!" message and let the player know what the number actually was. Nifty!
- For completeness sake, here is the full code for the SUPER Number Guessing Game project:

```
import random
number = random.randint(1, 10)
guess = 0
```

```
while guess < 3:
        playerGuess = input("Guess a number between one and ten ")

        if (int(playerGuess) == number):
                print("You Guessed Correctly!")
                break
        elif (int(playerGuess) > number):
                print("Your Guess was Too High!")
                guess += 1
        elif (int(playerGuess) < number):
                print("Your Guess was Too Low!")
                guess += 1

print("Game Over!")
print("The number was," number)
```

LEARNING OUTCOMES

Participants will:

- Learn about repetition, the third and final pillar of programming, with the use of while loops.
- Understand what a loop control variable is, why it is needed, and how to implement it.
- Learn about break statements and when to use them in a loop.
- Expand their knowledge of if statement by implementing elif statements.
- Gain a deeper understanding of data conversion and concatenation characters covered in the Creating Silly Story project.

RECOMMENDED NEXT PROJECTS

- Chapter 36: Choose Your Own Adventure: Bring Coding to Life with Interactive Storytelling by Kaitlin Frick and Grace Zell
- Chapter 40: Using Bloxels to Teach Storytelling and Video Game Design by Danielle Arnold
- Chapter 30: Beginner Video Game Coding and Design by Annamarie Carlson

27

Coding Music with Exceptional Learners

Mission Possible

MELANIE TORAN

Lead Librarian | Heritage High School, Newport News (Virginia) Public Schools

PROJECT DESCRIPTION (THE MOTIF)

What do your exceptional patrons come to the library to do? Access the computer to listen to music? Or watch the new song and dance challenges that have gone viral? Why not have these patrons be their own favorite artist? It is possible; the Mission is Possible!

Making music now is not what it used to be. In years past, making music was as simple as cutting on the 1980's Casio PT-1 keyboard and jamming to tunes. Music theory was embedded in the brain because melodies were pre-set and instruments were pre-selected to give the user an appreciation for music. However, users did not have to know anything about music to create instrumental melodies from the limited selections pre-loaded on the keyboard; they just knew that they needed one to make their own music. Now, making music is as easy as getting on your electronic device and coding musical phrases by using computational thinking (CT) to design what you want to hear. And you're no longer confined to monophonic sounds and limited rhythms that are pre-set.

Exceptional learners are motivated by music because music encompasses sensory modalities! Music is what one makes it; their own. Making music involves using CT to code musical phrases and music loops on an electronic device and not being confined to monophonic sounds.

Age Range

- Tweens (Ages 8–12)

Type of Library Best Suited For (The Choir)

- Public libraries
- Academic libraries
- School libraries

Cost Estimate

- $29–$2,500
- Packages and annual subscriptions to GROOVECODERS.COM are available at a discount price for schools and organizations.
    - An individual subscription costs $29 per user annually.
    - A school package (minimum of 10+ seats) costs $25 per user annually, including more than 25 lessons, student activities, and a teacher guide.

OVERVIEW
(The Prelude)

GROOVECODERS.COM inspires users to create original songs and learn the basics of programming vocabulary through CT and coding using computer science. There are more than 25 interactive lessons and assignments in each unit to help users arrange musical phrases and grooves by coding commands and experimenting through investigation. After completing tutorials, users can effectively write short codes to play grooves and beats from a custom music library.

This project can be a great summer program, an after-school club that can be held throughout the school year, or a program during school hours on select computers in the library for exploration. One student or multiple groups of students can participate and become coders through self-paced exploration or individualized instruction from librarians.

Software/Hardware Needed
(The Rehearsal)

- Apple- or Windows-based electronic device such as an Android tablet, iPad, Chromebook, or personal computer)
- GROOVECODERS.com web app installed on each electronic device (instrumental)
- Headphones (a cappella)

STEP-BY-STEP INSTRUCTIONS
(The Etude)

Preparation

- Make sure that all users who have expressed interest in the program have their own unique log-in.
- Keep all log-in information on hand in case someone forgets his username and password.
- Keep extra headphones on hand in case they become misplaced, mishandled, or mistakenly taken.

PROJECT INSTRUCTIONS

- Students log in using their unique user password and username.
- Use the teacher guide to describe to users the program's focus and to build your objectives for the session's intended outcome.
- Have students watch each short tutorial to get an understanding of coding basics.
- After watching the tutorial video, students must complete the exercises at the end of each module as a means of formative assessment. They have to write 2 sentences in a reflection box about what they learned from the video or answer a question by filling in the blank or using a drop-down box. Even though students are wearing headphones while they are working, they are not discouraged by being incorrect by hearing loud dings and buzzes. The next lesson will not load until the correct answer is submitted. This confirms the student uses computational thinking to understand coding basics. For students who have difficulty expressing themselves about what they learned, they can use an emoticon smiley face if they understand or a sad face if they do not understand or use colors (green if they understand, yellow if they think they "got it," or red if they don't understand).
- After students have gained understanding of the coding basics, they can move into song writing. This program not only introduces coding vocabulary and coding commands, but it also reinforces English skills of rhyming, patterns, and forms of poetry. Here is where students' creative juices can start to flow. Students will write a song using the song-writing techniques included in the program.
- After students have written a song using rhyming techniques (by making use of the rhyming dictionary embedded in the program) and coded a rhythm (by using the library of custom beats and grooves), they can listen to their original work by using the built-in audio recorder.

- Students can share their original work with others in the GROOVECODERS community. Users can create community posts, enter contests, and participate in group challenges as part of this online community.
- At this point, users determine their outcome. Students may wish to add music to their playlist from what they coded, or they can embed what they created onto their social media accounts, make videos, or create their own library of grooves.
- If they can **code** a **groove,** *mission accomplished!*

LEARNING OUTCOMES
(The Cadenza)

Participants will:

- Develop 21st Century Skills by collaborating with others through creativity and critical thinking.
- Become familiar with computational thinking through computer science.
- Transition from school to post-secondary opportunities using computer coding to explore options in the computer science field.

RECOMMENDED NEXT PROJECTS
(The Encore)

- Connecting youth to learning opportunities beyond the program is an excellent way for students to showcase what they have learned and can do. Sometimes the best teachers are students. Students in the program can instruct younger students how to code music using computers. When students become confident in the different levels of coding, they can become peer tutors to other students. This could serve as an introduction to coding techniques to younger students while building the student tutor's confidence.
- Involving the community in the implementation of the program allows other students, teachers, and stakeholders to see all the great things students are doing in and outside of school. Students who are more tech savvy can blog about their adventures in coding by creating posts, uploading clips of music they have created using code, and posting videos of their journey as they become coders. The surrounding community and the GROOVECODERS community can provide feedback and ask questions. Hopefully, the blog will inspire students with exceptional abilities to begin coding.
- Who says students with exceptional abilities can't teach? *Mission complete!*

28

Build an Automated Puppet with Arduino

JAMIE BAIR

Senior Public Services Librarian: Experiential Learning

Fort Vancouver Regional Libraries, Vancouver, Washington

PROJECT DESCRIPTION

Kids will learn how to use a microcontroller to attach a motor to a pull-string "jumping puppet." This project can be expanded to include the creation of other items powered by a motor. No prior microcontroller or coding experience necessary.

Age Range

- Tweens (Ages 8–12)
- Young adults (Ages 13–18)
- Adults

Type of Library Best Suited For

- Public libraries
- Academic libraries
- School libraries

Cost Estimate

- $30–$220
- $22 for Arduino Uno
  - https://store.arduino.cc/usa/arduino-uno-rev3/
- $4.10 for EMax ES08A Mini Servo Motor or a similar small servo motor
  - https://www.emaxmodel.com/es08a-ii.html#product_tabs_description_tabbed/

- The cost for pull-string puppets varies
  - We usually find these at yard sales or thrift stores. You can build your own inexpensive puppet: http://www.ucandostuff.com/Guide-895-How%20to%20make%20a%20jumping%20puppet%20from%20cardboard%20and%20string.aspx/
- $3/95 for a pack of male/male jumper wires
  - https://www.adafruit.com/product/758/

OVERVIEW

Participants will use the Arduino microcontroller to build automated puppets. Most Arduino projects begin with lighting a light, which teaches a lot of great fundamental concepts of wiring and coding microcontrollers. Participants new to microcontrollers are initially impressed with controlling lights, but their real interest lies in creating things that move. The Mini Servo is an easy-to-program motor that allows participants to quickly become comfortable with coding precise movements for inanimate objects.

There is an initial cost for this project, but Arduino Unos are great for prototyping and can be rewired and coded for multiple projects. A classroom set of 6 is recommended, with the expectation that up to 4 kids can work together on 1 board. The instructor has an additional Arduino to wire with the group. No breadboard is necessary for this project as participants will wire their motor directly to the Arduino.

Software/Hardware Needed

- Device to access Arduino IDE such as laptops or desktop computers
- Mini-screwdrivers to attach servo horn (white plastic tips)
- Paperclips or other small flexible metal object to fit into servo horn holes and attach to puppet strings
- Cardboard or craft supplies to construct a mechanism to hang puppets
- Arduino
- Mini Servo Motors (1 per board)
- Pull-string puppet
- Jump wires to connect motor to Arduino

STEP-BY-STEP INSTRUCTIONS

Preparation

- Play with an Arduino before leading this project. Get familiar with the resources available through the Arduino website at https://www.arduino.cc/en/Guide/HomePage/.
- Gain a basic understanding of circuits and how servo motors work. There are several great examples online.
- This project utilizes the sample code "Sweep" provided by Arduino. Find the code in the Arduino software:

  File → Examples → Servo → Sweep
- Assemble a demonstration version of the project ahead of the workshop so participants can observe the mechanisms.
- Attach clear plastic servo horns to all motors ahead of the workshop.
- Plug Arduinos into computers ahead of the workshop so the driver software can download.
- Divide supplies per group:
  - Arduino board
  - Arduino USB cord
  - Servo motor
  - Puppet supplies
  - Paperclip/wire
  - 3 male/male jumper wires (NOTE: any color is fine, but you can minimize confusion by providing wire colors that correspond to the motor wires (red/brown/orange).

PROJECT INSTRUCTIONS

- Have patrons observe the working puppet.
  - Potential observations will likely identify the basic components of this project: a motor, wires, microcontroller, and power.
  - The servo motor motion is 180 degrees. Discuss how many degrees are in a circle.
- Instruct patrons to open the Arduino software and load the Sweep code.
  - Take a moment to explore the comments (indicated with //) provided

in the code and discuss how comments help you understand how the code functions.

- Have participants predict how the code functions on the puppet.

- Next, ask patrons to observe the microcontroller board and motor wiring.
  - Have them compare the physical components to the code.
  - Patrons can predict how the motor may be wired to the microcontroller.
  - "myservo.attach(9)" indicates the servo will be attached to Pin 9 on the Arduino microcontroller board,
- Instruct patrons to wire the motor to Arduino.
  - Note: to avoid electric shock, do not plug Arduino into USB/power source while working on wiring.
  - Mini Servo Motors have 3 wires: red, brown/black, yellow/orange.
    - Red == power (think of the + side of a battery)
    - Brown/black == ground (think of the – side of a battery)
    - Yellow/orange == signal (how the Arduino talks to the motor)
    - Attach the male/male jumper wires into the female end of the motor wire.
    - Plug the red wire into 5V (5 volt) pin on Arduino.
    - Plug the brown/black wire into GND (ground) pin on Arduino (there are 2, either works).
    - Plug yellow wire into pin 9 (Digital Pin 9).
- Have patrons load the code onto Arduino.
  - Plug the USB cable into Arduino and computer.

    Verify the Sweep code, then Send to the Arduino.

    1. If you have trouble, check the port settings in Arduino.
       a. Tools → Board (Arduino Uno)
       b. Tools → Port (look for the COM with Arduino attached)
- They can then observe working motor. Once the motor is working, participants can attach a pre-made puppet or make their own.
- Using the paperclip or other thin, flexible wire, anchor the puppet string to the motor using a hole in the servo horn (figure 28.1).
- Patrons can observe the motion of their puppet and make adjustments to the physical rig.

- Next, they can then go into the code and edit the range of motion (in degrees).
- Discuss how to troubleshoot the code and make fine adjustments to the servo motor.
- Patrons can prototype the mechanism to make the puppet freestanding.
- Have patrons test the rig and adjust components.

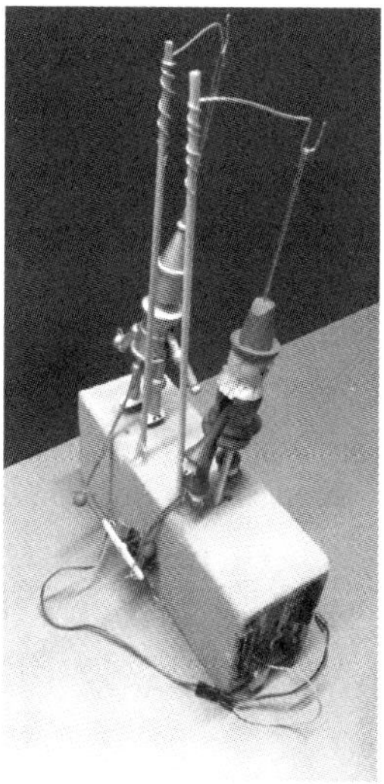

FIGURE 28.1

Wired and rigged freestanding puppet

LEARNING OUTCOMES

Participants will:

- Learn the basics of microcontrollers.
- Learn how to build a simple circuit.
- Learn how to program a servo motor.
- Learn to troubleshoot physical and digital components in a moving project.

RECOMMENDED NEXT PROJECTS

- Combine 2 puppets on 1 motor.
- Work together to combine motors and make several independent moving parts.
- Create a narrative to go with the puppets.
- Remove the servo horn and attach a toy or 3-D printed wheels to the servo motor.

29

Coding Camp for Tweens

ANNAMARIE CARLSON

Youth Librarian | Westerville (Ohio) Public Library

PROJECT DESCRIPTION

Technology is cool. Patrons of all ages want to learn what coding is and how to teach a robot to follow their commands. However, librarians may struggle with engaging tween patrons in deeper learning. In a standard 1-hour coding program, tweens will spend about 20 minutes defining basic coding vocabulary and discussing the applicability of coding in their everyday lives. Due to limited resources, students will spend the remaining 40 minutes shuffling between various activities, never spending more than 8–10 minutes with a single project. Even though this kind of program can inspire interest in coding, students who return for another coding program a week or a month later often forgot everything they learned previously. This lack of skill building, combined with new students at every program with varying knowledge levels, spurs the need to look for a new direction to focus technology programming.

To combat this lack of focused learning and skill development, consider creating a Coding Camp. This 4-day experience will allow 16 students to complete increasingly difficult coding challenges by regularly reviewing and building on skills learned the day before. Each day of the camp will focus on a different element of coding including:

- how computers work and computational thinking through unplugged activities;
- computational thinking and block-based coding;
- block-based coding with loops and conditionals; and
- using coding skills beyond programming robots to do tricks.

Age Range

- This program was designed for tweens, but the structure could be adapted for any age group.
- Tweens (Ages 8–12)

Type of Library Best Suited For

- Public libraries
- School libraries

Cost Estimate

- $1,400
- We created this program based on specific technology purchased through a grant. This program could be adapted based on robots, tablets, and computers a library may already own.
- The price estimate does not include access to 8 tablets with bluetooth capabilities and 8 laptops or computers with headphones.
- The above cost is based on 16 students working in pairs. The program cost could be reduced significantly if fewer students participated in the program or if students worked in larger groups (3 or 4 students per robot).

OVERVIEW

Coding Camp is a 4-day program with 16 students attending a 1.5 hour-session each day. Each session reviews and builds on material from the day before, so it is important to encourage students to attend every day. Each day focuses on a different topic:

Day 1: How Computers Work, Computational Thinking, and Unplugged Coding

Day 2: Block-Based Coding Introduction

Day 3: Block-Based Coding: Loops and Conditionals

Day 4: Applying Coding Skills Beyond Robots

This program could succeed with groups of 1–4 students, but the most learning will come from pairs of students sharing 1 tablet and 1 robot. Group work allows students to work through problems on their own and gain teamwork skills.

This program can be run with just 1 staff member, although having at least 2 people (such as 1 staff member and 1 teen volunteer) is ideal.

Software/Hardware Needed

Equipment

- 8 tablets with bluetooth capabilities
- 4 Dash robots and the Blockly app

- 4 SPRK+ Sphero robots and the Sphero Edu app
- 8 laptops or personal computers with access to the Internet
- 16 sets of headphones
- 8 sets of headphone splitters

Materials

- An open computer tower with individual computer components such as a CPU, RAM drive, hard drive, and power supply, although having additional computer components is beneficial)
- Jar of jelly
- Loaf of bread (may want multiple)
- Paper plates, paper towels, plastic knives, cleaning wipes
- 100 cups of the same size
- Paper and pencils
- 5 surfaces to write on (trays, books, etc.)
- Masking tape
- 48 empty plastic water bottles
- Large white paper (butcher paper or poster board)
- 4 Crayola markers
- 10 rubber bands
- *I Spy* books (optional)

Files

Day 1 PowerPoint: https://www.slideshare.net/aecarlson/coding-camp-day-1/

Day 1 Small Group Coding Activity Sheets: https://csedweek.org/files/CSEDrobotics.pdf

Day 2 PowerPoint: https://www.slideshare.net/aecarlson/coding-camp-day-2/

Day 3 PowerPoint: https://www.slideshare.net/aecarlson/coding-camp-day-3/

Day 3 SPRK+ Animal Guessing Game Introduction Packet: https://www.slideshare.net/aecarlson/day-3-sprk-animal-guessing-game-introduction-packet/

Day 3 SPRK+ Animal Guessing Game Explanation Packet: https://www.slideshare.net/aecarlson/day-3-sprk-animal-guessing-game-explanation-packet-116766739/

Day 4 PowerPoint: https://www.slideshare.net/aecarlson/coding-camp-day-4

Day 4 Scratch Introduction Packet: https://www.slideshare.net/aecarlson/coding-camp-day-4-scratch-introduction-packet/

Day 4 Scratch Building Challenge Project Sheet: https://www.slideshare.net/aecarlson/coding-camp-day-4-scratch-building-challenge-project-sheet/

Coding Resources Take Home Bookmark: https://www.slideshare.net/aecarlson/coding-camp-take-home-resources-bookmark/

STEP-BY-STEP INSTRUCTIONS

Preparation

- Before putting your program on the calendar, think about:
    - Staffing availability, including time for setup and cleanup
    - Ability to have a program at the same time on 4 consecutive days
    - Limiting the number of attendees based on the number of materials you have and the number of students your staff can handle
- Between a week and a month before the program:
    - Start collecting materials, especially an open computer tower with individual computer components to pass around to participants.
    - Explore the Blockly app and Dash robot and the Sphero Edu app and SPRK+ robot until you are comfortable with them. Test some of the activities listed in "Project Instructions" and make sure you are comfortable teaching them.
- Each day of your program:
    - Set out materials based on activities listed under "Project Instructions" for that day.
    - Set up a laptop and projector to show a PowerPoint with images and vocabulary focused on that day's activities.
    - Charge your Dash and SPRK+ robots with their mini-USB cables (days 2 and 3).
    - Charge your tablets (days 2 and 3).
    - Charge your laptops (day 4) (if necessary).

PROJECT INSTRUCTIONS

DAY 1

How Computers Work, Computational Thinking, and Unplugged Coding

Room Setup

- PowerPoint displayed
- One table at the front of the room for the group coding activity
- Students and instructors will sit on the floor in a circle until the small group coding activity when students will break into groups of 3.
- Space for 5 groups of 3–4 students to work on small group activities

Materials

- Introduce/Learn
    - PowerPoint (https://www.slideshare.net/aecarlson/coding-camp-day-1/)
    - An open computer tower with individual computer components such as a CPU, RAM board, hard drive, and power supply, although having additional computer components is beneficial
- Practice: Group Coding
    - Loaf of bread (may want multiple)
    - Jar of jelly
    - Paper plates, paper towels, plastic knives, cleaning wipes
- Practice: Small Group Coding
    - 5 sets of 20 cups
    - 5 instruction sheets (Page 9: https://csedweek.org/files/CSEDrobotics.pdf)
    - 5 sets of coding cup challenges (Pages 10–12), cut so that each group receives only one image at a time: https://csedweek.org/files/CSEDrobotics.pdf
    - 5 sets of paper, pencils, and a surface to write on

Activities

Introduce. Introduce the program by talking about the daily schedule and expectations.

Learn.

Talk about how computers work:

- Discuss the difference between physical hardware and software.
- Talk about the physical hardware found in a computer. Ask for examples. Pass around the open computer tower and the individual computer components and talk about what each part does. Typically, students have a lot of questions about the hardware.
- Talk about types of software. Ask for examples. Connect software to coding—coding is what makes computer software work and what tells those hardware components how to work together.
- Talk about basic coding vocabulary that you will be using throughout the program. Some attendees may know these words, so try to make most of this part of the program a discussion (instead of a lecture). Include words such as *algorithm, code/program, coding/programming, bug,* and *debugging.*

Practice: Group Coding. Students will "code" their instructor to make a jelly sandwich. Be as ridiculous as you like with this activity. For example, if a student tells you to "open the bread," you can tear the loaf in half, causing pieces of bread to fly everywhere. Students quickly catch on that they need to make their instructions very specific to get the desired result, and sometimes they need to work together to undo errors (debug their program). After this activity is complete, discuss as a group what students learned and how this might apply to coding.

Practice: Small Group Coding. Explain to students that now they will be coding one another in small groups. During this activity, 2 student coders will work together to write an algorithm to show a third student "robot" how to build a specific type of cup tower. The "robot" only understands 6 specific arrows, shown on page 9 of the activity guide (https://csedweek.org/files/CSEDrobotics.pdf).

- Break students into groups of 3–4.
- Give each group a basket of supplies, including 20 cups of the same size, blank pieces of paper, a few pencils, and a surface to write on.
- Each group will decide who will be their "robot" first. The robot will leave the other 2 group members and move to a different part of the room. Provide the robots with *I Spy* books while they wait.
- The remaining 2 coders will be given a picture of a simple cup pattern (typically involving no more than 4 cups). Cup patterns can be found on pages 10–12 of this packet: https://csedweek.org/files/CSEDrobotics

.pdf. Coders will write down instructions for the robot using just the 6 arrows on the instruction sheet. Coders cannot test their code using the cups—only the robot can touch the cups.

- When coders think they are ready, they will call the robot back to the group. The robot can only make the motions written on the paper. The robot cannot listen to any verbal instructions. The robot should not be able to see the picture of the cup pattern provided to coders.
- If the code works, then the group selects a new robot. That robot moves to the robot waiting area, and the 2 remaining coders receive another, more difficult cup image. Groups will repeat this cycle until you are out of time for the day.
- If the code does not work, the robot will return to the waiting area, and the coders will try to debug their program. They will repeat this cycle until the code is successful.

Discuss: At the end of each day, the group members come together and talk about what they learned and how the different activities connected to one another.

DAY 2

Block-Based Coding Introduction

Room Setup

- PowerPoint displayed
- Students will sit at the front of the room for the overview, facing the PowerPoint before moving to 1 of 4 Dash grids or 1 of 4 SPRK+ mazes.
- Dash setup
    - Create 4 5'×5' grids out of masking tape. Each grid square should be approximately 1'×1', although this will have to be adapted based on your space. Put 12 empty plastic water bottles on random grid intersection locations. Tape a masking tape "X" on the floor in front of each grid where you would like Dash to start.
    - Place a Dash robot and tablet near each grid. Connect each robot to its appropriate tablet in the Blockly app right before the program begins.
- SPRK+ Setup
    - Create 4 mazes on the floor out of masking tape. These do not need to be too difficult (ours typically involved 4–5 simple turns). Tape a masking tape "X" on the floor in front of each maze where you would like SPRK+ to start.

- Put another masking tape "X" near, but not overlapping, each SPRK+ maze. Make a small cup tower about 3' diagonally away from this "X."
- Place a SPRK+ robot and tablet near each maze. Connect each robot to its appropriate tablet in the Sphero Edu app right before the program begins.

Materials

- Introduction/Review/Learn
    - PowerPoint (https://www.slideshare.net/aecarlson/coding-camp-day-2/)
    - Dash robot and tablet opened to a new program in the Blockly app (to be put out for a group to use during practice)
    - SPRK+ robot and tablet opened to a new block-based program in the Sphero Edu app (to be put out for a group to use during practice)
- Practice: Dash
    - 4 Dash robots
    - 4 tablets with bluetooth capabilities opened to a new program in the Blockly app
    - Masking tape (taped down in 4 grids, as described under "Room Setup")
    - 48 empty plastic water bottles
- Practice: SPRK+
    - 4 SPRK+ robots
    - 4 tablets with bluetooth capabilities opened to a new block-based program in the Sphero Edu app
    - Masking tape (taped down in 4 mazes, as described under "Room Setup")
    - 4 sets of 6 cups

Activities

Introduce. Introduce the program by talking about the daily schedule and expectations.

Review. Review what you discussed the previous day. You could start the review by asking "what did we do yesterday?" and lead the conversation from there. Review specific concepts from the previous day, including the difference between hardware and software, identifying various parts of a computer and what they do, and defining coding vocabulary.

Learn.

Introduce the Dash and SPRK+ robots. Discuss what each can do. For example, Dash can talk, but SPRK+ does not make sound. Dash moves based on distance (in centimeter intervals), while SPRK+ moves based on speed and time (tell him how fast to drive and for how long). Ask if anyone has experience with either robot.

- Talk about block-based coding. In addition to holding up a tablet and showing the Blockly and Sphero Edu apps in action, show screenshots of the apps via that day's PowerPoint. Connect a tablet to the projector to show the apps in action that way as well. Talk about how to find blocks, how to add blocks, how to connect blocks to one another, how to edit the details of a block (such as how far students want Dash to go), and how to delete a block. Students picked up on how to do this on their own through their hands-on practice later on.
- SPRK+ adds an extra challenge because students cannot easily program it to move a certain distance and it is a sphere, so they have to check each time they give it a new set of code to make sure the robot is facing the direction they want it to move. To figure out how to tell the robot how far to move, instructors could teach students how to calculate distance based on time and speed. Another option is to instruct students to use trial and error, which encouraged the mindset that a program will not always go right the first time—and that is okay. To check the direction SPRK+ is going to move, each robot comes with its own protractor. Students can use this to measure the angle they would like SPRK+ to point toward, or they can select the "AIM" button in the top right corner of the Sphero Edu app and make sure that the robot's taillight (a little light that shines when the "AIM" button is pressed) is pointed away from the direction they want the robot to move. The "AIM" approach only works if participants are writing 1 line of code at a time as they work to complete the maze (instead of writing an entire program at once).

Practice: Split the group of 16 tweens into pairs. Four pairs will start with Dash, and 4 pairs will start with SPRK+. Split the remaining time between the 2 robots. Each pair should have about 20–25 minutes per robot. As you divide the groups into these activities, expect to need to check on each robot to make sure it is still linked to the appropriate tablet.

Activity 1: Dash

Challenge one: Make Dash talk. The first challenge is simply to get students comfortable using the tablets and block-based coding. In their pairs, students will figure out how to make Dash say "okay" and then how to make Dash say "Huh?" after a student speaks to Dash. This activity should take no more than 5 minutes.

Challenge two: Robo bowling (figure 29.1). This challenge should take up the bulk of students' time. Students need to create code that makes Dash knock down all of the water bottles on the grid in 1 try. They will mostly use blocks from the "Drive" category, including "Forward," "Backward," "Turn Left," and "Turn Right." If students are struggling, they can try to complete this activity using individual lines of code instead of writing the entire program at once. If students move through this activity quickly, place the leftover cups from the SPRK+ groups in select spaces on the masking tape grids with some of the original water bottles. Tell the group that they still need to knock down the water bottles, but they cannot touch the cups. Before rotating, ask each group to clear out any created program to provide a blank screen for the next group.

FIGURE 29.1

Three coders watch Dash successfully knock down the majority of the bowling pins (toilet paper tubes) during the robo bowling activity

Activity 2: SPRK+

Challenge one: Make SPRK+ knock down the cup tower. Each group should place the robot on the masking tape "X." The goal is to use coding blocks to drive SPRK+ to knock down the cups. This activity is meant to help students get used to this robot, particularly because the move forward and turn blocks are not as intuitive as Dash. This activity should take no more than 5 minutes. If students are struggling with it, suggest they move on to the next challenge.

Challenge two: Complete the maze. This challenge should take up the bulk of students' time. Students should place SPRK+ at the "X" at the entrance to the maze and create code that allows SPRK+ to navigate through the masking tape. Students should try to create 1 set of code that allows the robot to complete the entire maze with 1 press of the start button. If students are struggling, they can try to complete this activity using individual lines of code instead of writing an entire program that can be run at once. If students move through this activity quickly, have 2 groups switch mazes if each maze is different. Alternatively, give a group a roll of masking tape and encourage students to make their own maze. Before rotating, ask each group to clear out any created program to provide a blank screen for the next group.

SPRK+ tip: The Sphero EDU app has a free drive feature that students will find easily. They cannot turn off this feature, and they can access it from the screen where they are creating their programs. SPRK+ robots can travel across a large meeting room in seconds, very easily becoming a distraction for other students. Discourage students from using the free drive feature. We often gave students a few minutes at the end of their SPRK+ time to free drive.

Discuss. At the end of the day, the group comes together and talks about what they learned and how the different activities connected to one another.

DAY 3

Block-Based Coding: Loops and Conditionals

Room Setup

- PowerPoint displayed
- Students will sit at the front of the room for the overview, facing the PowerPoint.
- Dash setup
  - Spread out 4 pieces of large white butcher paper or poster board on the floor along with a marker and a few rubber bands.
  - Place a Dash robot and tablet near each piece of paper. Connect each robot to its appropriate tablet in the Blockly app right before the program begins.
  - Have 4 extra pieces of white poster board or butcher paper nearby to replace the used paper after the groups rotate.
  - Place a copy of Dash Loopy Shapes Challenge Cards near each robot.
- SPRK+ setup
  - Place 4 SPRK+ robots around the room. Connect each robot to its appropriate tablet in the SPRK+ app right before the program begins. The robots will not need to move around extensively, so a large amount of space is not needed.
  - Place an SPRK+ Animal Guessing Game Sheet near each robot.
  - Have copies of the SPRK+ Animal Guessing Game Explanation Packet on hand.

Materials

- Introduction/Review/Learn
    - PowerPoint (https://www.slideshare.net/aecarlson/coding-camp-day-3)
- Practice: Dash
    - 4 Dash robots
    - 4 tablets with bluetooth capabilities opened to a new program in the Blockly app
    - 8 pieces of white butcher paper or poster board
    - 4 markers
    - 8–12 rubber bands
    - 4 sets of self-created Dash Loopy Shapes Challenge Cards
- Practice: SPRK+
    - 4 SPRK+ robots
    - 4 tablets with bluetooth capabilities opened to a new block-based program in the Sphero Edu app
    - 4 SPRK+ Animal Guessing Game Sheets (https://www.slideshare.net/aecarlson/day-3-sprk-animal-guessing-game-introduction-packet/)
    - 4 sets of Animal Guessing Game Explanation Packets (https://www.slideshare.net/aecarlson/day-3-sprk-animal-guessing-game-explanation-packet-116766739/)

Activities

Introduce. Introduce the program by talking about the daily schedule and expectations.

Review. Review what you discussed the previous 2 days. Start by asking "what did we do yesterday?" and lead the conversation from there. Review specific concepts from the previous days, including coding vocabulary, the abilities and limitations of both Dash and SPRK+, and details about how to check and change SPRK+'s direction.

Learn.

Introduce loops by asking if anyone knows what a loop is. After defining a loop as the "action of doing something over and over again," ask for a volunteer. Instruct the volunteer to "walk around the room." Repeat this exact phrase 4 times.

Ask students what you could have said to make this process easier. Draw the connection between a person saying "walk around the room" 4 times and "Repeat(4) [Walk around the room]."

Continue the conversation by asking: if "Repeat(4) [Walk around the room]" means walk around the room 4 times, what does "Forever [Walk around the room]" mean?

- Introduce conditional statements. After defining conditional statements such as "If one condition exists, then it commands the program to do something," talk about the phrasing of conditional statements as "If ________, then do ______ else (if NOT this), then do ________."

  Practice the concept of conditionals with the If/Then backyard coding game (Source: https://leftbraincraftbrain.com/if-then-backyard-coding-game-for-kids/). The instructor is the programmer, and students are the computers. The programmer gives computers a command such as, "If I point to the sky, then you jump up and down." Once this level is mastered, continue the game with harder commands such as "If I point to the sky, then you jump up and down, else stand on one foot." If you want to make it more challenging, have speed rounds where computers sit down if they do not follow commands correctly.

Practice: Split the group of 16 tweens into pairs. Four pairs will start with Dash, and 4 pairs will start with SPRK+. Split the remaining time between the 2 robots. Each pair should have about 20–25 minutes per robot.

After you divide the groups into their first stations, expect to have to check on each robot to make sure it is still linked to the appropriate tablet.

Activity 1: Dash and Loopy Shapes

Students should attach a marker to Dash with the rubber bands so that when Dash moves, the uncapped marker draws a line on the ground. During this activity, students will use loops to make Dash create different shapes in as few lines of code as possible. We provided students with challenge cards that included squares, rectangles, hexagons, octagons, and circles.

If students are struggling, they can try to complete this activity using individual lines of code instead of writing the entire program at once. If students move through this activity quickly, encourage them to try to code Dash to write their name in as few lines of code as possible. Before rotating, ask each group to clear out any created program to provide a blank screen for the next group.

Activity 2: SPRK+ and Animal Guessing Game

Students will use conditionals to create the Animal Guessing Game (figure 29.2) based on Sphero Edu's "Block 2: If/Then, Else" activity (https://edu

.sphero.com/cwists/preview/2143x/). When the program is completed correctly, every time SPRK+ is lightly tossed (or shaken), he will turn green and play a random animal sound. When caught, SPRK+ will turn red and not play a sound. When students have completed their code and are playing the game, they will gently toss SPRK+ from player to player. When a player catches the robot, she will guess what animal sound it just made. If she gets the animal sound correct, she will toss the robot to the next player. If she does not get the animal sound correct, she will have to act out the correct animal. The instructor can act as a judge to determine if the animal sounds were guessed correctly.

FIGURE 29.2

Three coders work together to create the Animal Toss Game using SPRK+

The Sphero Edu website provides videos with step-by-step explanations about how to make this program. We did not show students these videos. Instead, we provided them with this packet: https://www.slideshare.net/ae carlson/day-3-sprk-animal-guessing-game-introduction-packet/. This packet lists all of the blocks that students will need to use to create their code, plus details on the accelerometer feature, which tells SPRK+ when it is being tossed.

If students are struggling with this program, provide them with the following packet, which, working with the introduction packet, provides step-by-step instructions on how to create the code: https://www.slideshare.net/aecarlson/day-3-sprk-animal-guessing-game-explanation-packet/. If students move through this activity quickly, encourage them to brainstorm ways to make the game more challenging and figure out how to implement those challenges in their code, such as adding a timer that will end the game after a specific amount of time. Before rotating, ask each group to clear out any created program to provide a blank screen for the next group.

SPRK+ tip: The animal sounds will play from the tablet, not from the robot. Make sure the tablet's sound is turned up.

Discuss. At the end of each day, the group comes together and talks about what they learned and how the different activities connected to one another.

DAY 4

Applying Coding Skills Beyond Robots

Room Setup

- PowerPoint displayed
- Students will sit at the front of the room for the overview, facing the PowerPoint.
- 8 laptops or computers will be spread around the room with 2 chairs at each computer. Each computer will also have 2 sets of headphones attached to the computer with a splitter, plus a Scratch Building Challenge Project Sheet.
- Have copies of the Scratch Introduction Packet on hand for any groups that need extra help learning how to use Scratch.
- *Optional:* Have chairs set up facing the PowerPoint for parents to sit in approximately 15 minutes at the end of the program so they can see what their tweens learned all week.

Materials

- Introduction/Review/Learn
  - PowerPoint (https://www.slideshare.net/aecarlson/coding-camp-day-4/)
- Practice
  - 8 laptops or computers
  - 16 sets of headphones
  - 8 headphone splitters
  - 8 Scratch Building Challenge Project Sheets (https://www.slideshare.net/aecarlson/coding-camp-day-4-scratch-building-challenge-project-sheet/)
  - 4–8 Scratch Introduction Packets (https://www.slideshare.net/aecarlson/coding-camp-day-4-scratch-introduction-packet/)
- Optional Parent Showcase
  - 16 Coding Resources Take-Home Bookmarks (Westerville Library specific sample found here: https://www.slideshare.net/aecarlson/coding-camp-take-home-resources-bookmark/)

Activities

Introduce. Introduce the program by talking about the daily schedule and expectations.

Review. Review what was discussed during the previous 3 days. Start the review by asking "what did we do yesterday?" and lead the conversation from there. Review specific concepts from the previous days, including the difference between hardware and software, what specific computers parts do, coding vocabulary, the abilities and limitations of both Dash and SPRK+, and the difference between a loop and a conditional statement.

Learn.

Talk about how the block-based coding skills and coding concepts students practiced worked with both Dash and SPRK+, even though the robots speak different coding languages. These same skills can be translated to other coding platforms, such as Scratch (https://scratch.mit.edu). Introduce Scratch. Show screenshots of the website via the PowerPoint or bring up the website and show students how to navigate it via your computer and projector setup. Show students how to switch between collecti. ns of blocks, add blocks, and delete blocks.

Practice. Split the group of 16 students into pairs. Each pair will work together at a laptop to create a Scratch project of their choice that uses the skills they learned that week. Students can make whatever they want, but they must use a minimum of the blocks specified on the Scratch Building Challenge Project Sheet (https://www.slideshare.net/aecarlson/coding-camp-day-4-scratch-building-challenge-project-sheet/).

If students are unfamiliar with Scratch, offer everyone or specific groups the Scratch Introduction Packet (https://www.slideshare.net/aecarlson/coding-camp-day-4-scratch-introduction-packet/). These provide simple step-by-step instructions that help students become familiar with the platform. Students should work on these for no more than 15 minutes before moving on to the main assignment.

Scratch is an excellent tool for a variety of coding ability levels. If students work through the main activity quickly, encourage them to explore new features of Scratch to make their project more advanced.

Optional Parent Showcase. In place of the closing discussion, we invited parents to stop by about 15 minutes before the end of the program so their students could show them what they created in Scratch. During this show-and-tell, we displayed pictures of the students working on their projects throughout the week. After students showed off their work, parents and students moved to the front of the room so we could explain the concepts we learned that week through a final group review and through more photos of their daily activities. We provided students with a certificate at this time recognizing that they completed a week of coding camp as well as the Coding Resources Take Home Bookmark (https://www.slideshare.net/aecarlson/coding-camp-take-home-resources-bookmark/), which provides a list of future technology programs at the library along with books, websites, and apps to inspire future learning.

LEARNING OUTCOMES

Participants will:

- Learn basic technological skills that build confidence in their ability to experiment with coding and computer science in the future.
- Understand at a basic level how computer hardware works and what these hardware components do.
- Develop computational thinking skills that allow them to break down complex problems into more solvable parts.
- Be able to define and use loops and conditionals in block-based programming.
- Recognize how coding skills transfer between different types of robots, platforms, and languages.

RECOMMENDED NEXT PROJECTS

- Students can continue to work on their Scratch projects individually or create new projects on their own.
- Students can explore websites, books, and apps that teach text-based coding skills, such as beginner Python tutorials or Apple's Swift Playground, which acts as an excellent stepping stone between block-based coding and text-based coding.
- Libraries could offer more advanced programs for this age group, such as an Intermediate Coding Camp focusing on text-based coding or a program that explores these concepts in more depth. See Chapter 37: LEGO Sumobots: Programming Robots with LEGO MINDSTORMS by Chad Clark.

30

Beginner Video Game Coding and Design

ANNAMARIE CARLSON

Youth Librarian | Westerville (Ohio) Public Library

PROJECT DESCRIPTION

Library patrons of all ages spend hours on public computers playing Roblox, Minecraft, Fortnite, and the like. Libraries can capitalize on this interest by creating a 1-hour program during which 16 tweens can learn about video game coding and design by using Scratch and Bloxels. Even though this program is designed to use physical Bloxels building boards and manipulatives, it could be easily adapted to just use tablets and computers that a library already owns.

Age Range

- This program was designed for tweens, but the structure could be adapted for any age group.
- Tweens (Ages 8–12)

Type of Library Best Suited For

- Public libraries
- School libraries

Cost Estimate

- $0–$200
- The price estimate does not include access to 8 tablets and 8 laptops or computers with headphones.
- The above cost is based on 16 students working individually. The program cost could be reduced significantly if fewer students participated in the program or if students worked in larger groups (2 or 3 students per Bloxels board).

- The Bloxels app essentially provides the same functions as the physical board. Even though there is a lot of value in having students use physical components when learning about video game design, this program could be completed without any additional purchases.

OVERVIEW

Beginner Video Game Coding and Design is a 1-hour program designed for 16 tweens to use Bloxels and Scratch. While we generally encourage group work to create higher levels of thinking and problem solving in coding programs, we have students work individually during this program. Pairs or groups tend to become more caught up in debating what color a background should be than the bigger-picture challenges librarians are trying to engage them in.

After an overview about the different components of video game design, attendees will split the remaining time between 2 activities: video game design with Bloxels and video game coding with Scratch.

Software/Hardware Needed

Equipment

- 8 tablets
- 8 Bloxels kits with the Bloxels app
- 8 laptops or personal computers with access to the Internet
- 8 sets of headphones

Files

- Video Game Design PowerPoint: https://www.slideshare.net/aecarlson/video-game-design-presentation/
- Scratch Fish Ball Packet: https://www.slideshare.net/aecarlson/fish-ball-scratch-instructions/

STEP-BY-STEP INSTRUCTIONS

Preparation

- Before putting this program on the calendar, think about:
    - Staffing availability, including time for setup and cleanup
    - Limiting the number of attendees based on the number of materials you have and the number of students your staff can handle

- Between a week and a month before the program:
  - Explore the Bloxels kit and Bloxels app. Make sure you are familiar with how they work together and feel comfortable troubleshooting problems that students will run into.
  - Explore the Scratch website (https://scratch.mit.edu). Make sure you are comfortable with the interface and can troubleshoot problems that students will run into.
- On the day of the program:
  - Gather the materials.
  - Charge the tablets.
  - Charge the laptops (if necessary).
  - Set up the programming space:

    Display a PowerPoint with a computer and projector to show the video game design video, screenshots of the Bloxels app, and the Scratch interface. (PowerPoint: https://www.slideshare.net/aecarlson/video-game-design-presentation/).

    Set up 8 laptops (with headphones) open to the Scratch website.

    Set up 8 tablets open to the Bloxels app. Place a Bloxels kit (board and pieces) nearby.

PROJECT INSTRUCTIONS

Introduce. Introduce the program by providing a brief overview of what participants will be doing and the program expectations.

Learn.

- Talk about video games. What are students' favorite video games? Why are these games their favorites? What kind of interfaces do students play video games on?
- Watch this Khan Academy video: https://www.khanacademy.org/partner-content/mit-k12/eng-and-electronics/v/mit-explains-how-to-make-a-video-game/) about how video games are made. This video focuses on coding and Scratch and provides a good overview of different elements of video game creation.
- Explain that in today's program participants will focus on 2 elements of video game creation: design and coding. Discuss what this means and how these elements are different.

Demonstrate how the Bloxels app and kit work. The Bloxels kit comes with a black board and a variety of multi-colored blocks. Each color represents a different element of a video game. For example, green blocks represent terrain and blue blocks represent water.

Students will place these blocks into the empty spaces on the black board to create a Mario Bros.–style game screen. In addition to creating terrain and water, students can use these blocks to add hazards, coins, enemies, power-ups, exploding blocks, and story blocks to make their games more elaborate. When students have created a board they are happy with, they open the free Bloxels app to a new game on the tablet and take a picture of their board. The app will turn the camera image into a playable game board on the tablet that students can move a virtual character around on.

Students can also use the board to design their own characters, enemies, power-ups, backgrounds, and more. Each game can include up to 169 different screens that all connect together to form 1 giant game.

- Demonstrate how the Scratch website works. Show students how to find new blocks, add blocks, delete blocks, and start a program. Scratch is a block-based coding interface that allows students to make a "sprite" character interact with other characters and the environment the user creates.

Practice: Split the group of 16 students into 2 groups of 8. Eight students will start with Bloxels, and the remaining students will start with Scratch. Each pair should have about 20–25 minutes per activity.

- **Activity 1: Bloxels.** Students will make their own video games using the Bloxels kits and app. Instead of providing students with a specific challenge or instructions, feel free to leave this activity open ended. Students become quickly immersed in building their own digital games using this tool. Encourage students to try to create a playable game with at least 3 screens and a self-designed character. Students often need to focus on thinking about how to make a game simple enough to be winnable. Creating a game full of enemies and hazards may be fun, but it does not result in a game that other people want to play. Before they rotate, ask students to exchange boards with a partner and give feedback on their partner's game.

  Ask each group to save any created games and open a new, blank game for the next user.

- **Activity 2: Scratch.** Students will use block-based coding in Scratch to create a game of their choice. At each program, there will be students attending who have never heard of coding, as well as students who have built extensive projects in Scratch. To provide a good experience for all students regardless of skill level, provide them with 3 options during the Scratch portion of the program:

Fish Ball Game. If students have no coding experience, encourage them to try the Fish Ball Game. Provide students with packets of step-by-step instructions to create a soccer game with a fish—"fish ball." This activity is adapted from the book *Coding in Scratch: Games Workbook* by Jon Woodcock and Steve Setford. Activity packets can be found here: https://www.slideshare.net/aecarlson/fish-ball-scratch-instructions/.

Game-Based Scratch Tutorial. If students have some experience with Scratch, but they do not want to create their own program, encourage them to try one of the Scratch tutorials. There are a variety of Scratch-based tutorials that focus on game making. Encourage students to explore the "Create a Pong Game," "Race to the Finish," "Hide and Seek Game," and "Catch Game" activities.

Free Building. If students have Scratch experience and are self-motivated to create their own game, encourage them to build something themselves. This often works best if students already have their own Scratch accounts and are comfortable using the website.

Before they rotate, have students show their work to a partner and give their partner feedback on their creation.

Ask each group to save any created games and open a new, blank program screen for the next user.

Discuss: At the end of the program, everyone comes together and talks about what they learned and how the different activities connected to one another.

LEARNING OUTCOMES

Participants will:

- Learn the basics of video game creation and about 2 of the main elements behind their creation: design and code.
- Develop technological skills that allow them to break down complex problems into more solvable parts.
- Be inspired to create something meaningful with their new skills.

RECOMMENDED NEXT PROJECTS

- Students can continue to work on their Scratch projects individually or create new projects on their own.
- Students can use the free Bloxels app on any smartphone or tablet to continue to develop their own video games.
- Libraries could offer more advanced video game–focused programs, including multi-day programs delving more deeply into these concepts, particularly using interfaces such as Scratch and more advanced coding languages.

31

Outreach Programming with Robots and Coding

ANNAMARIE CARLSON

Youth Librarian | Westerville (Ohio) Public Library

PROJECT DESCRIPTION

Even though in-library technology programs always fill up as soon as registration opens, libraries may not be reaching students in their service area who have the least access to coding and robotics activities at home and in their classrooms. To combat this issue, why not partner with the local school district to bring robots and introductory coding activities to students? These 1-hour sessions provide a brief introduction to coding with a variety of robots.

Age Range

- This program was designed for tweens, but the structure could be adapted for any age group.
- Tweens (Ages 8–12)

Type of Library Best Suited For

- Public libraries
- School libraries

Cost Estimate

- $900–$1,100
- We created this program based on specific technology we purchased through a grant. This program could be adapted based on robots, tablets, and computers your library already owns.
- The cost estimate does not include access to 2–4 tablets with Bluetooth capabilities and a container to move the robots in.

OVERVIEW

Outreach Programming with Robots and Coding is a 1-hour program designed for 15–20 tweens to receive a brief introduction to coding as well as hands-on time with different robots outside of the physical library. After a coding overview, pairs of students can rotate through 4 activities:

- Unplugged Coding
- Dash Robots and App-Based Coding
- KIBO Robots and Writing Programs
- Code-a-pillar and Problem Solving (third graders) *or* SPRK+ and Block-Based Coding (fourth graders)

Two librarians can work with each class, roving between the stations to provide assistance.

Software/Hardware Needed

Equipment

- 2–4 tablets with bluetooth capabilities (2 for third graders, 4 for fourth graders)
- 2 KIBO robots with ear sensors and coding blocks
- 2 Dash robots with the Wonder app
- 2 Code-a-pillars with start/stop markers and extra segments (for third graders)
- 2 SPRK+ Robots with the Sphero Edu app (for fourth graders)

Materials

- Group Coding
    - Loaf of bread (may want multiple)
    - Jar of jelly
    - Paper plates, paper towels, plastic knives, and cleaning wipes
- Unplugged Coding
    - Twister board with 4 paper circles (2 purple circles, 1 with the number "1" and 1 with the number "2" and 2 similar orange circles)
    - 4 small traffic cones or alternative obstacle objects
    - 2 colored balls, preferably purple and orange
    - Blank paper
    - 2 pencils

- SPRK+ and block-based coding: (for fourth graders)
    - 15 cardboard or wood blocks or alternative "robot blocking" tools
    - Masking tape
- At least 12 extra AA batteries (for KIBO and Code-a-pillar)
- 1 Phillips head and 1 flat head screwdriver
- Something in which to transport your materials, such as a set of travel suitcases
- Files
    - Unplugged Coding Challenge Cards: https://www.slideshare.net/aecarlson/unplugged-coding-challenge-cards/
    - Dash Coding Challenge Cards: https://www.slideshare.net/aecarlson/dash-coding-challenge-cards/
    - KIBO Challenge Cards: http://resources.kinderlabrobotics.com/resource/cards-for-kibo-independent-exploration/
    - Code-a-pillar Challenge Cards (for third graders): https://www.slideshare.net/aecarlson/codeapillar-challenge-cards/
    - SPRK+ Challenge Cards (for fourth graders): https://www.slideshare.net/aecarlson/sprk-coding-challenge-cards/

STEP-BY-STEP INSTRUCTIONS

Preparation

- Before putting this program on the calendar, think about:
    - Staffing availability, including time for travel, setup, and cleanup and how many staff members are needed to manage an unknown space and potentially unknown number of attendees
    - Limiting the number of attendees based on the number of materials you have and the number of students your staff can handle
    - How to safely transport the needed equipment
- Between a week and a month before the program:
    - Explore the Unplugged Coding activities. Make sure you are familiar with how they work and that you feel comfortable troubleshooting problems that students will run into.
    - Add 2 "start" and 2 "stop" circles to the Twister board. Create 2 purple circles: 1 with a number "1" inside and 1 with a number "2" inside. Place each on diagonal corners of the Twister board. Do the same with 2 numbered

orange circles on the opposite corners. Students use these spaces as start and end points during their unplugged activities.

- Explore each robot's specific activities and create new challenge cards as needed. Practice connecting Dash and SPRK+ to their tablets and apps. Make sure you are familiar with how each device works and feel comfortable troubleshooting problems that students will run into.

- The day before the program:
  - Charge the tablets.
  - Charge the robots, including Dash and SPRK+.
  - Gather and pack all materials, particularly if you need to leave early the next morning.
- On the day of the program:
  - Set up the programming space.
  - Leave a space for students to sit facing you while you lead the introduction and learning portions of the program. Bring 1 robot and its appropriate supplies from each station to the front of the room.
  - Block off 4 spaces for students to work with the various activities. Each activity station will have 2 pairs of students working on the same activities with separate robots and challenge cards. Each device will need a different type of space:

Unplugged Coding. Lay out the Twister board with the colored and numbered circles taped on top of each corner circle, as described under "Between a Week and a Month Before Your Program" in the "Preparation" section. Leave 1 set of the following supplies next to each number 1: 1 set of Unplugged Challenge Cards, 2 small traffic cones (or other obstacle items), a colored ball, blank paper, and a pencil.

Dash Robots and App-Based Coding. Place 2 Dash robots and tablets with bluetooth capabilities on the floor. Robots will not move around extensively, so they do not need a lot of space. Connect each tablet to a robot in the Wonder app. Open the app to the first of the pre-set Wonder tutorials called "Scroll Quest" and "Wonder Workshop."

KIBO Robots and Writing Programs. Place 2 sets of KIBO materials on the floor, including 1 set of KIBO Challenge Cards, 1 KIBO robot base, 2 motors, 2 wheels, an ear sensor, and a set of programming blocks. Make sure the programming blocks include at least 1 start, 1 end, 2 forward, 1 backward, 1 turn left, 1 turn right, 1 spin, 1 shake, and 1 wait for clap block. The robots will need room to move, but not extensively, so they do not need a lot of space. Push KIBO's triangular button to turn him on.

Code-a-pillar and Problem Solving (third graders). Place 2 sets of Code-a-pillar materials on the floor, including the Code-a-pillar Challenge Cards, Code-a-pillar start and stop markers, Code-a-pillar head, a collection of Code-a-pillar segments, and obstacles (as available). Code-a-pillars need space to move, so provide as much space as you can for this activity. Code-a-pillars can travel long distances and are loud, so they can be distracting to other coders. Keep Code-a-pillars as separate from the other activities as space allows. Make sure each Code-a-pillar head is switched to "on."

SPRK+ and Block-Based Coding (fourth graders). Instead of using Code-a-pillars, which teach rudimentary coding concepts, use SPRK+ robots with fourth graders. Tape down 2 masking tape mazes to the floor. These should include simple turns and directions.

Place 2 sets of SPRK+ materials on the floor, including the SPRK+ Challenge Cards, a SPRK+ robot, and a tablet with bluetooth capabilities. SPRK+ robots need space to move. Try to use wooden or cardboard blocks, or any available materials, to create a sectioned-off area for SPRK+ robots. SPRK+ robots can travel long distances very quickly and can easily be distracting to other coders. Keep SPRK+ as separate from other activities as space allows. Connect each tablet to a robot in the Sphero Edu app. Open the app to a blank Blocks program screen.

PROJECT INSTRUCTIONS

Introduce. Introduce the program by providing a brief overview of what participants will be doing and the program expectations.

Learn.

- Talk about coding. What is coding? How do computers work? What experience do students have with coding and robots? Explain that coding is a set of step-by-step instructions written in a language a computer can understand that tell a computer what to do.

- Explore coding more deeply by practicing group coding. Students will "code" their instructor to make a jelly sandwich. Be as ridiculous as you like with this activity. For example, if a student tells you to "open the bread," tear the loaf in half, causing pieces of bread to fly everywhere. Students quickly catch on that they need to make their instructions very specific to get the desired result, and sometimes they need to work together to undo errors (debug their program). After this activity is complete, discuss as a group what students learned and how this might apply to coding.
- Introduce 4 different activities and provide a brief overview of what students will be doing at each station. Demonstrate how some of these activities work, particularly how to make each robot move. Talk about how each robot speaks its own language and receives commands a little differently, but the idea of simple, step-by-step instructions is universal.

Practice. Ideally, split the group of students into 8 pairs. Two pairs of students will start with Unplugged Coding, 2 with Dash, 2 with KIBO, and 2 with Code-a-pillar or SPRK+ depending on the grade. If there are more than 16 students, each group will need to include more than 2 students. Each group should have about 10 minutes per activity.

Activity 1: Unplugged Coding. Two pairs of students will complete coding challenges on the same Twister board (figure 31.1). One pair of students, "Team Purple," will start on the purple 1 taped to the Twister board. The other pair of students, "Team Orange," will start on the orange 1 taped to the Twister board.

All activity instructions are in the Unplugged Coding Challenge Cards, provided to each group (https://www.slideshare.net/aecarlson/unplugged-coding-challenge-cards/). Students will instruct each other how to move from the start circle to the end circle by giving each other step-by-step instructions. Challenges will become increasingly more difficult, involving obstacles and stops along the way.

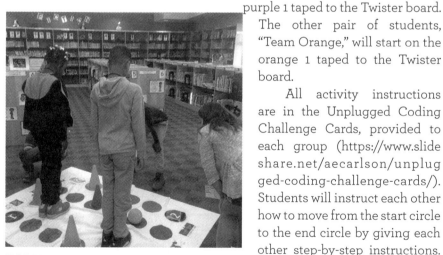

FIGURE 31.1

Two groups of students practice unplugged coding challenges using a Twister board and obstacles

If students complete these activities quickly, they can work on the final coding challenge: coding each other to write letters of the alphabet.

Activity 2: Dash Robots and App-Based Coding. A pair of students will work with a Dash robot and the Wonder app to develop coding skills. Students will work together to complete the Dash tutorials found in the Wonder app under "Scroll Quest" and "Wonder Workshop."

We provided students with challenge cards to help them figure out how to navigate the app if a librarian was not nearby (https://www.slideshare.net/aecarlson/dash-coding-challenge-cards/). There are dozens of tutorials under "Scroll Quest," so students will have something to do for the entire time they work with Dash.

Activity 3: KIBO Robots and Writing Programs. A pair of students will work with a KIBO robot and the KIBO Challenge Cards. We used cards created by Rivka Heisler and the SAR Academy, found on KIBO's educational resources website: KinderLab Robotics (http://resources.kinderlabrobotics.com/resource/cards-for-kibo-independent-exploration/). Students will need to insert the 2 motors (with the green dot visible through the clear bottom of the robot), attach a wheel to each motor, and attach the ear sensor to 1 of the ports on top of the robot.

Students will use the challenge cards to make KIBO move in a circle, make letters, and do the Hokey Pokey. The final card in the set is "What letters can you make with KIBO?" so students will not run out of things to do in their 10 minutes with KIBO.

Ask each group to take the robot apart so that everything will be set up for the next group.

Activity 4: Code-a-pillar and Problem Solving (third graders). A pair of students will work with a Code-a-pillar to practice predicting what will happen when they attach different instructional segments. Students can rearrange segments and attach new segments easily because each segment connects to the next via a USB port. When students are ready to test their program, they will press the "start" button behind the Code-a-pillar's head.

Students will use challenge cards (https://www.slideshare net/aecarlson/codeapillar-challenge-cards/) to direct the Code-a-pillar make letters, draw shapes, and dance. The final card asks students to program the Code-a-pillar to make letters so they will not run out of things to do in their 10 minutes with the Code-a-pillar.

Students may just want to attach as many segments to the Code-a-pillar as possible. You may find that this station will require a lot of redirection to the more focused activities suggested or any activity that allows for prediction of where the Code-a-pillar will end up based on the instructions he was provided.

Ask each group to remove the segments they attached to the Code-a-pillar so that everything will be set up for the next group.

Activity 5: SPRK+ and Block-Based Coding (fourth graders). To provide a more advanced experience, we used SPRK+ robots with fourth-grade students instead of Code-a-pillars. A pair of students will work with SPRK+ and the Sphero Edu app to help SPRK+ navigate a masking tape maze (figure 31.2). Because this may be many students' first time using block-based coding, we did not ask students to create 1 code that moved SPRK+ through the entire maze at once. Instead, we encouraged students to create individual lines of code to gradually work the robot through the maze.

As with the previous activities, we provided a set of challenge cards (https://www.slideshare.net/aecarlson/sprk-coding-challenge-cards/).

Students may need help with the AIM feature. To check the direction SPRK+ is going to move, students can select the "AIM" button in the top right corner of the Sphero Edu app and make sure that the robot's taillight (a little light that shines when the "AIM" button is pressed) is pointed away from the direction they want the robot to move. Ask each group to delete any created program to provide a blank screen for the next group.

Discuss. At the end of the program, everyone comes together to talk about what they learned and how the different activities connected to each other.

FIGURE 31.2

Students learn how to use the Sphero EDU app to make the SPRK+ robot move

LEARNING OUTCOMES

Participants will:

- Realize that they are smarter than the technology they are using and that they have the power and ability to make that technology do what they want.
- Be inspired to pursue more courses and activities related to math, science, coding, and robotics.
- Become familiar with the term *coding* and how it relates to their everyday lives.

RECOMMENDED NEXT PROJECTS

- Students can continue to explore coding concepts at home through free websites like Code.org and Scratch as well as through library programs.
- Your library could offer repeated visits with more structured activities that focus on specific tasks, preferably with all students using the same robot for more than 10 minutes.

32

Scratch Art

Create and Animate Characters Using Scratch

MARY CARRIER

Digital Services Trainer | Clifton Park-Halfmoon Public Library, Clifton Park, New York

PROJECT DESCRIPTION

In this project, participants will learn the basics of Scratch programming and experience a unique opportunity to create an original character or background. Scratch programming is known as visual or block programming and can be accessed at www.scratch.mit.edu. Blocks of code are found in the Scripts area and dragged to the work area to create coding that animates a sprite (character). The Scratch Art class inspires creativity and allows participants to draw their own sprites and backdrops (backgrounds).

Age Range

- Tweens (Ages 8–12)
- Young adults (Ages 13–18)
- Adults

Type of Library Best Suited For

- Public libraries
- School libraries

Cost Estimate

- $0

OVERVIEW

Scratch Art is a particularly popular class because students use their imagination to draw original sprites and backdrops, and all skill levels are welcome. Young children enjoy changing the colors of Scratch sprites or finding projects to color. Older children and adults create illustrations, animated art, or stories. This is a 1.5–2-hour class, offered monthly.

Software/Hardware Needed

- Computers or laptops with Internet access
- Adobe Flash Player

STEP-BY-STEP INSTRUCTIONS

Create a Scratch Account (this allows you to save your projects)

- Go to www.scratch.mit.edu.
- Have students click Join Scratch.
- Have all participants create a username and password to use each time they log in to Scratch.
- Complete the registration process, which includes providing an e-mail address.

Welcome to Scratch

- Click Create (on the blue strip at the top, to the right of the word *Scratch*).
- Review the Scratch environment—pointing out the Scripts, Sprites, and Backdrops.
- Show a simple example of coding Scratch the cat to move across the screen:
    - From the **Scripts** area, click **Motion**, drag the *move 10 steps command* to the right side to the work area.
    - Click in the white circle and change the 10 to 50.
    - Scroll down in the **Motion** scripts, click and drag the *if on edge, bounce* script and click it to the *move 50 steps* script.
    - Test Scratch's movement by clicking on the move script in the work area.
    - Now add the *forever* loop (found in the **Control** scripts) around the 2 motion scripts.
    - Go to the **Events** scripts and drag the *when green flag clicked* to the top of the *forever* loop.
    - Click the green flag on the screen to the left of the Scripts area. Watch Scratch go!

- Kids may experiment with the number in the white circle. If the number is too high, Scratch may disappear off the screen. To get Scratch back, click the *set X to 0* and/or *set Y to 0* (found in the **Looks** scripts) to bring Scratch back to the center.
- Currently in a forever loop, Scratch runs upside down from right to left. To correct this, click the Scratch character (on the left side, listed as Sprite1). Click the white **i** with the blue background.
- Locate the **rotation style**—change the rotation from the curved arrow to the straight line (figure 32.1). Click the white arrow in the blue circle to close this space and check the results by clicking the green flag again.

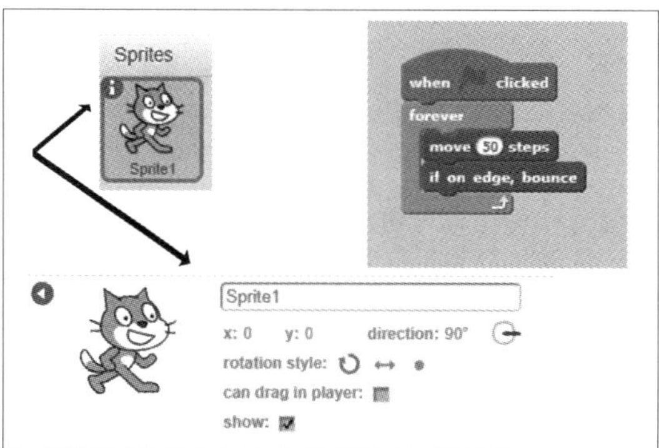

FIGURE 32.1

Change the rotation style

- Title the project. All projects are saved automatically. To find their saved projects, participants click their username in the top right. Click My Stuff. All of their projects will be listed. Click see inside to edit a project or delete projects from here.

HINT: Participants click **File, New** when they're ready to start a new project. **Delete** the Scratch cat by clicking on the scissors (above the red stop sign), then click Scratch. This deletes Scratch and the coding.

Remember to click File, New for each of the following projects.

Modify a Sprite

- Explain to students that they can add a new sprite by clicking the little fairy to the right of the words **new sprite**. This brings them to the Sprite Library. Click on a sprite, then click **OK** at the bottom right of the screen. Each sprite needs its own scripts. Click and drag commands to the right into the work area to make this new sprite move.
- Modify the look of any sprite by clicking the **Costumes** tab to the right of the **Scripts** tab.

- In the **Costumes** area, participants need to make sure they are in **Bitmap mode** (noted in the bottom right corner). In Bitmap mode, tools will be on the left side.
- Click the paintbrush in the tools, then draw a hat or cape on the sprite. If participants want to color in (fill) the shape, they will need to make sure the drawn lines are attached in each part. For example: Draw a straight line, draw a curved semi-circle above the straight line to represent a hat. Each end of the curved semi-circle must touch the line for the shape to be filled in with color. Participants' work is shown immediately as they create it and automatically saves.
- Use the **Zoom** magnifying glass symbol plus (+) to zoom in or minus (-) to zoom out. Use the curved **Undo arrow** to remove unwanted actions.
- Click the **paint can** in the tools, click on a paint color from the palette, and click on the hat to fill in the color.

Create a Sprite

- Have students delete the Scratch character or other sprite.
- Instruct them to draw their own sprite. Click on the paintbrush to the right of the little fairy. Adjust the paintbrush width using the lever on the bottom left. Adjust the color by clicking on a color square. Next, participants click the paintbrush and then draw and create their own sprite.
- Use the **Zoom** magnifying glass symbol plus (+) to zoom in or minus (-) to zoom out. Use the curved **Undo arrow** to remove unwanted actions. Click on **Clear** to erase the entire canvas to start over.
- *Remember to complete the lines to use fill color.* Click on the color you want, click on the paint can, and then click on the part of the sprite to fill in.

Animate a Sprite

- Next, have students animate their sprite. They will need a series of costumes. Right-click on the original sprite, left-click on **duplicate**. They will see costume 1 and costume 2. They are identical.
- Use the eraser and paintbrush to make changes to costume 2. For example: Change the sprite's mouth from a happy smile to a surprised mouth.
- Continue making duplicate costumes and change each of them.
- It's time to animate! Click on costume 1. Click on the **Scripts** tab at the top to move from the Costumes area and go back to the project work area.
- Drag the following scripts to the right and click them together:
    - When green flag clicked (from the Events scripts)

  - Wait 1 second (from the Control scripts)
  - Next Costume (from the Looks scripts)
  - Wait 2 seconds
  - Next Costume
  - Wait 1 second
  - Next Costume
  - Add the forever loop below the green flag (around the remaining commands).
- Run the code by clicking the green flag. You can change the wait time or add other commands such as *Say* or *Think* from the **Looks** script.

Create Backdrops

- Now that they understand how to make their own sprite, participants can try making their own backdrop.
- Click on the **paintbrush** on the bottom left side under the words *new backdrop*:
- This will bring participants into the same drawing area that they saw with the costumes. But this time they are in the **Backdrops** tab and each scene will be labeled backdrop 1 and backdrop 2, etc., similar to costume 1 and costume 2.
- Fill in the entire backdrop with color—click on a color on the palette, click on the **paint can** in the Tools area. Click on the Backdrop canvas. Draw scene 1 on the background.
- Right-click the mini backdrop 1 and duplicate it.
- Draw scene 2 on backdrop 2—draw trees or buildings, clouds, etc.
- Continue to duplicate the backdrops and add to each scene.

Animate the Backdrops

- It's time to animate! Click backdrop 1. Click on the **Scripts** tab at the top to move from the Backdrops area and go back to the project work area.
- Drag the following scripts to the right and click them together:
  - When green flag clicked (from the Events scripts)
  - Switch backdrop to backdrop 1 (from the Looks scripts)
  - Wait 5 seconds (from the Control scripts)
  - Switch backdrop to backdrop 2

    - Wait 5 seconds
    - Switch backdrop to backdrop 3
    - Add the forever loop below the green flag (around the remaining commands).
- Run the code by clicking the green flag. Participants can change the wait time.

LEARNING OUTCOMES

Participants will:

- Learn the basics of sequencing and coding in Scratch.
- Be introduced to Scratch vocabulary and the environment, including the Scripts tab, Costumes tab, and the Backdrops tab.
- Use techniques needed to use the Bitmap mode tools to create and draw costumes and backdrops in Scratch.
- Create commands needed to animate sprites and backdrops
- Participants are allowed to move at their own pace and spend their time in the area that interests them:
    - Modify sprites from the Sprite Library.
    - Modify backdrops from the Backdrop Library.
    - Draw original pictures—this can be a sprite or backdrop.
    - Animate sprites and backdrops.
    - Experiment with the various tools not used for the lesson—line, circle, rectangle, and text.
    - Remix and color other people's projects.

RECOMMENDED NEXT PROJECTS

- Provide examples in class—type these key words into the search bar in Scratch
- Remix or create originals:
    - Speed art
    - Scribble art
    - Pixel art
    - Circle art
    - Coloring book or contests
- Create how-to instructions using animated backdrops and the text tool

33

Program A-mazing Finch Robots with Scratch

MARY CARRIER

Digital Services Trainer | Clifton Park-Halfmoon Public Library, Clifton Park, New York

PROJECT DESCRIPTION

Scratch programming is used to command Finch robots as they move, dance, chirp, change beak color, and maneuver their way through a maze. The A-mazing Finch robot class rewards problem solving and teamwork with fantastic results.

Age Range

- Tweens (Ages 8–12)

Type of Library Best Suited For

- Public libraries
- School libraries

Cost Estimate

- $600
- Each Finch robot costs $99 ($89 with an educational discount)—available at www.birdbraintechnologies.com or www.finchrobot.com.
- Additional costs include the cost to print instructional material and the instructor's time.

OVERVIEW

The A-mazing Finch Robots class is a hit! Students learn how to transfer coding to a physical robot. The Finch takes on a life of its own. It is rewarding for participants to see it do what they command it to do. We originally purchased 6 Finch robots for a class of 12. As interest in the program grew, we purchased 6 more and allowed them to circulate. We now have 14 Finch robots and offer classes during school breaks and during the summer. The class runs 1.5–2 hours.

Software/Hardware Needed

- Laptops for portability (computers will work if you don't have laptops)
- Hard-surface floor (robots works best on a hard surface, but they can run on carpet)
- Items to create a maze
- Cardboard boxes/blocks
- Styrofoam or plastic cups
- Masking tape
- Tablet, smartphone, or watch with a timer (optional)

STEP-BY-STEP INSTRUCTIONS

Pre-Class Prep

- Download the BirdBrain Robot Server to each laptop—this allows access to Scratch or Snap software. The download includes Scratch 2.0 offline (so Internet access is not necessary during class). Go to www.finchrobot.com, click the Learning drop-down arrow, click Software, click Scratch, and click on the appropriate installation—Windows, Mac, or Chromebook. Click the download link to get started.
- Test that the Finch and Scratch work together—Plug the cable into the Finch and then into the laptop. The Finch beak will light up briefly.
- Double-click the BirdBrain icon and then click the Open Scratch button. Look in the center of the screen for the Scripts and locate the last command, More Blocks.
- Follow these trouble-shooting tips before and during class:
    - While using the Finch, if the software is unresponsive, or you do not see the black commands under More Blocks, unplug the cable and plug it back in, and look for the beak to light up. (See the Troubleshooting link under the Learning tab at www.finchrobot.com.)
    - Click and drag the commands to the work area on the right side of the screen. Drag the move command to the work area (add 100 to each of the white circles).

- Move Finch left: 100, Move Finch right: 100
- Click the command line and the Finch will move forward.

Beginning-of-Class Intro

- Explain the goals and structure of class—exploring commands, races, and mazes.
- Participants will work independently or with a partner (depending on the number of participants).
- Remind participants to take turns and handle the equipment with care.

Exploring Commands

- Students will work independently or with a partner (watch to see that no one is getting frustrated or distracted). Students may experiment with other Scratch commands such as sounds and sprites. Curiosity and experimentation is not discouraged, but continue to check their progress with the following exercises.
- Locate the More Blocks area and ask students to try these commands (figure 33.1):

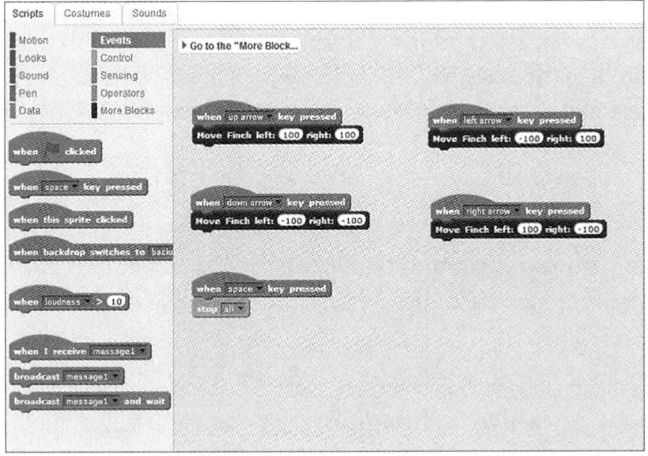

FIGURE 33.1

Set up move commands with arrow keys

Motion Commands (Use a separate command line for each—click on the command to make it run.)

- Move Forward—Move Finch left: 100, Move Finch right: 100
- Move Backward—Move Finch left: -100, Move Finch right: -100

- Move Right—Move Finch left: 100, Move Finch right: -100
- Move Left—Move Finch left: -100, Move Finch right: 100

LED Commands (Light up the beak.)

- Finch LED color R:20 G:40 B:40 (Try different numbers between 0 and 100.)

Sound Commands (Finch will buzz or chirp)

- Finch buzz at 100 Hz for 1000 ms (Try different numbers range 20–20,000) 1,000 ms = 1 second

Arrow Commands

- Write these instructions on the board and ensure that each laptop has the commands correctly programmed.

- Find the commands in the Events scripts:

Use Up Arrow to move forward—click the Up Arrow command and the Move forward command together.

Use Down Arrow to move backward—click the Down Arrow command and the Move backward command together.

Use Left Arrow to move left—click the Left Arrow command and the Move left command together.

Use Right Arrow to move right—click the Right Arrow command and the Move right command together.

Use Spacebar to stop—click the Use Spacebar command and the stop all command (from the Control scripts) together.

For the next 2 exercises, be sure to have a method to get everyone's attention. I use clapping hands, "Finches Quiet," and a laminated sign—one side with a green light and the other side with a red light.

Ready for the Races

- Place a straight line of tape on the floor from wall to wall for each pair.
- Before the race begins, ask each student to add the "when green flag clicked" command to the Move Forward script. Use the green flag on the screen to start and the stop sign to stop.
- Students need to work in partners. One person drives the laptop and the other person holds the cable for the Finch. Both students need to stand and move with the Finch.
- The "driver" clicks the green flag to start the forward command. The cable holder walks with the Finch. The Finch stays straight and moves forward

better if students hold the cable closer to the Finch plug-in versus holding the cable farther from the plug-in or laying the cable on the floor.

- Do a practice run, do a real race, and then switch roles—as an option, use a timer to record the races, create team names, and provide prizes. Note: Some students do not like the competitive nature or get frustrated that the Finch is not staying on course. Encourage fair play—do not pull the Finch across the floor or lift and correct it.

Through the Maze

Split the class into 2 groups (students will remain with their partners). Group 1 builds a maze and rebuilds it after the Finch goes through. Group 2 takes turns going through the maze with the Finch (figure 33.2). One student drives the laptop using the arrow keys and the other holds the cable to help the Finch stay on track. Remind students about fair play.

- Laptop drivers use the arrow keys to move the Finch through the maze while their partner holds the cable (for better control). When partners make it through the maze, the maze is rebuilt and the next team goes. All drivers go through the maze first, and then they switch roles to have the next set of drivers go through.

FIGURE 33.2

Kids work in teams and encourage fair play

- Some students don't like the noise, crowd, or competitive nature of the maze. There should be an opportunity for "practice" with additional blocks and obstacles that can be set up for smaller groups or individual "dry runs." Styrofoam or plastic cups can be set up like traffic cones. Shoeboxes can be used as garages.

LEARNING OUTCOMES

Participants will:

- Learn to code the Finch robot with Scratch programming.
- Understand troubleshooting techniques needed when coding and using robots.
- Collaborate and learn from each other.
- Use teamwork to design a maze, take turns, and resolve any conflicts.

RECOMMENDED NEXT PROJECTS

- Program the Finch to dance to music.
- Create a story starring the Finch.
- Program the Finch to sense obstacles.
- Try other programming languages such as Snap or Python.
- See www.finchrobots.com for additional instructions and ideas.

34

A Crash Course in Robotics

LOREN McCLAIN
Administrative Specialist III | Muncie (Indiana) Public Library

PROJECT DESCRIPTION

Who would not want their own robot? Something that could pick up after you, do what you told it to do, and even help you create a video game? In this crash course, patrons will learn how to build Vernie the LEGO BOOST Robot, as well as learn how to communicate with him and all his friends using block coding language.

Age Range

- Tweens (Ages 8–12)

Type of Library Best Suited For

- Public libraries
- School libraries

Cost Estimate

- $130–$600
- The cost of LEGO BOOST runs $130–$160. The application runs better on iOS devices and provides a more mobile experience for participants. The cost of the project depends on how many sets you will purchase for participants. Students can work together in groups of up to 4 to build the robot sets.

OVERVIEW

The popularity of LEGOS has surged so far that oftentimes suppliers cannot keep up with the demand for them. However, what was once a child's building toy set has now bridged the gap from play to education. LEGO BOOST lends itself to more than just basic math, science, and building. It pushes students toward coding, robotics, physics, measurements, and even the humanities.

Using basic commands, a poem, and the LEGO BOOST set, students can begin to decipher and learn what makes humans different from machines. From this conversation, students will be able to gather information based on how society programs people to behave and how they can, in turn, program their robots.

The coding language used by LEGO BOOST is block based and allows youth to learn and understand basic concepts such as parameters, conditionals, loops, and functions simply by dragging boxes around and seeing how they link together. LEGO BOOST comes with 5 complete projects in 1 box, and kids can modify them over time and add additional packs.

Software/Hardware Needed

- LEGO BOOST core set
- A tablet or computer; LEGO BOOST Creative Toolbox app is compatible with iOS, Android, Kindle, and Windows 10 devices
- LEGO BOOST Creative Toolbox app
- A copy of the poem "Lift Your Right Arm" by Peter Cherches

STEP-BY-STEP INSTRUCTIONS

Preparation

- Make sure electronic devices are fully charges and have the LEGO BOOST Creative Toolbox app downloaded and installed.
- Allow the LEGO BOOST Creative Toolbox app access to the microphone and camera on the device.

PROJECT INSTRUCTIONS

Building Vernie

- Open the LEGO BOOST Creative Toolbox app. Select Vernie the Robot from the opening screen (he is the second option from the left).
- Talk to students about building Vernie.
- Students have only 1 option available in the beginning because they must build Vernie prior to advancing. Pro tip: There are 3 stages to each level of

building and interacting with Vernie. Students won't be able to progress to the next level without completing all of the previous stages. Each beginning "stage" is marked with an asterisk (*)—so tell them to keep their eyes peeled!

- Instruct students to tap the top option with the yellow triangle.
- Tap the first ID badge on the next screen.
- Have students follow the on-screen instructions to build Vernie.
- Tell students to take their time and try not to get frustrated. There are 154 steps to follow!

Making Vernie Mobile: Adding the Tank Wheels

- Once Vernie is built, have students insert batteries in the Move Hub. Make sure they turn on the Move Hub by pressing the green button.
- Switch on the bluetooth. Wait a few seconds to make sure the Move Hub pairs with the LEGO BOOST Creative Toolbox app.
- Once Vernie is turned on, have students tap the first ID badge again. They will now see a yellow block at the bottom of the screen. Drag and drop the yellow block onto the center of the dashboard screen.
- The yellow block will be the "play" button to test their coding set.
- Action options on the bottom of the toolbar make Vernie move his head left, right, down (to nod), say "hello" (this option will also be used to make Vernie wave in the next session), move forward, or power down (turn off).
- Instruct students to drag the purple icon with the orange hand on to the yellow block. They will see a white block appear under each action you drop into the sequence. By adding a number into this white block, Vernie will perform that specific action that number of times before moving on to the next action in the sequence.
    - For this part, make sure Vernie only says "hello" once by adding a 1 in the white box.
- Next, return to the previous screen. Students should tap the orange and white arrow in the upper left corner to go back to the stage selection screen.
- Students will have now unlocked the second set of Vernie build instructions: tank wheels. Tap on the second ID badge, which contains instructions for building Vernie's tank wheels.
- Students will build Vernie's tank wheels by following the instructions. There are 53 steps, but actually they are going to do the same 26 twice. So, once they get the first wheel pair done, they just have to replicate it. It is a lot easier than it appears!

- On the final step of putting Vernie's wheels together, be sure students apply the small red nut to the outside of the wheel cage to make sure Vernie's wheels do not fall off.

Adding Vernie's Arms

For steps 54 to 85, instruct students to be very careful because they are going to put together Vernie's arms and there are many small parts. When they push the parts together, they will want to hear a "click" not a "snap." Advise them to apply gentle but firm pressure to Vernie's arms so they do not break him!

Building the Tire Track

- When students have made sure Vernie's arms are secure on his torso, they should turn him face down. They'll continue to follow the steps provided on the LEGO BOOST Creative Toolbox app. When they reach step 106, they will have to connect 19 tire track pieces together to create the tread of Vernie's wheels.
- Step 107 takes a while to complete. Students must put 19 of the orange plugs into the 19 holes on the outside lane of the tank tire track. Put Vernie, right side up (meaning wheels down), on the tank tire track and hook the pieces together to complete (and enclose the tire track).
- Students repeat steps 107 to 109 for the other tire. Make sure that the orange tracks are on the outside (not the inside) of the wheels.

Building Smaller Robots

- Next, instruct students to follow steps 113–117 to make 2 smaller Vernie-like bots.

Programming Vernie

- When complete, have students tap the second ID badge again on the dashboard.
- Students will program Vernie, and, just as they did in the first programming test, drag the yellow block onto the coding dashboard.
  - Add a purple "greeting box" to the right of the yellow box; add a 1 in the white box, below the purple box.
  - Add a green, upward arrow, the "forward arrow," to the right of the purple box; add a 1 in the white box below the green box. This will make sure Vernie moves forward only 1 space.

- Students can program Vernie to move around the 2 smaller Vernie bots they made previously.
- Students will follow the on-screen instructions to maneuver Vernie around the smaller bots. Explain to them that when they use the right or left turn commands, the number they place in white box will correspond to the number of degrees they want Vernie to move. So, a number of 90 means Vernie would make a complete left or right turn at a 90 degree angle.
    - Pro tip: Students will have to make Vernie turn left twice and right twice. So, make sure the left and right turn commands are not next to each other, otherwise Vernie will turn around in a circle!

Make Vernie Follow Commands with "Lift Your Right Arm"

- Read the poem "Lift Your Right Arm" by Peter Cherches to students.
- Ask them to think about how they can make Vernie follow their code to replicate the commands in the poem.
- Have them take 1 line at a time and break down the function Vernie can do.
- Code each into Vernie's program.
- When students are finished, celebrate because they have done incredible work!

LEARNING OUTCOMES

Participants will:

- Work on resilience and perseverance through the development of planning skills.
- Demonstrate the process of testing solutions through investigative means.
- Optimize design solutions based on scientific process.
- Learn by doing.

RECOMMENDED NEXT PROJECTS

1. LEGO BOOST AutoBuilder
2. LEGO BOOST Frankie the Cat
3. LEGO BOOST Guitar4000
4. LEGO BOOST M.T.R. 4
5. LEGO MINDSTORMS Education EV3 Robotics: Robotic Arm H25, Color Sorter, Puppy, Gyro Boy, or Educator Vehicle (with attachments)

35

Unstructured Learning

Using Drop-In Technology Programs to Engage More Patrons and Support Learning Through Play

JULIA CLARK

Library Experience Manager | Evansville Vanderburgh (Indiana) Public Library

PROJECT DESCRIPTION

Many factors affect library programming, including lack of time, available staff, space, and funding. Technology programming can be especially intimidating to library staff who may not be comfortable with many new technology concepts and tools. One possible solution to providing technology programming in the face of these potential pitfalls is unstructured, drop-in programming. In this model, staff are not experts but facilitators of learning. Children, parents, and staff work and learn together through play and exploration.

Age Range

- Kids (Ages 3–7)
- Tweens (Ages 8–12)
- Young adults (Ages 13–18)

Type of Library Best Suited For

- Public libraries
- School libraries

Cost Estimate

- $1,520
- This estimate includes the cost for 8 LEGO WeDo kits; however, the price will vary depending on technology and supplies used.

OVERVIEW

This is a drop-in technology program for children ages 5–12, with parents assisting if the child is under 8 years of age. It is designed to allow children a time of unstructured exploration with various technologies. Staff serve as facilitators; however, participants direct how they choose to interact with the technologies. Through play and exploration, children build problem-solving skills as well as confidence in their abilities.

Sessions can be held for 2-hour periods. Participants should be allowed to sign up at the beginning of the program for 30-minute time slots, with a recommended limit of 8 participants allowed in the room at any time. At the end of their 30 minutes, participants are allowed to continue exploring if other patrons are not waiting. Typically, 2 to 3 library staff members should be present in the room at all times. Acting as facilitators, staff members will give brief introductions to the equipment and help with troubleshooting. Using the drop-in model instead of the registered class model allows staff to engage a higher number of patrons during any given session, increasing not only the attendance number but also the cost effectiveness of the program.

Drop-in technology programming is adaptable to any age group, library size, budget, and staff skill. The following instructions will detail Tech-It-Out: LEGO WeDo Robotics, one of the more popular iterations of a drop-in technology program. This program has also been run using Snap Circuits, Code.org, Ozobots, and more.

Software/Hardware Needed

Necessary Equipment

- A room or dedicated space that can be monitored, with tables and chairs
- Laptops or desktop computers—preferably 1 per participant, but the program can be run with 1 computer per 2 participants
- Computer mice—1 per laptop
- LEGO WeDo kits—1 per laptop
- Whiteboard and markers for sign-in
- Paper, cotton balls, and miscellaneous supplies for participants to use with their robots
- Enthusiastic staff

STEP-BY-STEP INSTRUCTIONS

Before the Program

- Make sure LEGO WeDo software is loaded onto the computers or laptops participants will be using.
- Familiarize yourself and assisting staff with LEGO WeDo Robotics software. This can be done through guided training or open exploration time for your staff. Try building a few of the robots to see how they work. This will help program facilitation.
- Decide how to advertise the program and address registration. You may find it beneficial to have sign-up on the day of the event to eliminate no-shows. However, pre-registration is also an option.

Room Setup

- Make sure laptops are fully charged or are close to accessible outlets.
- Plug in mice to all computers. Younger participants sometimes struggle with only a trackpad.
- Set up tables, chairs, and laptops in stations around the room. There should be enough room for staff to walk around.
- Turn on computers, plug in the LEGO WeDo USB hub, and make sure the driver is installed properly.
- Turn up the volume on the laptops—some robots make sound.
- Open the LEGO WeDo software. Guided robot builds can be found by clicking the LEGO head in the top corner.
- Depending on registration, setting up a whiteboard at the entrance of the room might be helpful. Use this board to record participant names, time in, time out, and number of patrons in the room at a time.

Running the Program

- At the beginning of the program, open the doors and let the first number of participants come in and find a station.
- As participants come in, remind them that they will have a set time to interact with the technology, but that they may be able to continue exploring at the end of their time if there is not a wait.

- As participants enter, staff should introduce the technology either to each individual or to the group as a whole, depending on how quickly participants come in and get settled.
- Once participants have been introduced to the technology enough to start exploring, staff can begin circulating around the room.
- As staff walk around, encourage them to talk with participants. Ask participants what they are building, why they picked that robot, etc.
- Sometimes participants will run into an issue with their build. Encourage staff to work through the problems with participants rather than fixing it for them. This will encourage critical thinking and creativity on the part of the participant.
- If participants finish with their robots and still have time left over in their session, encourage them to try to add on to or modify their robot. Have supplies like paper, cotton balls, cups, and more for patrons to try out with their robots.
- Near the end of the first session, if others are waiting, let current participants know that it is time for them to finish up and begin dismantling and cleaning up their stations.
- Once stations are reset, begin signing in the next set of participants and repeat the steps above.

LEARNING OUTCOMES

Participants will:

- Increase their problem-solving and critical thinking skills by finding solutions and trying new things.
- Gain greater comfort and familiarity with technology as they explore with facilitator help.
- Increase communication and collaboration skills as they work with other participants and facilitators.

RECOMMENDED NEXT PROJECTS

- Try this model with other technologies. Kids love exploring.
- Once participants have explored on their own with this model, they may be ready for more in-depth projects with the technology. Why not try:
    - Programming with LEGO WeDo

  - Programming robots with LEGO MINDSTORMS
  - Chapter 41: How to Give Successful Coding Workshops for Ages 8–12 by Karima Kafif
  - Chapter 38: Digital Dress-Up: Creating Drag-and-Drop Games in Scratch by Olivia Horvath
- If you have enthusiastic participants, but insufficient staff time or knowledge, try this project: Tapping into Community Knowledge and Youth Interest to Create a Successful Technology Mentorship Program.

36

Choose Your Own Adventure

Bring Coding to Life with Interactive Storytelling

KAITLIN FRICK and GRACE ZELL

Children's Librarians | New York Public Library, 53rd Street Branch

PROJECT DESCRIPTION

In this project, kids will pave their own path through a Choose Your Own Adventure–style story created by the program leader with a computer science twist: Each choice will lead participants to a problem the protagonist faces that they must help solve by using tech tools—from coding their way out of a fairy glen to lighting their way through a dark forest. This project is an adaptable blend of problem solving, creative exploration, and storytelling that can be customized to suit the materials you have on hand and your own fun story. Kids will learn basic coding and STEM concepts, will grow as problem solvers and creative communicators, and will work with peers to navigate technology challenges on the fly, such as coding through an asteroid field (figure 36.1).

Age Range

- Kids (Ages 3–7)
- Tweens (8–12)

Type of Library Best Suited For

- Public libraries
- School libraries

Cost Estimate

- $0–$2,000 (depending on the supplies used)

OVERVIEW

FIGURE 36.1

Coding through an asteroid field

The Choose Your Own Adventure STEAM program is designed to let young patrons create their own story (the adventure) using problem-solving skills and innovative thinking, as well as various tech tools and resources. It is adaptable to the supplies available at your library, but the project may require some significant preparation on the part of the program leader.

Each program revolves around a story—created by the program leader—that participants will navigate to its conclusion. Stories should begin with a bit of exposition setting up the central problem participants are tasked with solving. For example:

> You are a member of the royal family of the Kingdom of Librarylandia. You have been away on a grand tour of the kingdom while your parents have been busy taking care of your 6 younger brothers and sisters. As the crown prince or princess, you are the next ruler of the kingdom and have been entrusted to represent the king and queen on all official business. You are just finishing a speech to the villagers of a coastal town when you get the terrible news: Your parents and younger siblings are being held hostage by an evil dragon that has captured the castle in the capital city. You must return home and rescue them!

Participants will then be faced with a series of choices—and creative coding or STEM tasks—following the theme of the overall story. For example, program leaders may tell participants they've reached a fork in the road and must choose to go either left into a dark forest or right into the mountains. Participants who choose the path to the left might then face a life-size "fairy glen" coding grid, where they must program a path to avoid the impish fairies and escape the glen. Participants who travel right could find a boulder in their path and be asked to build a device using simple cardboard, string, and LEGOS to produce a simple machine (like a pulley) to move the obstacle. The program leader will act as a narrator and guide—telling participants the story, offering options for next steps, and helping kids explore coding and STEM concepts with a few guiding questions. Participants should be allowed to puzzle things out on their own or in groups with minimal guidance from the program leader. Participants can be encouraged to work through snags in their projects with open-ended, leading questions.

Materials List

- Your imagination
- Flexibility
- A room or dedicated space, along with tables and chairs
- Building supplies (cardboard, pipe cleaners, yarn, scissors, straws, glue, tape, etc.)

Examples of Recommended (but Optional) Materials

Refer to our example script when reading this list. The materials are broken down into specific uses for the challenges. Of course, your adventure may be different from ours, but you can use these tools (and alternatives) to accomplish anything you dream up! The beauty and the challenge of this program is that you have complete creative control in designing the challenges and the skill sets you want the kids to use. The Guiding Questions in the Appendix at the end of this chapter may also be helpful when choosing your materials. What materials will work best to get participants thinking like a programmer?

Fairy Glen Coding Materials

- Painter's tape: for creating a life-size game board or grid
- Directional Coding Cards: cardstock or construction paper cards that have arrows or other directions, e.g., STOP, GO, DANCE on them. We used a Sharpie marker to write and draw, but you can print them if you'd rather.

Alternative Materials

- Other programmable coding toys that allow kids to plug in directions, e.g., Left, Forward, Right, Spin
    - Code & Go Robot Mouse
    - Code-a-pillar
    - Sphero
    - Dash and Dot
    - Robot Turtles board game

Dark Forest Lighting Challenge Materials

- littleBits: for creating a basic light-up circuit using several connecting bits

Alternative Materials

- Cheap, basic electronics for lighting crafts, e.g., LED lights, coin cell batteries, copper tape, paper

Underground Cavern Pattern Challenge Materials

- Magna-Tiles, for creating a pattern that kids try to identify

Alternative Materials

- Beans, colored paper, blocks, or any other material to make a pattern with

Perilous Peaks, Dungeon, and Castle Building Challenge Materials

- Enough cardboard for the group
- Makedo kits for connecting and cutting cardboard pieces
- Tape for connecting cardboard pieces
- LEGOS or blocks
- Pipe cleaners
- Craft sticks
- Cups
- String or yarn

Alternative Materials

- Anything—really, anything—in your supply cabinet your kids can use to build simple machines or a shield (Let participants stretch their creative muscles.)
- Tape for securing cardboard pieces together
- Adults-only scissors or box cutter for cutting cardboard

STEP-BY-STEP INSTRUCTIONS

Preparation

To get started, create a story with several branches. Pick a combination of coding and STEM activities that fit into the story (use our example or make your own), and settle on what materials to use for each activity. Although activities can leverage high-tech tools (such as littleBits) if you have them, those tools can easily be subbed out for simpler and cheaper solutions like coin cell batteries and LEDs. Lastly, you want to feel confident in your ability to help kids explore the coding and STEM concepts behind each activity, so do some light reading as needed and have a few guiding questions and definitions ready.

- Take stock of what tools and supplies you already have that support STEM and coding activities and then start brainstorming a Choose Your Own Adventure (CYOA) story that will make use of these tools.
- Review your initial brainstorm and decide if there are additional tools or materials you need or would like to bring in.
- Build a personal familiarity with your tools (littleBits, Code & Go Robot Mouse, etc.); know how they work and be comfortable educating others on how they work.
- Create a story. This can be a simple story or as heavily narrated and as detailed as you want. However, come up with at least 2 separate paths for each task accomplished. The original CYOA books are a great idea resource! *An example CYOA script with accompanying challenges is included in the Appendix at the end of this chapter.*
- Make sure each choice has a corresponding coding or STEM-related task. Participants might be asked to navigate a life-size coding grid, decipher an ancient language (coded message), complete a color/shape pattern, build a structure or device to answer an engineering problem, etc.
- For each task, jot down some key STEM and coding concepts for kids to explore during that activity, as well as a few guiding questions you can use to prompt exploration. Examples may include branching (If/Then statements), sequencing, the engineering process, etc.
- Make sure all your tools are working and you have enough materials for everyone in the program (not necessarily to use at the same time but to have each child interact with everything at some point in your adventure).
- Determine how best to set up the space for the story and interactive challenges.

PROJECT INSTRUCTIONS

Engage

In this opener for the day, gather kids together to discuss what a Choose Your Own Adventure Story is. If you have any of the classic books by Edward Packard, this would be a great opportunity to read a passage from one and discuss how it's organized. During this initial circle time, you may also begin to assess participants and determine the size of the groups they will be working in. Introductions and "icebreakers" can also be done during this time.

- Ask participants if they know what a Choose Your Own Adventure story is.
- Read the exposition of your story and present participants with their first choice.
- If your group is large and you don't have enough materials for all kids to work on the same activity at the same time, consider breaking kids into small groups and having each group start with different activities. You'll have to get creative with how you present the story in this scenario. For example, you can present 2 separate storylines after your exposition that diverge before coming back together at the end.

Explore

Exploration is the heart of this program. Have your key concepts and guiding questions in mind, and then let participants run with the challenges. Remember: The goal is to let participants problem solve on their own, offering only minimal guidance when necessary. And if an activity seems too challenging (or too easy) for the entire group, be prepared to make adjustments.

- Help participants navigate through the story as the narrator and ask questions when they get stuck on a task.
- Encourage caregivers, if present, not to solve the problem for participants.
- Be prepared to adjust activities or paths on the fly if necessary.

Empower

Once participants have completed the story, it's time to talk about what they've learned. Taking time to discuss their process allows participants to take charge of their learning and become the experts, while also giving them time to review key concepts. Further empower participants by providing them with additional activities to try at home.

- Ask participants what they learned, have them show off their creations, and/or have everyone talk about their favorite parts of the adventure, what was most challenging, etc.
- If you had a life-size coding grid, go over the grid as a group to reinforce learning and see if participants came up with multiple solutions.
- Empower participants by giving them additional challenges or tasks to try at home or the next time they come to the library. For example, a bingo card that includes experimenting with Scratch at home or in the library to code a story related to the theme that week, or encouraging them to take pictures of simple machines that they see while they are walking around their hometown to "show and tell" next time they see the program instructor.
- Promote related library materials and resources:
    - Lost in Space theme, e.g., books about space, physics, the solar system, etc.
    - Fantasy theme, e.g., fairy tales, books about castles and knights
    - Coding books, e.g., *Secret Coders* by Gene Luen Yang
    - The Edward Packard or R.A. Montgomery Choose Your Own Adventure Books
- Tidy up your space.
- Make sure all tech tools are still in working order before putting them away.

LEARNING OUTCOMES

This is a very open-ended program, so many learning outcomes will be determined by the program leaders as they craft the adventure story. However, some outcomes should be universally expected.

Participants will:

- Leave with a basic understanding of coding and/or STEM concepts.
- Grow as problem solvers and creative communicators by utilizing code and different tech tools in innovative ways.
- Gain independence to make their own choices.
- Develop storytelling abilities using the tools available.
- Work with peers to navigate challenges and difficulties.
- Be challenged to use their imaginations and think creatively to solve problems on the fly.

RECOMMENDED NEXT PROJECTS

If you noticed participants were really pumped about a particular aspect or tech tool, make a note of it:

- Your kids loved building with cardboard? Try a cardboard challenge program.
- Your tweens went crazy for coding? A Google CS First club could be a great next step for them.
- Based partly on this program idea, Kristin McWilliams, a youth manager with the Houston (Texas) Public Library, created a Super Mario Bros.-themed coding adventure, where participants were given character identities and tasked with navigating a life-size grid using the Directional Coding Cards. The program was a success, and she was able to combine a game the young patrons were passionate about with a new skill set for them to use and build on. Well done, Kristin!

APPENDIX

Example CYOA Story, Challenges, and Guiding Questions

Below is a full example—including an opening scenario, individual choices, and technology challenges—of how to run a Fantasy CYOA program. All of the *italic* instructions indicate the task to complete. Again, this is just what we did; you can change it up however you want!

MISSION: FANTASYTHEME RESCUE

The Scenario

You are a member of the royal family of the Kingdom of Librarylandia. You have been away on a grand tour of the kingdom while your parents have been busy taking care of your six younger brothers and sisters. As the crown prince or princess, you are the next ruler of the kingdom and have been entrusted to represent the king and queen on all official business. You are just finishing a speech to the villagers of a coastal town when you get the terrible news: Your parents and younger siblings are being held hostage by an evil dragon who has captured the castle in the capital city. You must return home and rescue them!

The First Choice

You and your companions plot the fastest routes back to castle, but the fastest routes turn out to hold the most dangers. You have charted 2 paths: one through the Dark Forest and the other over the Perilous Peaks mountain range. Which route do you choose?

A: Dark Forest

B: Perilous Peaks mountain range

A: You leave the seaside town at a full gallop on your horse and arrive on the outskirts of the Dark Forest. The forest is so dense and thick with trees and vines that it is nearly impossible to see! You have some supplies with you but will have to be creative to put together a device to see through the pitch black. *Use the littleBits to create something that will light your way.*

——> You are finally able to see! As you follow the winding path through the forest, you come upon a dark grove where the path splits. Do you go left or right ?

B: You leave the seaside town at a full gallop on your horse and soon arrive on the base of the Perilous Peaks mountain range. There is a twisting narrow path that will hopefully lead you across the mountain range. You start the slow climb to the highest mountain pass but soon find your way is blocked. A large boulder is in your way! You find some timber and hiking equipment and ropes that have been abandoned by some climbers. Can you build a simple machine (pulley or lever/catapult) to lift the rock? *Provide cardboard, craft sticks, rubber bands, paper cups, yarn, etc., to build simple machines.*

——> You lifted the rock! Well done! You continue your journey up the peaks. The path is becoming almost impossible to see. Soon you reach a fork. Do you go left or right?

Forest Left

You find yourself drawn toward a glowing light up ahead—a fairy glen! But these are no ordinary fairies; they are trickster spirits who want to confuse you into getting lost. The fairies have positioned themselves in certain spots in the glen, and you have to move around them to keep them from touching and confusing you. *Code your way out of the glen using the Directional Coding Cards.*

——> You did it! You found your way out of the fairy glen unharmed and may continue on the path to the castle. Go to the Castle.

Forest Right

You find yourself slowly descending into a sunken part of the forest that dead ends into a cave. Inside the cave, you see different color crystals growing in strange shapes. You suddenly remember a story your mother told you about a secret passageway to the castle from a cave. She said something about completing a pattern, but you don't really remember the rest. what will you do? That's when you notice the crystals. . . . *pattern matching with the Magnatiles or Magz-Bricks*

——> The side of the cave swings open to reveal . . . a passageway! The stories are true; this will lead you to the castle dungeon. Go to the Dungeon.

Mountain Left

You continue the climb up to the highest peak and soon find yourself in a clearing. Before you can cross the pass to head down the mountain again, you notice something up ahead: It's a mountain sprite gathering! Sprites are trickster spirits who want to confuse you into getting lost. The sprites have positioned themselves in certain spots in the clearing, and you have to move around them to keep them from touching and confusing you. *Code your way out of the clearing using the Directional Coding Cards.*

——>Well done! You can head back down the mountain toward the castle! Go to the Castle.

Mountain Right

You continue to climb up the mountain when all of a sudden the path gives way and you drop into an underground cavern. The walls of the cavern are covered in strange writing and the cavern is illuminated by glowing crystals. The crystals all seem to have a pattern, but you notice some of the pieces are missing. you find some shards among the rubble from the cave in. You wonder what will happen if you put them back together? *pattern matching with the Magnatiles or Magz-Bricks*

——> The side of the cave swings open to reveal . . . .a passageway! You follow it out of the cavern and find yourself at the base of the mountain with the castle in front of you. Go to the Castle.

The Dungeon

You find yourself in the deepest part of the dungeon. How will you ever get to your family? The dungeon is locked, but you may be able to break out if you can build a machine/structure to either get you over the walls or break through a door. *Provide cardboard, craft sticks, rubber bands, paper cups, yarn, etc., to build simple machines.*

——> You did it! You are free! You run toward the highest tower where you think your family will be hiding out from the dragon. The door to the tower is locked with some sort of magic spell code. *Crack the code (see below) to release your family.*

The Castle

As you run toward the front gate of the castle, the dragon suddenly appears! Just before he sends a jet of flames toward you, you roll into the moat and swim under the bridge. You find some materials that have been caught in the drain. *You'll need to build a shield to get past the dragon. Your shield must allow you to leave 1 hand free to open the gate or wield a sword (aka must build a shield with a handle of some sort).*

——> Great shield! Now, on to free your family! You run past the dragon and to the tower where your family is surely hiding out! The door to the tower is locked. *Crack the code (see below) to release your family.*

The Final Challenge: Crack the Code to Rescue Your Family

The code is the backward alphabet code.

Code to present to kids: HZB: "WIZTLM YV TLMV!"

Solution: SAY: "DRAGON BE GONE!"

KEY CONCEPTS AND GUIDING QUESTIONS

Fairy Glen

1. Key Concepts
   a. Sequencing—the order in which commands are executed by a computer
2. Guiding Questions
   a. How does a computer know to run the code you sequence? How does it know when to stop?
   b. What order should the commands be entered in? Why does the order matter?
3. Quick Background
   a YouTube Video: "Sequence Programming: How It Works" by Kodable, https://www.youtube.com/watch?v=StY_kQujls4/

Dark Forest

1. Key Concept
    a. Building a simple circuit
2. Guiding Questions
    b. Where do you think power for the LED light comes from?
    c. Electrical current moves in a path! What path do you think it follows?
    d. What might be preventing the LED light from lighting?
3. Quick Background
    a. YouTube Video: "The Power Of Circuits" by SciShow Kids, https://www.youtube.com/watch?v=HOFp8bHTN30/

Perilous Peaks Mountain Range, Dungeon, and Castle

1. Key Concept
    a. Building simple machines to solve given challenges
2. Guiding Questions
    b. What sort of design will help you move a large object with minimal effort? (Work smarter, not harder!)
    c. What sort of simple machine will move you vertically (to escape the dungeon)?
    d. What could you use as protection against the dragon? How would it work?
3. Quick Background
    e. YouTube Video: "Simple Machines Song" by Science4Us, https://www.youtube.com/watch?v=yNUgbdsWSm4/

Underground Cavern

1. Key Concept
    a. Pattern Matching—checking a given sequence for the presence of the same pattern
2. Guiding Questions
    b. A successful match must be exact, so remember to double-check the given pattern on all sides. Did you check all the angles or sides of this pattern?
    c. This may only be applicable if you are building in 3-D, like with Magna-Tiles.

37

LEGO Sumobots

Programming Robots with LEGO MINDSTORMS

CHAD CLARK

New Media Services Manager | Highland Park (Illinois) Public Library

PROJECT DESCRIPTION

Participants will build and program robots that face off in head-to-head matches just like in real-life sumo matches! They will learn the universal coding concepts of loops and conditional If/Then statements by programing a robot that can push their competitors' robot out of a ring. In addition to learning basic programming constructs, participants will gain an understanding of the engineering design process and consider robot structure, weight, and gear ratios in their designs to make robots push as hard as possible. No prior experience with computer programming or LEGO MINDSTORMS is necessary to participate in LEGO Sumo.

Age Range

This project can be easily tailored to accommodate many ages.

- Tweens (Ages 8–12)
- Young adults (Ages 13–18)
- Adults

Type of Library Best Suited For

- Public libraries
- School libraries

Cost Estimate

- $800–$1,600
- Cost is based on 2 to 4 LEGO MINDSTORMS EV3 Core Sets (5003400) at approximately $400 each.[1]

OVERVIEW

For this challenge, participants will assemble and program in teams a LEGO MINDSTORMS robot that can push other teams' robots back and eventually make them go outside of a marked area. Each LEGO MINDSTORMS robot includes a small computer called an intelligent brick that controls the system, a set of modular sensors and motors, and LEGO BLOCKS. For this challenge, programs will be written on iPads using the EV3 Programmer app and sent to the robots via bluetooth. The EV3 Programmer app is a drag-and-drop programming environment that allows users to select BLOCKS that contain commands, logic, variables, and more and then connect them together to create the rules for their program. In a drag-and-drop programming environment, users don't have to worry about making syntax errors and things like that and can concentrate on learning programming logic first. Building a "Sumobot" involves a physical design component as well as a programming component, thus requiring participants to consider multiple parameters and numerous approaches in their designs.

Software/Hardware Needed

- LEGO MINDSTORMS EV3 Core Set (2 or more)
- iPad tablet with bluetooth capabilities (2 or more)
- 3'×3' minimum flat surface
- Black markers and a large role of white paper to mark the challenge ring on the floor
- Paper and pencils for brainstorming and drawing designs

STEP-BY-STEP INSTRUCTIONS

Preparation

- Build 2 or more super bare-bones robots. LEGO calls these the "Driving Base Robot." The Driving Base Robot is basically just the "intelligent brick" (i.e., the robot's brain), 2 motors, and 2 wheels. Put these pieces together and plug in the cables from the motors into ports B and C on the intelligent brick. Build instructions for the Driving Base Robot are included in every EV3

Core Set. Participants will expand, modify, and personalize these bots later when competition time arrives.

- Open the EV3 Programmer app on a tablet and dive in. It's a drag-and-drop programming environment. The open white space is called the Canvas and at the bottom is the Palette, where different colored BLOCKS are located. Each BLOCK represents a command that can be customized. BLOCKS are dragged on to the Palette to create programs. (See figure 37.1.)

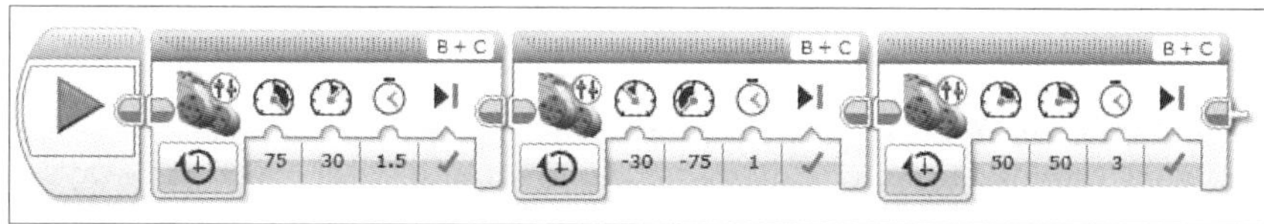

FIGURE 37.1

Programs should be read from left to right

Basic Movement

- The first BLOCK is a "Start" BLOCK.
- The second BLOCK is a Move Steering BLOCK with mode set to Rotations. The steering value is set to 0 so the robot will move in a straight line, the power is set to +50 so the robot will move forward at 50 percent power, the number of rotations is set to 2, and the option to apply the brake after the motion is set to On. Thus, this BLOCK will make the robot move 2 wheel rotations forward in a straight line. Note:the blue ovals in the image highlight values that have been changed from their default values.
- The third BLOCK is a Wait BLOCK. Its mode is set to Time, and the time is set to 1 second so the robot will pause for 1 second.
- The fourth BLOCK is a Move Steering BLOCK with mode set to Degrees. The steering value is set to 0 so the robot will move in a straight line, the power is set to -50 so the robot will move *backward* at 50 percent power, the angle is set to 720 degrees (2 rotations), and the brake option is set to On. Thus, this BLOCK will make the robot move 2 rotations (of the wheels) *backward* in a straight line, bringing the robot back to its starting position.
- The fifth BLOCK is a Wait BLOCK, set like the third BLOCK to make the robot pause for 1 second.
- The sixth BLOCK is a Move Steering BLOCK with mode set to Seconds. The steering value is set to 0 so the robot will move in a straight line, the power is set to +50 so the robot will move forward at 50 percent power, the number of *seconds* is set to 1, and the brake option is set to On. Thus, this BLOCK will make the robot move forward in a straight line at 50 percent power for 1 second.

Day of the Program

- Charge the LEGO MINDSTORMS robots using the mini-USB cables.
- Charge your tablets and make sure the EV3 Programming app is installed and can connect via bluetooth to the LEGO MINDSTORMS.
- Set up the playing field. Mark out the competition ring (about 75 cm in diameter). We used black marker on large sheets of white paper. Starting lines for each Sumobot should be placed in the center.
- You will also want a timer that is large enough so everyone can see it.

Getting Started

- A great way to start things off is to pull out the Driving Base Robot and iPads and have the group attempt to command robots to move in a pattern that forms a repeatable shape (for example, a triangle or a square).
- After a few minutes, encourage participants to explore different ways of turning the wheeled robot and the effect that altering the power on each motor has.

Exploration

- First, the facilitator will have to decide how teams will be formed. Sometimes participants arrive with partners they expect to collaborate with and sometimes they don't. Whatever the case and once teams are formed, discuss with the group the rapid nature of the competition. Building and programming time between matches should be timed and kept relatively short. We do 2 minutes of building and programing time before teams are required to be on the starting lines inside the ring. This pace is maintained so that participants are encouraged to constantly evaluate and debug their programs and build designs. Emphasize to the group that the design process is iterative, meaning that participants should repeat the steps as many times as needed, making improvements along the way as they learn from failure and uncover new design possibilities to arrive at great solutions.
- Before any bouts begin, define the rules:
    - Robots must be completely autonomous after the bout has started.
    - If it is determined by the judge that both robots are stuck in an entanglement or deadlock for at least 15 seconds, the facilitator will call for a Reset. If the facilitator declares a Reset, the clock is stopped, robots are put back in starting positions, robots will be reactivated, and the clock restarted.
    - A match is over after 2 minutes or after 1 "win" occurs.

Discussion

Questions to ask:

- Could you use an almost flat front sheet to slide under an opponent's wheels?
- Could you use more than 2 powered wheels (to give robots more "oomph")?
- Could you use smaller or bigger wheels? Which would be best?
- Could you use tracks instead of wheels? Would this help?
- Could you use some sort of battering ram (a third motor to knock your opponent sideways)?

LEARNING OUTCOMES

Participants will:

- Learn basic programming constructs such as control flow, loops, branches, and conditions as they engage within a visual programming environment.
- Be able to see connections between coding in a computer and real-life experiences.
- Learn to recognize failure as a form of information gathering.
- Use technology and coding to communicate effectively and express themselves creatively.
- Improve their collaborative skills in a hands-on, team learning environment.

RECOMMENDED NEXT PROJECTS

- **Gold Digger Project:** Find 3 pieces of randomly placed yellow paper on a table using the color sensor, without falling off the table.
- **The Maze Challenge:** Create a maze on the floor with painter's tape. Participants solve the maze using basic move BLOCKS to go forward and turn using rotations/degrees.
- **First LEGO League (FLL):** Participate in an international competition organized by FIRST for elementary and middle school students.

NOTE

1. At https://education.lego.com/en-us/products/lego-mindstorms-education-EV3-core-set-/5003400/.

38

Digital Dress-Up

Creating Drag-and-Drop Games in Scratch

OLIVIA HORVATH
Digital Services Specialist
Prince George's County (Maryland) Memorial Library System

PROJECT DESCRIPTION

Participants will create a drag-and-drop–style game using Scratch in this easy and fun project. The inspiration comes from the JavaScript doll maker, a ubiquitous and unabashedly feminine presence in early 2000's Internet culture. This hour-long workshop gives a comprehensive introduction to Scratch, and the code behind this project is simple and endlessly customizable. Once participants learn the coding concepts behind this project, they will have the tools to create an endless number of interactive, remixable games and interactive stories.

Age Range

- Tweens (Ages 8–12)

Type of Library Best Suited For

- Public libraries
- School libraries

Cost Estimate

- $0–$700

OVERVIEW

If you used the Internet in the late 1990s, you've probably seen them. And if you were a young person involved in chatroom culture, chances are you know them well! Hands tucked behind their backs, feet pointing out from flared jeans or fairy gowns, mischievous smiles surrounded by GIF-animated décor and pithy pixel sayings—Dollz were everywhere. Web artist Melicia Greenwood created the original Dollz as customizable chatroom avatars in 1995 (figure 38.1). Dollz quickly became ubiquitous in online spaces in the late 1990s to early 2000s, showing up as avatars, on website banners, and in interactive "doll maker" dress-up games across the web.[1]

FIGURE 38.1

Some of Melicia Greenwood's original Dollz. image from www.shatteredinnocents.com via Internet Archive

Doll makers were (and are) an easy entry point to digital art for many Internet users, and many women involved in digital art and game development have acknowledged the doll maker's impact.[2] Though Greenwood's Dollz are largely homogenous in their physicality (primarily white and Barbie-thin), dress-up games and doll makers have continued to expand as a genre. DollDivine (www.dolldivine.com), a website collecting hundreds of free doll maker games, features games celebrating a spectrum of body types, skin tones, genders, and cultural experiences.

Why has the digital doll maker held such lasting appeal? Doll makers are not a game in the traditional sense—there's no point system, winning, or losing. The goal is set by the players, who customize their doll for as long or short of a time as it takes until they are satisfied with the end product. The doll maker is more of a digital toy or even an exploratory tool. There is an element of exploration and persona creation inherent in its function. Whether taking a sartorial risk or stepping into a new identity, the doll maker allows the participant to switch between visual signifiers in a playful and safe environment. No outcome is wrong, and any end product can be saved to a desktop, shared on the web, or erased by simply refreshing the browser.

A doll maker or dress-up game, is, at its heart, a very simple piece of code applied to any number of assets. The basics of drag-and-drop functionality require some objects to be "draggable" and some to be stationary. Scratch makes this functionality easy, with the option to make any sprite draggable with the check of the box. Complexity beyond this point is up to you and participants. This workshop is a great introduction to Scratch and can be held in an hour, leaving participants with a simple game they can expand as their skills in Scratch grow.

Software/Hardware Needed

Equipment

- Personal computer or laptop with Internet access or with Scratch Offline Editor installed
- *Optional:* Colored paper and scissors for prototyping

STEP-BY-STEP INSTRUCTIONS

Preparation

Slip into something comfortable.

- Make sure you're familiar with Scratch and its basic controls, including the sprite editor and sensing and operator block types. This project is simple on its surface, but it has the potential for more complexity as each draggable object and property is added.
- Decide on a perspective from which participants will come to this project. This tutorial is for a dress-up–style game, but drag-and-drop functionality can be utilized to create many different kinds of games. The following are suggestions for thematic approaches to this project.

  Self-Portrait: Participants draw themselves and create their ideal wardrobe.

  Halloween/Cosplay: Create costumes from favorite books and movies.

  Past/Present/Future: What would someone my age wear throughout history or 200 years from now?

  Build-a-Monster: Attach legs, horns, tails, and tentacles to a basic beast body.

  Fantasy Library: Start with a photo of the library and create exciting new additions. Water slide? Hot dog stand? Unicorn rides? Why not!

PROJECT INSTRUCTIONS

Set the Scene (5–10 minutes)

- Introduce the project and its goals. Have participants brainstorm characters and costumes, introducing thematic parameters if you have decided to use them. Generate a list of ideas as a group, or experiment with cut paper as a way to think about creating clothing with basic shapes.

- Start participants with a blank canvas. Using the paint tool on backdrop 1, draw a line down the middle of the canvas. Use the fill tool to paint each side in a different solid color. The left side will function as the wardrobe (where draggable objects will live by default). The right will be the active area (where participants will dress their character).

Create a Character (10–15 minutes)

- Create a new sprite and give it a name (the example sprite is named "Buffy"). Depending on the theme and goals, guide participants in drawing their own character. A simple base is a good base—forward-facing bodies with arms to the side will be the easiest to dress. For learners who need a starting place, the Scratch sprite library also contains editable, age-appropriate bases under the Dress-Up category. Refer to this sprite as participants' "character."
- Place the character sprite on the right side of the canvas, within the active area. In the sprite information window, make sure "can drag in player" is *not* checked. The character will be stationary throughout the game.
- Avoiding the language of "dolls" at this stage opens students to exploration and encourages thinking further than idealized body images.

Accessorize (20–30 minutes)

- Participants are now ready to create their first "draggable" object. To ensure a good "fit," duplicate the character sprite and draw an article of clothing or an accessory onto the character. When it is finished, remove the character using the erase tool.
- In the sprite information menu, check "can drag in player" and give the sprite a descriptive name, like "Jacket." Place the object inside the wardrobe on the left side of the screen (figure 38.2).
- Turn the green flag into a "reset" button, returning the object to its place in the wardrobe. The motion block "go to x/y" automatically takes the coordinates for wherever the sprite is. Follow the "when green flag clicked" event block with the "go to x/y" motion block, and the canvas and character will clear when the flag is clear.
- Repeat this process at least 3 times to create a number of outfits and accessories for the character sprite.
- At this point, participants have the ability to create more complex code allowing the object to "snap" to selected points. "Snap to wardrobe" keeps objects organized by moving them to a set coordinate within the wardrobe

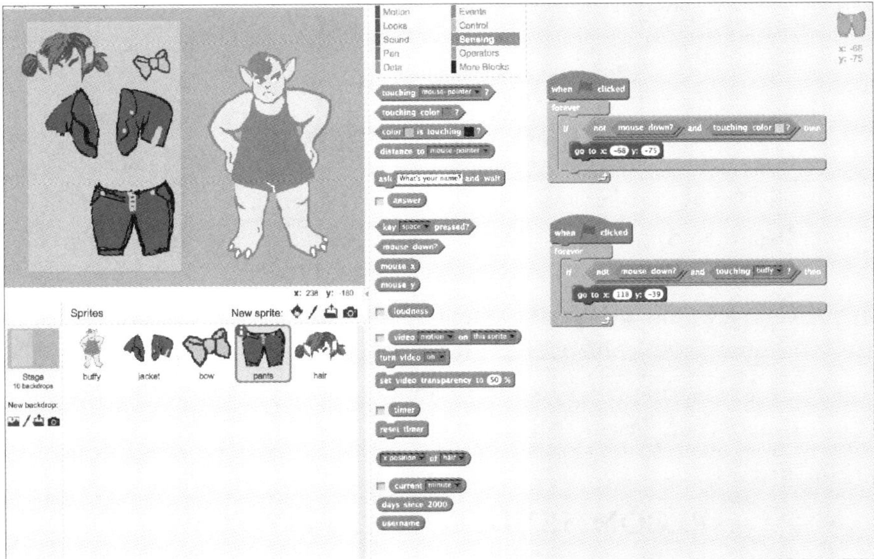

FIGURE 38.2

The top line of code snaps the clothing to wardrobe coordinates. The bottom line of code snaps the clothing to the character sprite

if the mouse is released when the object is touching the wardrobe. "Snap to character" code will move the object to a precise position if the mouse is released when the object is touching the character.

- To snap to wardrobe: When green flag clicked -> forever -> if [not [[mouse down?]]] and [[touching color (background color of wardrobe)?]] then -> go to x/y (object's position in wardrobe)
- To snap to character: When green flag clicked -> forever -> if [not [[mouse down?]]] and [[touching (name of character)?]] then -> go to x/y (object's position on character)

Both functions make game play smoother and more immersive. Snapping to the wardrobe keeps the canvas clean, a necessity in a game with many draggable objects. Snapping to the character ensures an exact "fit" for objects that look best on a specific part of the character.

Explore (5–15 minutes)

- Give time at the end of the project for participants to talk about what inspired them and to experiment with each other's creations. This project lends itself to remixes and collaboration. Participants may be inspired to replicate objects from other projects in their own game or make new outfits for each other's games. The possibilities are endless.

LEARNING OUTCOMES

Participants will:

- Design and code an interactive game with their own distinct character and wardrobe.
- Gain a working understanding of control (If/Else statements), sensing (mouse down), and operator (and, not) blocks in Scratch.
- Understand sprite-specific attributes, a basis for understanding the concepts of classes and IDs in coding languages.

RECOMMENDED NEXT PROJECTS

- Take your game to the next level! This workshop can easily be expanded into 2 or 3 sessions by adding more complex code. Participants can expand their skills in Scratch and enhance their project by animating an intro screen or adding a second character, a color slider for garments, or sprite reactions to certain outfit combinations.
- After completing this project, participants will be ready to explore more coding-intensive projects in Scratch and beyond. Build skills and expand horizons with:
    - Chapter 32: Scratch Art: Create and Animate Characters Using Scratch by Mary Carrier
    - Chapter 22: Scratch Coding for Tweens: Creating Cartoons by Karlene Tura Clark
    - Chapter 39: Remix a Meme Using Scratch by Olivia Horvath
- If participants have enjoyed the character creation aspect of this project, they may enjoy:
    - Chapter 40: Using Bloxels to Teach Storytelling and Video Game Design by Danielle Arnold

NOTES

1. Greenwood, M. (2003). *The Originz of Dollz*. Retrieved from https://web.archive.org/web/20031009132317/http:/www.shatteredinnocents.com:80/dollz/originz1.html.
2. Carpenter, N. (2018, March 29). "On 'the Palace,' You Can Be Anyone You Want to Be." *The Outline*. Retrieved from https://theoutline.com/post/3964/the-palace-game-history.

39

Remix a Meme Using Scratch

OLIVIA HORVATH
Digital Services Specialist
Prince George's County (Maryland) Memorial Library System

PROJECT DESCRIPTION

What is a meme? You may not be able to call up a definition, but if you've used the Internet in the last 15 years, chances are you've experienced them in all their perplexing ubiquity. The universality, comedy, and infectiousness of the visual meme makes it a perfect starting point for creative exploration of digital tools. This project is a lightning-fast introduction to Scratch for middle grade patrons with little to no coding experience. Participants will be introduced to basic computer science principles and create looping animated pieces using viral images, simple Scratch blocks, and their senses of humor.

Age Range

- Tweens (Ages 8–12)

Type of Library Best Suited For

- Public libraries
- School libraries

Cost Estimate

- $0–$700

OVERVIEW

So, what is a meme? Derived from a term used for cultural criticism, the word *meme* has come to represent an image or idea that takes on a life of its own through replication, imitation, and manipulation.[1]

Art historian Alice Bucknell traces the Internet meme's lineage from Dada and Postmodernism, calling them "the democratizing medium of our collective digital present. Easy to make, easy to share; instantly recognizable and a little nonsensical [. . .] nothing escapes the meme's comic gaze, and the form is being recognized as an artistic medium for this interconnected online moment."[2]

Participants with relative digital literacy will almost certainly have experience with viral images, and many will know the word *meme*. The easy transition from meme consumer to meme creator holds appeal even for students more reticent to dive into creative and coding projects.

This project is flexible in both scale and scope. An introduction to the Scratch coding environment and its simplest blocks, it is designed to run about an hour in length. The project is comfortable with 1 facilitator and 10–12 participants but can easily run larger, although you may want to encourage pairs or small groups. The images used can be tailored to fit your setting, and they can be used to enrich other thematic offerings.

A note on content: Bringing viral content into a learning environment can be fun, but it has the potential to shift participants' focus from the project to the Internet. This project opens with participants away from their own computers and engaging in a generative activity to jumpstart creativity and keep attentions from wandering outside the project space. Additionally, the world of memes, for all its creative potential, has played host to unsavory and downright offensive imagery and language. To maintain focus and respect in the space, it is recommended to create a meme "canvas" for participants to begin from rather than having them search for their own images. An encyclopedic knowledge of memes is not at all necessary for this project, but some research is recommended so that images and phrases with harmful intent can be avoided. Know Your Meme (knowyourmeme.com), a wiki-like database of viral phenomena, hosts thousands of meme images and research on their origins. If using a pre-existing meme, take care to understand its context.

Software/Hardware Needed

A computer or netbook with Internet access or with Scratch Offline Editor installed

STEP-BY-STEP INSTRUCTIONS

Preparation

Create your canvas:

- Before introducing participants to Scratch, brainstorm ideas for format and content. You can promote a theme beforehand (popular books, holidays, and historical events are all good subjects to riff off of) or encourage participants to choose their own.

- Select 5–10 "subject" images for participants to choose from. This activity works best with a headshot of an animal, well-known character, or historical figure with a clear facial expression and an uncluttered background. Tailor images to your learning environment, or use known visual memes or "reaction images."
- In a new Scratch project, upload each image as a sprite. Uncheck the "show" box for each sprite so the canvas is blank.
- Title the new project and share it to make it remixable by the Scratch community.

PROJECT INSTRUCTIONS

Introduce the Format and Brainstorm a Concept (5–10 minutes)

- As a group, have participants share their knowledge of memes. Participants may be familiar with the term and able to give examples, but a definition may be more elusive.
- Show some recent examples of viral images or videos and discuss their similarities.
- Generate a working definition (e.g., "A meme is an image or idea that is passed around by many people and changes as it is passed.") or a list of descriptors (e.g., funny, repetitive, fast, parody, digital, collage).
- Discuss how humor was used in the memes viewed earlier. Ask participants to think about how they will use image and text to convey information. Will they be making absurd collages or sharing relatable emotions? There's no wrong answer!

Select a Subject (5–10 minutes)

- Participants will follow the link to your project and click the See Inside button to make their edits.
- Once inside, they will choose one image from your pre-loaded sprites, check the "show" box so it is visible on the canvas, and edit out the image background so they can add their own.
- Under Costumes, select the magic wand tool to remove as much of the background as possible. Use the erase tool to clean up any remaining parts. Edit the image in bitmap mode.

- Have participants create a new sprite for the meme's text. They may use the text tool in the sprite editor or Scratch's pre-existing alphabet sprites for more emphasis.

Remix (20–30 minutes)

Once the meme's subject and text are in place, challenge participants to add 3 or more behaviors to the piece using code blocks. The following are suggestions for simple looping behaviors. Tailor them to participants' skill levels and interests accordingly.

Subject

- When flag clicked, have subject say or think a funny phrase.
- Make a second sprite with the subject mirrored. When flag clicked, switch between costumes and loop.

Text

- When flag clicked, "wobble" text by rotating back and forth along y-axis.

Background

- Choose a background from the library or create one using the editor. When flag clicked, change color and repeat.
- Duplicate the background and rotate in the editor. When flag clicked, switch between costumes and loop to create a rotating effect.
- When flag clicked, play a song from the library and loop.

Advanced

- When flag clicked, move text around the screen at random intervals. If on edge, bounce.
- Create a visual effect (e.g., confetti, rain, balloons, stars) using the sprite library or drawing in the editor. When flag clicked, move up or down the canvas.
- Use conditional (If/Then) statements using control and sensing blocks to create an effect caused by a mouseover.

Go Viral (5–10 minutes)

- Bring participants together at the end of the program to share their creations, such as in figure 39.1. Through humor, guide participants in observing how ideas "went viral" in the microcosm of the project space. What ideas and images are shared, and what is unique in each participant's interpretation? What could happen next?

FIGURE 39.1
Example code

LEARNING OUTCOMES

Participants will:

- Discuss the phenomenon of the viral image as a digital native method of expression and collaboration.
- Use coding, images, and words to express themselves in a time-based digital art piece.
- Comprehend the layout and function of the Scratch coding environment.
- Have a working understanding of the use of events, control, and motion blocks in Scratch, laying the groundwork for the computer science concepts of **class** and **behavior.**

RECOMMENDED NEXT PROJECTS

- Encourage participants to expand their knowledge of Scratch and coding by using the sensing, operator, and data blocks with projects such as:
    - Chapter 32: Scratch Art: Create and Animate Characters Using Scratch by Mary Carrier
    - *Chapter 22:* Scratch Coding for Tweens: Creating Cartoons by Karlene Tura Clark
    - Chapter 38: Digital Dress-Up: Creating Drag-and-Drop Games in Scratch by Olivia Horvath

NOTES

1. Solon, O. (2013, June 20). *Richard Dawkins on the Internet's Hijacking of the Word 'Meme.'* Retrieved from https://www.wired.co.uk/article/richard-dawkins-memes.
2. Bucknell, A. (2017, May 30). *What Memes Owe to Art History.* Retrieved from https://www.artsy.net/article/artsy-editorial-memes-owe-art-history.

40

Using Bloxels to Teach Storytelling and Video Game Design

DANIELLE ARNOLD

K–8 School Library Media Specialist | Belmar (New Jersey) Elementary School

PROJECT DESCRIPTION

In this project, participants will learn how to write a story, while getting to design and play their own video game. The activity starts off by having participants write their own story. Afterward, they will peer-review one another's work, revise, and rewrite their final draft. Once their final draft is complete, participants will make their story come to digital life by creating a video game to mimic their story. Participants will see what it's like to be a game designer by creating and designing a story with characters, a setting, and challenges for the gamer to defeat. Participants will have the opportunity to peer-review one another's games to see if any unsolvable challenges arise in the game. To end the activity, you may choose to open your library and host a gaming day where designers can showcase their work!

Bloxels is an easy-to-use game design program that requires no gaming or design experience, just an imagination. Children and adults of all ages love seeing their video games come to life, and this program can easily be modified for any age range.

Age Range

- Tweens (Ages 8–12)

Type of Library Best Suited For

- Public libraries
- School libraries

Cost Estimate

- $35 and higher
- Costs depend on how many Bloxel boards and devices are purchased

OVERVIEW

This project is divided into 2 parts: Part 1 consists of participants writing their own story and Part 2 consists of participants designing a video game that represents their story. In Part 1, participants use the writing process to write their own story. Each story must include a beginning, a middle, and an end and have a problem and a solution. After participants write, revise, and complete their final draft, they will move on to Part 2, video game design.

FIGURE 40.1

Participant creating a character about a ballerina

During Part 2, participants design their characters, setting, and challenges using Bloxels and the Bloxels app. Participants use the color-coded blocks from the Bloxels game board for their design and upload them to the app using a device (figure 40.1). Once uploaded, participants can play their game live on the device. Having a showcase to conclude the project is a great way for participants to share their work with each other as well as family and friends.

The time frame of this project can vary depending on how long it takes to write the stories and design the games. It is recommended to have the full project completed within 2 weeks: 1 week for the writing process and 1 week for the game design. However, this can be shortened to meet your needs. The video game design works best if participants work individually or with a partner. It is not recommended to have more than 2 participants working on a Bloxels game at a time. Once participants understand the color-coded blocks, participants become very independent. However, if possible, have at least 2 staff members on hand for groups larger than 25. This will allow for participants to troubleshoot more easily if a problem arises.

Software/Hardware Needed

- Bloxels game board and blocks
- Device with Bloxels Builder app installed

STEP-BY-STEP INSTRUCTIONS

Preparation

- Determine whether participants can create anything they want or if you're providing a prompt or theme for them to complete.
- Determine if participants will work independently, with a partner, or in a small group.
- Pre-install app on devices.
- Have available writing paper to write a story or word processing program.

PROJECT INSTRUCTIONS

PART 1

- Begin by discussing video games and what they entail—characters, setting, problem, solution, etc., and compare/contrast them to stories.
- Demonstrate how to create a room/character for participants to see.
- Using the planning sheet or paper, have participants write a story or complete the writing prompt provided.
- Make sure the authors can answer the following questions: Where does the story take place? What are the characters? Emphasize that each story should have a beginning, a middle, and an end.
- Have participants peer-review each other's work. Authors will make any necessary changes.
- After revising is complete, participants will write their final draft.

PART 2

- Introduce Bloxels to participants. Explain the color blocks and what they represent. (red: hazard, blue: water, green: terrain, yellow: coin, orange: exploding blocks, pink: power ups, purples: enemies, white: story blocks).

- Participants create their story using the Bloxel game board and app. Participants write their story using the story blocks throughout their game.
- Encourage participants to take breaks and test one another's game. Designers can easily get caught up in designing a game but not see problems when they arise. Participants can provide peer reviews and feedback to make sure the game runs smoothly.
- If time is a factor, limit the number of rooms/characters participants can have.
- Once games are completed, have an author share so participants can read and play one another's game.

LEARNING OUTCOMES

Participants will:

- Write a story using the writing process.
- Peer-review each other's work.
- Use the design process to create a video game, including characters, setting, and challenges to correspond to the story.

RECOMMENDED NEXT PROJECTS

- Bloxels can be modified to be more or less challenging. Participants can continue to design their game or create a new one.
- After using Bloxels, create a story using Scratch.

41

How to Give Successful Coding Workshops for Ages 8-12

KARIMA KAFIF
Children's Programmer and Public Services Assistant
Ottawa (Ontario) Public Library, Greenboro Branch

PROJECT DESCRIPTION

Librarians and children's programmers will learn about all the logistics involved with running a coding workshop for kids and the different tools and tips that can support their project and lead to its success. Librarians will learn how to plan for the workshop and how to run it in a way that makes it easy and successful. All examples are driven from experience with Scratch, which is one of the most suitable programming languages for younger kids. However, the preparation steps can be modified for many other coding workshops.

Age Range

- Tweens (Ages 8–12)

Type of Library Best Suited For

- Public libraries
- School libraries

Cost Estimate

- $0
- The only costs involved include those for printing handouts and optional achievement certificates for participants.

OVERVIEW

This workshop is designed to be run in 3 sessions for children ages 8–12 and should involve prior registration. Limit the number of participants to 8–10 per session. Otherwise, get volunteers or colleagues to help you and make sure they are trained and familiar with the project you are teaching beforehand.

Although you may choose any programming language for your workshop, this project is specifically written for using Scratch because it is an easy language based on visual coding blocks and does not require any syntax writing. All that kids have to do to have fun and achieve quick results is to simply move around blocks of code.

A single session workshop may not reach its desired outcomes with children ages 8–12, which is why this program is designed to be a multisession workshop. One hour and half per session seems to be a right time to cover enough material at a convenient rhythm for young participants. If you can schedule the sessions close to one another, this will help maintain the continuity in learning.

Choose the right time to schedule your workshop. Depending on your environment, you may want to avoid having workshops during the school day. Spring break and the beginning of summer break are the best times to get kids interested. After-school programs can work well too.

Software/Hardware Needed

- Computers with Internet connection and updated Adobe Flash Player. It doesn't matter which operating system you have. However, if the connection doesn't work well, it would be better to install Scratch editor on computers and ask participants to bring a flash drive to save their work.
- 1 computer connected to a projector
- Papers and pencils or small booklets to encourage kids to take notes
- Access to a color printer for printing handouts

STEP-BY-STEP INSTRUCTIONS

Preparation

- If you are new to coding, familiarize yourself with the foundations of the language prior to the workshop. You can find some interesting courses about coding foundations on Lynda.com, and there are resources available on the Scratch main website at https://scratch.mit.edu.

- Become familiar with the Scratch platform and all of its features that display on the screen, even if you will not be using them. Children are curious, and you should be able to answer their questions. In general, the Help function is a good place to start and provides very easy and simplified definitions for most features.
- Reserve the computer room or the Chromebooks. Have mice connected to the Chromebooks to make it easier for kids. Some librarians give kids the choice to bring their own device. It is an option to consider, but keep in mind that you will have to help with a device that you may not be familiar with, and this can be time consuming.
- If you have a bad connection, install Scratch editor on computers and make sure Adobe Flash Player is updated.
- Check to make sure the sound is working or if headphones are needed.
- Create your own account online and get a few versions of your project ready at different steps of its development. When doing so, take a snapshot of each step. Make a Word document that includes all snapshots with explanations of the script, including which sprite it is for.
- Create a backup of your project on flash memory
- Use snapshots with simple instructions to create handouts.
- Prepare a glossary of all technical words you will use and have a printed copy with you.
- When advertising your program, make sure that the poster and online description of your workshop specify the age and level of difficulty. Also, send a letter to parents who registered their kids about what to expect. Ask them to open an account for their child by following the link you provide, or make sure that kids have access to an e-mail address with a password. Of course, if you are working offline, children can use a flash memory to save their projects.

Workshop Instructions

- The best way to get participants' attention right from the start is to present the results at the beginning of the session. Run a complete pre-tested version of the project you intend to teach, preferably a project with colors, animation, and music, and you'll pique everyone's interest and get their attention. For example, when I told kids, "today, you'll be able to make an electronic birthday card by yourself" and showed them the animated card on the projector, I immediately felt their interest and enthusiasm. (You will find more details about the birthday card project in the "examples" section.)

- Introduce the basic functions (for Scratch: stage, sprite, script, costume). Explain other concepts (for example, loop, condition, variable) only when you have the opportunity to use them. Some suggest that theory should be taught first and even propose that the first workshop doesn't need computers. However, I prefer to get hands-on from the beginning. Children are excited about the computer itself, and at this age they generally don't have much patience for theoretical explanations.
- Break down the code and don't give all the instructions at once because children may become overwhelmed. The code of a finished project shows many intricate blocks and can be difficult for a child to decipher. Presenting 1 step at the time makes it visually more accessible and easier to understand.

Exploration

- Throughout the workshop, it is helpful to seek interaction rather than revealing the correct answer right away. Similarly, don't reveal the entire script at the beginning of the workshop. Let participants get a feel for the problem and the need to resolve it. For instance, the size of the sprite is too big, or it is hiding at the edge, or it should show up later instead of at the beginning. Once the problem is identified, it is effective to help children find the solution.
- Be flexible about children's choice of sprite, stage, music, and written statements. The more a project is customized, the more participants feel enthusiastic to explore further.
- Let children explore other options and their effects. For example, if the instruction is "make the sprite 25 percent smaller," let kids try other sizes and test to see the result. Or, if the instruction is to repeat the action each minute, let them try a faster or slower timing. This will help them better understand the effects of their decisions.
- Encourage the fastest kids to try different options, or ask them to help others who are behind. Also, prepare and print a set of instructions that are more complicated. This is good to give to participants who are quicker with the coding than the rest of the group. Never let them feel bored.
- Allot enough time for setup, especially for the first session. Then, rove constantly to assist kids and verify that they were able to follow along.
- Alternate practice and theoretical explanations. Set aside enough time for participants to follow along with you and encourage them to name and save their project. Also, take time at the end of the session to wrap up with some information about what they will learn during the next session.

- Distributing handouts at the end of each session gives kids who couldn't finish their project another chance to catch up and helps them get ready for the next session.

Extending the Experience

- Explain how to find the right instructions for the right actions. Some kids will be tempted to blindly copy you because they want to get to the end results quickly. But it is by pushing them to resolve the problem themselves that they build their self-confidence.
- Extend the experience by allowing kids to elaborate more and try things that are not planned, especially the children who grasp concepts quickly and get the project done before others finish.
- Expand participants' vision by explaining how to reuse other projects. The power of most free platforms for coding comes from the community and the ability to share and reuse what others have already done. That's why you should schedule time, preferably near the end of the workshop, to teach kids how to build on others' work. This can be done gradually. For example, at the end of the first session, explain how to save the project and get back to it. During the second session, you can show participants how to copy the same code from 1 sprite to another. By the end of the workshop, kids should be able to remix other people's projects and customize them.
- Evaluate your work. By keeping notes of participants' questions, reactions, and feedbacks to each step of the project, you'll get to adjust your workshop as needed and empower yourself for future workshops.

LEARNING OUTCOMES

By completing this workshop, participants will:

- Become familiar with Scratch in particular and coding in general.
- Gain some knowledge about programming basics (logic instructions for actions, loops, variables, conditions).
- Be able to make some animations and multimedia programming.
- Gain self-confidence by developing critical thinking and problem-solving skills.
- Have fun using technology as a producer rather than a consumer.

RECOMMENDED NEXT PROJECTS

- After a first multi-session workshop, you have 2 options. You can go further with programming using Scratch and offer an intermediate-level workshop. This option requires in-depth learning to master complex functions and intricate instructions. It also implies that you will be working with children who already have an introductory knowledge of Scratch. Therefore, you can build on what you did before.
- The other option is to introduce another coding language like Ruby, Python, or Open Processing. This option helps to reach the same learning outcomes as the previous workshop and gives participants more opportunities to practice. Another benefit of this option is that participants don't need any prerequisite knowledge to attend the workshop.

Examples

For the first workshop, something as simple as a birthday card is appropriate because it doesn't need a lot of code, and the music and movement captivate kids (figure 41.1). You can find this project at https://scratch.mit.edu/projects/235941154/.

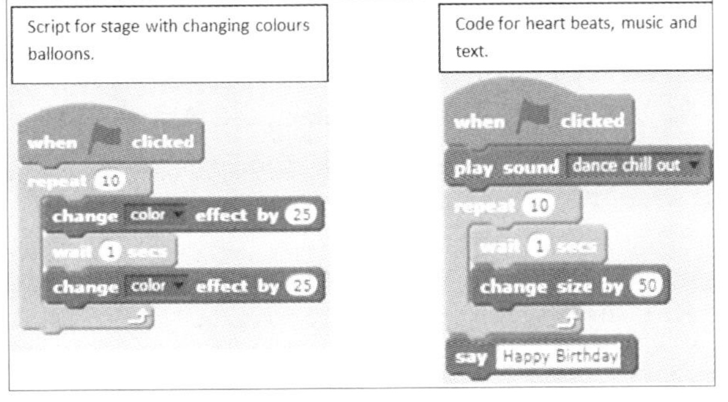

FIGURE 41.1
Code for Animated Birthday Card project

- One of the projects that works well during the second session is "Lost in Space" (figure 41.2). It's a project suggested by the Code Club website. It has the advantage of illustrating different ways to animate a few sprites. This is good practice for kids and helps them work at different rhythms. Presenting this project or something similar also allows beginners to assimilate the coding logic and gain some practice. It also gives faster participants enough material to go further without getting bored. For this project, see https://codeclubprojects.org/en-GB/scratch/lost-in-space/.

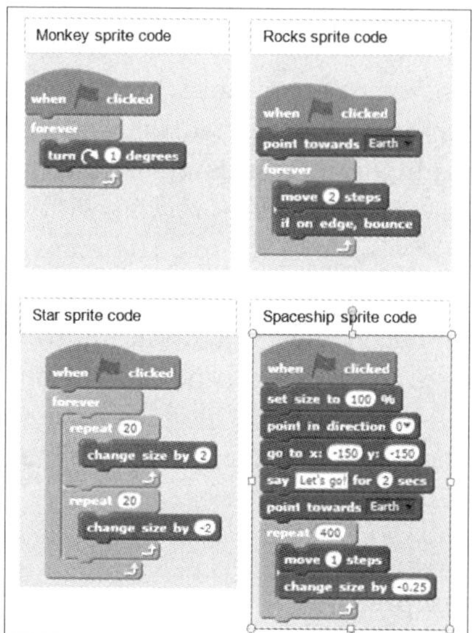

FIGURE 41.2

Code for Lost in Space project

- For the third session, assuming that participants are becoming more comfortable with the platform and the language, you may want to introduce the concept of game design. Kids are always impressed with the idea of creating interactive games themselves. One project that I found interesting is the "Hungry Shark" (figure 41.3). The stages and all the sprites for this project already exist in the Scratch library, and the project itself is shared by the community. For this project, see https://scratch.mit.edu/projects/237464468/.

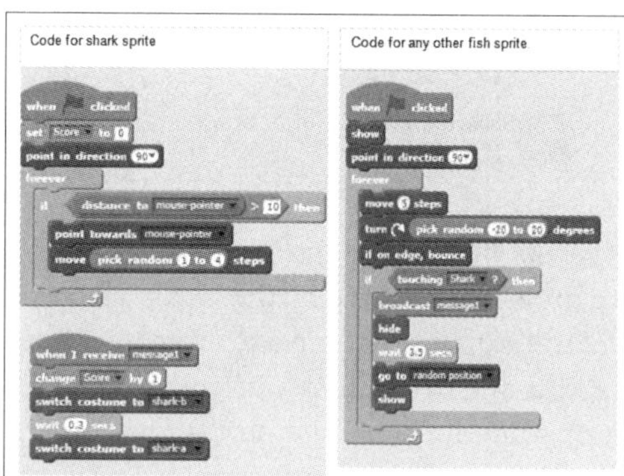

FIGURE 41.3

Code for Hungry Shark project

PART III

PROGRAMS FOR YOUNG ADULTS

(AGES 13–18)

42

Form a Hacker Club and Hacker Club Jr.

JESSICA FRANCO

Teen Librarian | Groton (Connecticut) Public Library

EMILY SHEEHAN

Children's and Emerging Technologies Librarian | Groton (Connecticut) Public Library

PROJECT DESCRIPTION

Hacker Club and Hacker Club Jr. are highly customizable programs that appeal to children of all ages. In this program model, teens in the Hacker Club meet once a month to learn new skills and familiarize themselves with different pieces of technology (figure 42.1). After exploring the new technology, teens meet with the program instructor to develop a lesson plan for Hacker Club Jr. Teen volunteers help implement the lesson with children participating in Hacker Club Jr. The lessons can be heavily modified to accommodate the available technology and instructors' skill level. The following lesson plans illustrate the range of activities available for the program series.

FIGURE 42.1

A teen participant programs a micro:bit using block-based coding

Age Range

- Kids (Ages 3–7)
- Tweens (Ages 8–12)
- Young adults (Ages 13–18)

Type of Library Best Suited For

- Public libraries
- School libraries

Cost Estimate

- $120–$1,440
- Ozobots range in price from $100 for a single robot to $1,200 for a classroom set with 12 robots and supporting materials. The micro:bits cost $20 for 1 unit and $240 for 12.

OVERVIEW

This program model has 2 general goals: to foster learning relationships in the library and to promote confident exploration of technology. The first half of Hacker Club should be an open exploration of the chosen skill or equipment. The second portion of the program will be a discussion of how to teach Hacker Club Jr. As a group, teens will identify what they want children to learn, activities that will have the strongest learning impact, and an essential question that will provide evidence of having completed the learning goal. In addition, expectations for teen volunteers should be outlined clearly and reviewed regularly. Teen volunteers should be taught how to instruct without taking over the project or task.

When teaching Hacker Club Jr., introduce teen instructors and allow them to teach as they feel capable. Depending on volunteers' comfort levels, it might be best to have staff introduce the program and allow teens to teach in small groups. At the end of the predetermined lesson, ask the essential question and record the answers to discuss later with teens.

Software/Hardware Needed

- Crackers
- Cream cheese or any type of spread (jelly, marshmallow creme, almond butter, etc.)
- Plastic knives
- Paper plates
- Paper
- Pencils
- Computers with Internet access
- Ozobots
- White or tan paper
- Green, red, blue, and black markers
- Micro:bits
- Computers with Internet access

STEP-BY-STEP INSTRUCTIONS

Computer Science Unplugged Session

- Introduce participants to the simple concepts of computer science and the importance of language when working with computers.

PROJECT INSTRUCTIONS

- Open with a brief discussion of how computers and robots interpret instructions.
- Conduct a brief demonstration of how a robot would interpret instructions in a literal sense by having participants guide the instructor through spreading cream cheese on a cracker and then successfully eating it. This exercise is a great icebreaker and will have everyone laughing at the results.
- Have participants break up into pairs or small groups to recreate the demonstration. Encourage them to write down the instructions and have their partner follow them. Everyone should get a chance at being the "robot" and giving/writing the instructions.
- End the session with "Digging Deeper" questions.

Digging Deeper

- How is language important when working with computers or robots?
- Is it easier to write down the instructions or speak them?

Resource Suggestions

- https://code.org/curriculum/unplugged/
- https://csunplugged.org/en/

JavaScript Session

- Participants are encouraged to try 2 gamified coding platforms so they can explore the usage of JavaScript as a coding language.

PROJECT INSTRUCTIONS

- Open with a brief discussion of programming languages such as Python, PHP, and JavaScript.
- Direct participants to computers and have them navigate to https://code.org/starwars/.
- Allow a half hour for participants to complete as many lessons as possible and then switch to www.codecombat.com.
- Be available to answer any questions or troubleshoot.
- End the session with "Digging Deeper" questions.

Digging Deeper

- Do you enjoy learning to code through gaming?
- Do you think you could create a game like the one you played?
- What were important elements you needed when working with JavaScript?

Ozobots Session

- Participants will explore coding and computational through color patterns.

PROJECT INSTRUCTIONS

- Open with a brief discussion of how computer code can sometimes come in various forms (letters, numbers, and colors).
- Introduce participants to Ozobots.
- Distribute Ozobots to participants or form groups (figure 42.2).
- Ask participants to create 3 lines of code using the Color Code Reference Sheet provided with Ozobots.
- Use Ozobots to test the code.

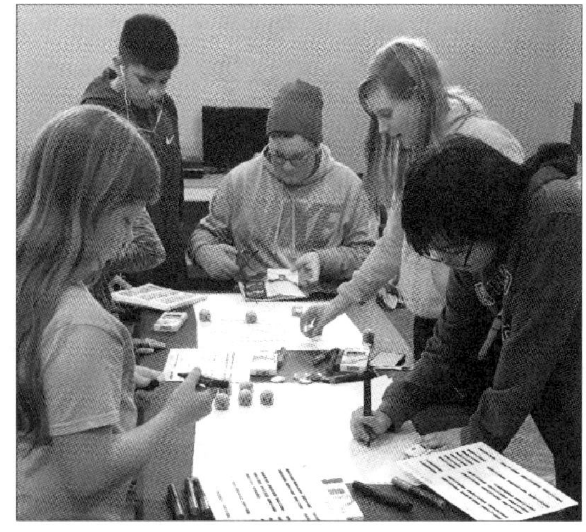

FIGURE 42.2

Teens work together to program Ozobots using markers

- If time permits, encourage participants to create race tracks or write their names.
- End the session with “Digging Deeper” questions.

Digging Deeper

- Was it important for the code to be precise? If yes, why?
- What was your favorite code?

Resource Suggestions

- https://ozobot.com/stem-education/stem-lessons/
- https://www.robot-advance.com/pj-94.pdf

Micro:bits Session

- Participants will utilize block coding to program micro:bits.

PROJECT INSTRUCTIONS

- Open with a brief demonstration and overview of the micro:bit.
- Distribute micro:bits to participants, allowing them to familiarize themselves with each part.
- Direct participants to computers and the JavaScript Blocks Editor: microbit .org/code.
- Walk participants through the blocks available to them and the code for displaying a smiley face.
- Allow participants to explore the code options or challenge the group to create a Rock, Paper, Scissors game using the micro:bit.
- End the session with “Digging Deeper” questions.

Digging Deeper

- What did you learn today?
- What did you code your micro:bit to do?
- How would you improve your code?

Resource Suggestions

- http://microbit.org
- https://www.microbit.co.uk/blocks/lessons/rock-paper-scissors/activity/

LEARNING OUTCOMES

Participants will:

- Demonstrate their ability to utilize computational thinking when writing instructions.
- Demonstrate good comprehension of loops and block coding.
- Write effective code using JavaScript.
- Recognize the importance of syntax in coding languages.
- Use color codes and patterns to demonstrate an understanding of coding and computational thinking.

RECOMMENDED NEXT PROJECTS

- **Mixing It Up:** Even though the program includes lessons that require specialized technology, it is not a necessary to successfully run the program. Evaluate your library's technology and look for opportunities using craft supplies and board games. We also recommend utilizing some of the lessons in this book for Hacker Club events.
- **Expand the Program:** Once the lesson plans have been developed, consider taking the program on the road. Take the lessons to local community center, schools, or youth centers to recreate the event. If your library allows it, have resident teens or teen volunteers meet you there to help facilitate the program.

43

Host a Teen and Tween App Development Camp in Your Library

JESSICA FRANCO

Teen Librarian | Groton (Connecticut) Public Library

EMILY SHEEHAN

Children's and Emerging Technologies Librarian | Groton (Connecticut) Public Library

PROJECT DESCRIPTION

This App Development Camp is a week-long series of programs for young adults and tweens. Using Thunkable or MIT App Inventor, participants can make apps for either iOS or Android devices, respectively. For those who are accustomed to using Scratch, both of these websites feature block-based coding, creating an easy-to-use and familiar environment.

Age Range

- Tweens (Ages 8–12)
- Young adults (Ages 13–18)

Type of Library Best Suited For

- Public libraries
- School libraries

Cost Estimate

- $0
- To successfully host this camp, the library needs to provide computers and reliable access to the Internet. Both Thunkable and MIT App Inventor provide opportunities for testing online, but having tablets or smartphones available allows for more reliable results. Participants can be asked to bring their own devices, but if the library has tablets to share, the program would be more accessible.

OVERVIEW

The camp walks participants through 2 predetermined apps. Through these lessons, participants will be exposed to the basic coding blocks required for creating a mobile app. The last 3 sessions of the camp are hosted as a workshop, allowing participants to create their own original app. During this time, the instructor acts as a resource and aids in troubleshooting any faulty code. At the end of the camp, participants are asked to showcase their finished product and receive feedback from peers.

Although this lesson includes tutorials for both Thunkable and MIT App Inventor, it is advised to teach them as separate programs. If taught side by side, we recommend having a small class size to make transitioning between the programs easier. Thunkable offers coding for both Android and iOS, with limited code options for iOS. MIT App Inventor is primarily for Android, although iOS is rumored to be in development. MIT App Inventor offers advanced options for design features. We recommend exploring both and choosing the one you are most comfortable with as the instructor.

Software/Hardware Needed

- Computers
- Internet access
- Mobile devices

STEP-BY-STEP INSTRUCTIONS

Introduction and Prediction App

Introduce participants to the new web application(s) and explore the available features by creating a prediction app.

PROJECT INSTRUCTIONS

- Open with a brief discussion of block coding and mobile applications. Define for the group what block coding is, emphasizing its puzzle-like nature. Here are some tutorials that explain block coding and its principles:
    - Thunkable—https://thunkable.com
    - MIT App Inventor—http://appinventor.mit.edu/explore/get-started.html/
- Discuss what apps you are using in your daily life, as well as apps you wish were available.
- At the MIT App Inventor or Thunkable websites, have attendees establish accounts, many of which can be connected directly to Google.

- Introduce MIT App Inventor or Thunkable and give an overview of the coding blocks that are available.
- Walk the group through creating the prediction app (Thunkable, shown in figure 43.1) or the Magic 8 Ball app (MIT App Inventor). Full tutorials are available online, or see this chapter's "Resource Suggestions" section.

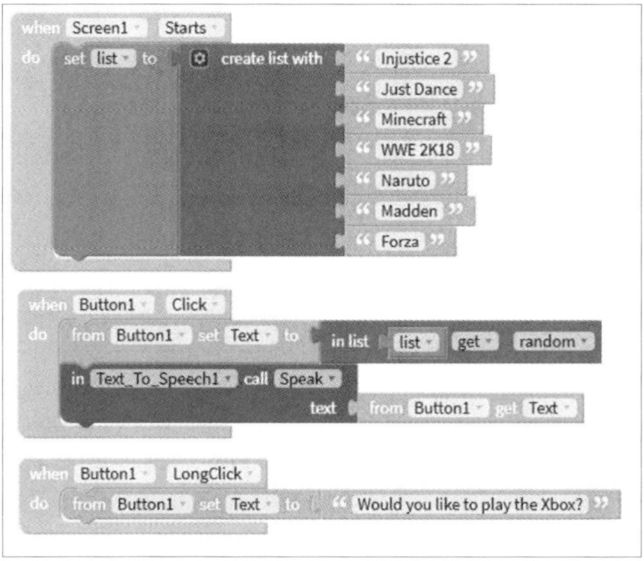

FIGURE 43.1

This is an example code for a prediction app on Thunkable. This code asked users if they wanted to play Xbox and presented them with a randomized game choice.

- Once the app has been created, install it on a mobile device and test it. A link with instructions for installation is available in this lesson's "Resource Suggestions" section or visit the tutorial section of Thunkable and MIT App Inventor websites.
- End the session with "Digging Deeper" questions.

Digging Deeper

- What did you learn today?
- Can you customize your app by adding sound effects, changing the color of the text or background, making each response appear in a different color, or having an instructional page?
- Can you use this code for something other than Magic 8 ball responses?

Resource Suggestions

- http://appinventor.mit.edu/explore/ai2/magic-8-ball.html/
- https://www.youtube.com/watch?v=sYmhosF-Ag8&list=PLB89L9PPGIrwy4Tfi1x9eu0LccH5Hsb3V/
- http://appinventor.mit.edu/explore/support/packaging-apps.html/
- https://thunkable.com/explore/ai2/share.html/

Variety App

- Continue exploring the features available on MIT App Inventor or Thunkable by creating a game or artificial intelligence app.

PROJECT INSTRUCTIONS

- Open with a discussion of the successes, challenges, and confusion from the previous session.
- Introduce the apps that will be created on each platform. MIT App Inventor users will make a game, and Thunkable users will make an artificial intelligence app.
- Split up the groups based on which individuals are using each platform. Allow 1 group to refine its app from the previous session, while the other learns about their new app, and then switch.
- Tutorials for the 2 apps are available in the “Resource Suggestions” section of this lesson.
- Once the app has been created, install it on a mobile device and test it.
- Remind students that the remaining sessions for the camp will be free code; discuss some of the ideas that they may have.
- End the session with “Digging Deeper” questions.

Digging Deeper

- What did you learn today?
- How could you customize your app?
- Can you use this code to create something original?

Resource Suggestions

- http://appinventor.mit.edu/explore/ai2/get-gold.html/
- https://www.youtube.com/watch?v=k9P0BIN3CUM/

Free Code and Showcase

Challenge participants to create an app or remix their previous code that meets their interests or needs. This lesson can be used multiple times until the end of camp when the apps are shared with the group.

PROJECT INSTRUCTIONS

- Open with a discussion of the successes, challenges, and confusion from the previous session.
- Ask students if they have any ideas for new apps. Discuss their ideas and help others get inspired. Ask participants if these apps will meet a need or an interest.
- Allow teens to begin working and provide encouragement and troubleshooting as needed.
- On the last day, celebrate the end of the camp with snacks and exploring each other's finished apps.
- Have teens introduce themselves (name, grade, and school), show their app (idea, goal, and thought process behind the app), and discuss their challenges/successes.
- Pass devices around so everyone can test them.
- End the session with "Digging Deeper" questions.

Digging Deeper

- What did you learn today?
- Encourage participants to provide expanded customization of color, sound, images, video, etc.
- Have you included any Easter eggs?
- Have you done any research into your app?
- What was your favorite code?

Resource Suggestions

- http://appinventor.mit.edu/explore/ai2/support/troubleshooting.html/
- https://docs.thunkable.com/thunkable-classic-android/troubleshooting/

LEARNING OUTCOMES

Participants will:

- Learn how to use either MIT App Inventor or Thunkable.
- Develop and demonstrate coding skills with a focus on creating lists, random generation of results, and text to speech.
- Hone their skills in either MIT App Inventor or Thunkable.
- Develop and demonstrate coding skills with a focus on visibility components using a timer, collision recognition, and design creation.
- Discover the importance of troubleshooting and perfecting code.

RECOMMENDED NEXT PROJECTS

- **Mixing It Up:** Both MIT App Inventor and Thunkable have an active online educational community. There are a number of tutorials, including projects and activities, that can be used to inspire and teach. Thunkable's content is primarily YouTube based, however it offers a variety of advanced code already condensed into blocks. In addition to the artificial intelligence, Thunkable users can create translation apps and incorporate social media. MIT App Inventor has more flexibility and allows for advanced game development.
- If you've already taught both programs, consider offering a hackathon challenge. Give participants a goal and set amount of time to complete it. Each person will approach it differently and create wildly different apps in the process.
- **Expanding the Program:** Reach out to local computer software engineers to visit the program as guest coders. Even though they may not be familiar with Thunkable or MIT App Inventor, they do have experience troubleshooting and using computational thinking in their daily lives. They also often have a user-oriented perspective that participants may be lacking. Guest coders can visit for the entire week or during 1 session to provide feedback and help as participants work. For the final session, invite the guest coders back to see the finished products. This real-world perspective—as well as representation of people from the community (be it geographical, gender, or ethnicity), making a career from these skills—may inspire young coders to further pursue computer science.

44

Host an Escape Room with a Robotic Twist

JOANNA SCHOFIELD

Branch Services Librarian-Generalist | Cuyahoga County (Ohio) Public Library

PROJECT DESCRIPTION

What do you get when you combine books, escape rooms, and robots? A technology-filled fun adventure. Tweens and teens enjoy trying to use clues and overcome challenges to work their way out of an escape room. For this program, we'll go high-tech by combining the traditional aspect of a timed escape room with LEGO MINDSTORMS robots (figure 44.1). For this particular escape room, we will focus on an *Escape from Mr. Lemoncello's Library* theme and highlighted book-related puzzles. Each puzzle will be followed by a robotics challenge ranging from following the line to parallel parking. To complete each challenge, participants must program their robot using LEGO software.

FIGURE 44.1

Students, along with librarian JoAnna Schofield, troubleshoot their MINDSTORMS robots to make them drive straight ahead

Age Range

- Tweens (Ages 8–12)
- Young adults (Ages 13–18)

Type of Library Best Suited For

- Public libraries
- School libraries

Cost Estimate

- $1,400
- Any LEGO MINDSTORMS kit can be used for this program. The latest models (LEGO MINDSTORMS EV3) cost $349.99. Two pieces of foam board (20"×30") (approximately $19.95 for 6).

OVERVIEW

This robotic challenge combines traditional riddle clues inspired by Chris Grabenstein's *Escape from Mr. Lemoncello's Library* with LEGO MINDSTORMS robots. Participants are challenged to do such things as complete paper puzzles involving everything from unscrambling classic book titles to filling in Sudoku math puzzles. The sky's the limit for the puzzles you can include. Customize the literature clues for a specific age group; for example, you could design an escape room challenge from *The Hunger Games* or *The Hobbit*. A good idea is to have a cart with all books referenced in the puzzles available in the room so that participants can use them to help solve the riddles (and hopefully check some of them out!). Between puzzles, participants are presented with robotics challenges that they must complete to move forward. These challenges are simple robotics moves that will introduce participants to LEGO MINDSTORMS robots and their capabilities. Then move up to slightly more challenging tasks such as the Follow the Line challenge, which uses a sensor that must be calibrated to work correctly.

The ideal number of participants for the program will vary greatly depending on how many robotics kits you have. Two people to a robot is the best fit for collaboration and equal turn taking. For this program, 8–12 participants are an appropriate number for 1–2 staff facilitators. This program should last approximately 90 minutes and should take place in a room with lots of open floor space so robots do not drive off of a table or crash into people.

At the end of this section a sample paper puzzle is included courtesy of Amy Dreger, Children's Supervisor at the Beachwood (Ohio) Branch of the Cuyahoga County Public Library. It is a great resource that can be used in the challenges.

After participants complete the entire escape room challenge, you can provide any prizes to reward the participants for a job well done.

Software/Hardware Needed

Each pair of participants requires:

- LEGO MINDOSTORMS EV3 robot or a LEGO MINDSTORMS NXT robot
- Computer equipped with LEOG MINDSTORMS EV3 software or LEGO MINDSTORMS NXT software, depending on the robot they are using

Materials List

- Copy of riddles from *Escape from Mr. Lemoncello's Library*; see http://chrisgrabenstein.com/books/escape-from-mr-lemoncellos-library/escape-from-mr-lemoncellos-library-extras/
- Extra riddles or puzzles
- 2 large pieces of foam board and contrasting tape designed for the Follow the Line challenge (see image below)
- Pencils and paper for riddle challenges
- Cart with books
- Contrasting tape (black electrical tape works well) to design the line for the Follow the Line challenge
- Completion award (We gave away a 3-D printer mini-robot. You could give away anything.)

STEP-BY-STEP INSTRUCTIONS

Preparation

- Read *Escape from Mr. Lemoncello's Library*.
- Download riddles from Chris Grabenstein's website or create your own. Three puzzles were plenty for the time allotted for the program.
- Decide which 3 robot moves you want students to master. For this challenge, we used Parallel Park, Follow the Line, and Drive Forward and Make a Sound.
- Using the large pieces of foam board, create a Dr. Zinchenko Follow the Line board.
- Charge the laptops (if you are using them).
- Charge the robots.
- Practice with the robots to ensure you can complete all of the robotic challenges before the program.

- Prepare yourself and any other facilitators to be able to quickly troubleshoot during the program. Practice recalibrating the sensors, connecting the robot to the computer, and other troubleshooting steps.
- Think about what you want to give away as a token for completing the escape room challenge.

During the Program

- Introduce yourself and explain the program's overall plan.
- Have participants make a name tag when they enter.
- Get them situated with a partner. Try to match participants in similar age groupings to prevent older students from monopolizing the robot from younger participants.
- Talk to them about their previous experiences with robots and ask if they are familiar with *Escape from Mr. Lemoncello's Library.*
- Inform participants that they have 1.5 hours to escape from Mr. Lemoncello's Library by completing 3 puzzles and 3 robotic challenges.
- Explain to the group that you will be alternating between puzzles and robotic challenges. Briefly go over the robotic challenges (Drive Forward and Make a Sound, Parallel Park, and Follow the Line). Reassure participants that you will be available to help if they get stuck.
- Work through the first puzzle and robotics challenge as a whole group.
- Hand out the first puzzle and begin.

Escape Room Timeline

To guide groups through the challenges, this schedule is helpful:

- 5 minutes: First Puzzle
- 5 minutes: Introduction to the Software
- 20 minutes: Drive Forward and Make a Sound Challenge
- 5 minutes: Second Puzzle
- 20 minutes: Parallel Park Challenge
- 5 minutes: Third Puzzle
- 20 minutes: Follow the Line Challenge

Tips for Working with the Robots with Kids

- Frequently remind students not to push the play button while the robot is on the table. This start feature should only be selected when the robot is on the floor and has plenty of room.
- For the Follow the Line challenge, participants may need to calibrate the sensor for the white space and colored space.
- Instruct students not to mix and match parts from other robotics kits. This will help tremendously with cleanup.

LEARNING OUTCOMES

Participants will:

- Be able to program a Lego MINDSTORMS robot to perform a specific task.
- Be able to solve word puzzles based on popular books.
- Work in a team to complete the tasks.

RECOMMENDED NEXT PROJECTS

After completing the specified tasks for the escape room, participants can program the LEGO MINDSTORMS robot to perform other actions not part of the escape room. Teens can also program more advanced MINDSTORMS challenges or create their own!

45

Advancing Beyond Scratch to Text-Based Coding with Pencil Code

JAMIE BAIR

Senior Public Services Librarian: Experiential Learning

Fort Vancouver Regional Libraries, Vancouver, Washington

PROJECT DESCRIPTION

Kids with block-based coding experience will practice writing text-based code to draw shapes using pencilcode.net. Kids will be challenged to practice using reference resources to build code and troubleshoot outcomes.

Age Range

- Tweens (Ages 8–12)
- Young adults (Ages 13–18)

Type of Library Best Suited For

- Public libraries
- School libraries

Cost Estimate

- $0

OVERVIEW

Scratch is a prevalent tool for teaching young people basic computational thinking. The drag-and-drop interface is accessible for many learners and leads to quick mastery. Transitioning to a text-based coding environment from Scratch can be a difficult adjustment for many kids.

Pencilcode.net, developed by a team led by David and Anthony Bau, is an open-source, educational tool to help participants transition from block-based to text-based coding. Pencil Code's web-based platform allows participants to return to their projects after the program from any location, making it a useful tool for public and school libraries.

This project focuses on building participants' confidence in using text-based coding and typically focuses on 2 or 3 basic challenges. The goal is to model the iterative learning process and encourage participants to observe code behavior, make incremental changes to the code, and predict how their changes will affect the outcome.

Participants also learn how to utilize resources to learn how to build code. In this project, participants are challenged to use the Pencil Code Quick Reference Sheet to determine the correct code for the desired outcome.

Software/Hardware Needed

- Device to access the Internet: Chromebooks, laptops, desktop computers
- Web browser: Firefox, Chrome, Safari, Internet Explorer
- Paper handout of Pencil Code Quick Reference Sheet

STEP-BY-STEP INSTRUCTIONS

Preparation

- Pencil Code has created an excellent education resource: https://guide.pencilcode.net. Workshop leaders may want to review the material ahead of leading this workshop for the first time.
- Play around on http://pencilcode.net.
- Get comfortable changing variables and making code observations.
- Print copies of the Pencil Code Quick Reference Sheet: http://pencilcode.net/material/reference.pdf.

PROJECT INSTRUCTIONS

- Survey attendees to find out who has coding experience and what programs they've used (Scratch, Hour of Code, Khan Academy, Code Academy, etc.).
- Direct participants to https://pencilcode.net.
    - If participants would like to save projects, they will need to create a free account (no e-mail required).
    - Participants will need an account to save projects if this is a multi-session program.

CHALLENGE 1

Boxes

- Click Let's Play and have participants review the existing code example.
- Have participants make observations about the block code and, using their experience with Scratch, hypothesize the code's purpose.
- When ready, click the play button at the middle of the split screen.
- Ask participants why the boxes are off-set.

    Solution == right turn value (rt 88)

- Challenge participants to make perfect squares.

    Solution == change right turn value (rt 90)

- Ask participants to change other variables within the existing code (change the speed, change pen color, change intervals).
- Have participants click the tab on the lower left side "Click for text."
- Moving forward, all participants will be working in text-based code. They should only toggle back to block-based code if they get *really* stuck.
- Hand out a copy of the Pencil Code Quick Reference Sheet to each participant.
- Have participants modify the code to create 1 complete square.

    Solution == change the loop value (for [1. .4])

- Now that participants have a basic understanding of the code, have them create comments to help remember the parts of the code (Setup, Drawing, Finish). Explain that commenting is a good practice to get into so other people know how your code is supposed to work.

    In CoffeeScript, commenting is designated with #. (See figure 45.1.)

```
#setup
speed 2
pen red
#drawing
for [1..4]
  fd 100
  rt 90
#finish
```

FIGURE 45.1

Basic solution for code comments

It is worth noting that #Finish is always the last piece of code. Any added commands need to be entered above #Finish.

CHALLENGE 2

Rectangle and Advanced Formatting

- Challenge participants to turn the square into a rectangle.
- Solicit suggestions from the group and work together.

- Remind participants to make small changes to their code and test before moving on. It's much easier to troubleshoot code as you go rather than after everything is written.
    - Solution:

```
#setup
speed 2
pen red
#drawing
fd 100
rt 90
fd 200
rt 90
fd 100
rt 90
fd 200
```

- Using the reference sheet, have participants identify the command to fill the shape with the color orange.
    - Solution:

Add new line after last `fd 200` (Fill orange)

- Challenge participants to create a duplicate rectangle with a different fill color (figure 45.2).

```
#setup
speed 2
pen red
#drawing
fd 100
rt 90
fd 200
rt 90
fd 100
rt 90
fd 200
fill orange
fd 100
rt 90
fd 200
rt 90
fd 100
rt 90
fd 200
fill red
#finish
```

FIGURE 45.2

Two rectangles code

CHALLENGE 3

Explore

Using the Pencil Code Quick Reference Sheet, have participants explore Pencil Code independently.

LEARNING OUTCOMES

Participants will:

- Identify similarities between commands in block-based and text-based code.
- Begin to develop an understanding of basic components of text-based code structure.
- Problem solve and troubleshoot text-based code.

- Learn how to communicate ideas and build projects using text-based code.
- Use resources to build their knowledge of code commands.

RECOMMENDED NEXT PROJECTS

- Create a drawing by inserting multiple rectangles.
- Use math to build different shapes (circle, triangle, star, etc.).
- Draw a stick figure person.
- Explore the Pencil Code Quick Reference Sheet to add new commands and observe the changed code.

46

Program a Scratch Guessing Machine

DAVID VANCE
Library Media Specialist | Glasgow (Kentucky) Middle School

PROJECT DESCRIPTION

Students in small groups create a Scratch program that is a Guessing Machine. The program will ask questions to a member of the group, and, based on the responses, it will figure out which member of the group is responding.

Age Range

- Tweens (Ages 8–12)
- Young adults (Ages 13–18)

Type of Library Best Suited For

- School libraries
- Public libraries

Cost Estimate

- $0

OVERVIEW

The librarian or teacher asks for 3 students to be volunteers and come to the front of the room. Students will play a version of the Guessing Machine created by the librarian for the purpose of modeling the activity. On the screen is a Scratch program with a rainbow unicorn.

The librarian clicks the green flag to begin. The unicorn asks the first volunteer, "Do you wear glasses?" She types "no." Then the unicorn asks, "Is your hair curly?" She types "no." Finally, it asks, "Do you love Harry Potter?" She types "yes." The unicorn says, "Hi Jessica! I knew that was you. Thanks for playing." The Guessing Machine correctly guesses the next 2 students—to everyone's delight and amazement. Although the first question was the same, the subsequent questions changed for each volunteer. Then the librarian announces that today everyone will learn to build their own Guessing Machine using Scratch.

Software/Hardware Needed

- Computer with Internet access
- Free Scratch account at https://scratch.mit.edu

STEP-BY-STEP INSTRUCTIONS

Preparation

- Place students in small groups, preferably of 3–5.
- Have the groups create questions and answers that help identify and differentiate each of them from their group mates. For example:
    1. Do you wear glasses?
    2. Do you have a little sister?
    3. What is your favorite book?

PROJECT INSTRUCTIONS

Setting Up the Code

- Provide students with the following instructions:
    - Create a new program in Scratch and choose either the default cat or a new sprite.
    - In the Events tab in the middle of the page, choose the block that says "When green flag clicked." Drag this block into the work area.
    - Next, in the Sensing tab, grab the block that says "ask and wait." Connect it to the bottom of the green flag block.
    - Under the Control tab, grab the block that says "if, then, else" and connect it to your code.
    - Inside the Operators tab, grab the "=" block. Place this inside the previous block between the "if" and "then."
    - Inside the Sensing tab, grab the block that says "answer." Place it inside the first square of the "=" block.

  - Finally, under the Look tab, grab the block that says "say and wait for secs." This will go inside the if statement in the first space.
  - Congratulations! You have created your template (figure 46.1).
- This code template will be used again and again in this project, so now is a good time to highlight it all and copy it. Draw a box around all of the code except for the green flag at the beginning. Then click CTRL + C to copy (Command + C on a Mac).

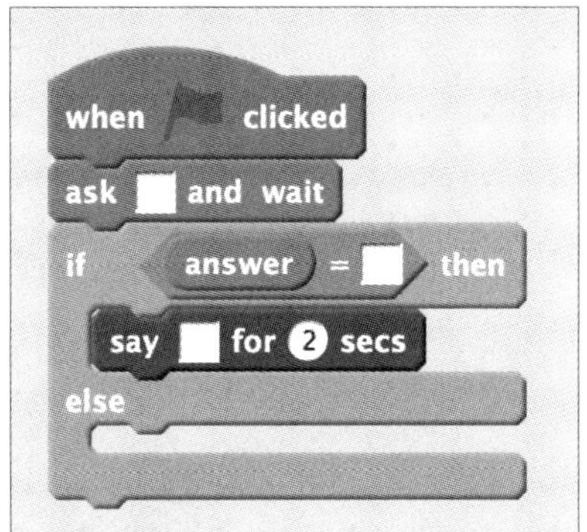

FIGURE 46.1

Guessing Machine code template

Personalization

- Now, students can personalize their projects by adding their first question. To do so, simply fill in the blanks of the code that is already written. For example, if a group has 4 students and 1 of them wears glasses, it might ask "Do you wear glasses?" and wait for an answer. If the answer=yes, then say, "Hi, Kelly! I knew it was you" for 2 seconds.
- The remaining 3 group members will need to ask a new differentiating question inside of the "else" case. To do so, paste the code that was copied above into the empty "else" section, and fill it in with the second question.
- Continuing to use the example questions from above, the code with the second question included would read as follows:

```
When the green flag is clicked
Ask "Do you wear glasses?" and wait
If answer = yes, then
Say "Hi Kelly! I knew it was you" for 2 seconds
Else
Ask "Do you have a little sister?" and wait
If answer = yes then
Say "Hi Arlo! Thanks for playing my game" for 2 seconds
Else
```

- Once again, the empty else statement will be used to ask another identifying question. This process of including if statements inside of another if statement is known as "nested if" statements. When you get to your last group member, she can simply be identified in the last else statement as seen here because the other members of the group have already been eliminated.

```
When the green flag is clicked
Ask "Do you wear glasses?" and wait
If answer = yes, then
Say "Hi Kelly! I knew it was you" for 2 seconds
Else
Ask "Do you have a little sister?" and wait
If answer = yes then
Say "Hi Arlo! Thanks for playing my game" for 2 seconds
Else
Ask "Do you love Harry Potter?" and wait
If answer = yes then
Say "Everett! I guessed you" for 2 seconds
Else
Say "Naomi! You almost stumped me" for 2 seconds
```

Feel free to use additional subheadings as well.

- The snippet of code above is sufficient for a group of 4 students and serves as a good size for modeling the process in front of a class.

Advanced Scenario

- With a larger group, naturally, there may be more than 1 person wearing glasses and more than 1 person with a little sister. In these cases, an extra question will be required. The code might look like that shown in figure 46.2.
- Because of these complications, it is better to start with small groups and allow students to gain an understanding of the process before combining groups or expanding groups to a larger size.

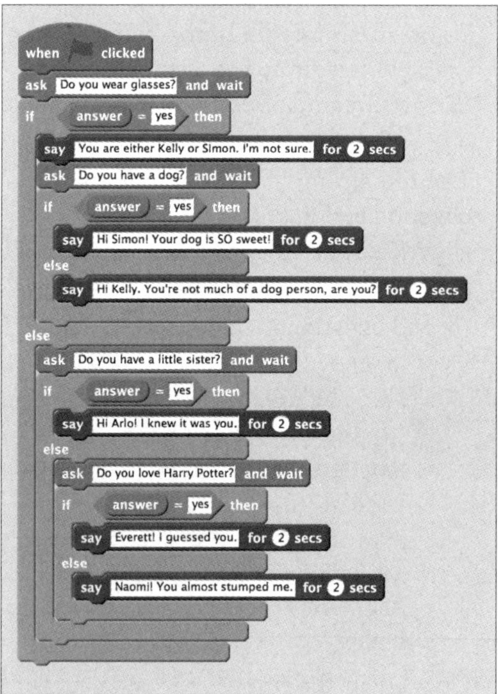

FIGURE 46.2

Differentiate between two students who answer "yes" by simply asking another differentiating question

LEARNING OUTCOMES

Participants will:

- Practice self-expression through project-based learning.
- Collaborate with a group.
- Learn to use the ask and answer block in Scratch.
- Use If/Else statements and nested if statements.

RECOMMENDED NEXT PROJECTS

Students who complete this project will be naturally inclined to create larger and larger guessing machines of their classmates, which is challenging and worthwhile. The real fun, however, is in the ideas and not in the code itself. Encourage students to branch out from guessing classmates into areas of their own interest. They might make machines that can guess.

- Superheroes,
- sports teams,
- library books, or
- YouTube stars.

47

Use HTML, JavaScript, and CSS to Create an Interactive Online Greet-Bot 3000

DAVID VANCE

Library Media Specialist | Glasgow (Kentucky) Middle School

PROJECT DESCRIPTION

This project combines HTML, CSS, and JavaScript to create a simple website showing an image of a robot. The website asks users their name, and then the robot gives a personal written greeting for each name given.

Age Range

- Tweens (Ages 8–12)
- Young adults (Ages 13–18)
  - This activity was designed for middle school students who had already completed Unit 2 (Web Development) of Computer Science Discoveries at Code.org. However, because some schools use this curriculum in high school, it could work for grades 6–10. It would be difficult for students to do this lesson without prior HTML experience. The exception might be in a small group or after-school club that focuses more on collaboration and less on grades and due dates.

Type of Library Best Suited For

- School libraries
- Public libraries

Cost Estimate

- $0

OVERVIEW

First, students use an image creating software or website to draw a robot. Then, they use HTML to create a website displaying the robot image. Next, they use CSS to position a div over the mouth of the robot. Finally, they use JavaScript to make the robot "speak" depending on who is visiting the site.

Software/Hardware Needed

- Computer with Internet access
- Software to create a robot image (figure 47.1). Free online editors like pixlr.com work great, but students could use Photoshop, Paint, or even draw an image by hand and take a photo of it with their phones and upload it.
- An HTML editor. Code.org's WebLab works, as will Notepad or Notepad++ on a windows machine or TextEdit on a Chromebook.

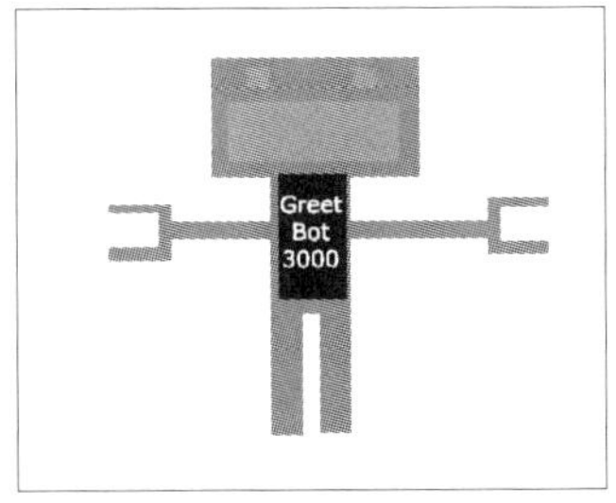

FIGURE 47.1

Greet-Bot 3000 robot

STEP-BY-STEP INSTRUCTIONS

- Students first need to come up with a robot. It doesn't have to look especially nice. In fact, sometimes the project is more fun when the robots look sort of clunky and homemade. This is an opportunity for self-expression and originality, but it's also not the project's primary focus. Try to be flexible with the finished product of the robot without letting this step drag on. The only very important element of the robot is that it must have a relatively large mouth, as that's where the personalized greetings will appear at the end of the project. This will make sense to students after they have seen an example in action.
- The next step is to create a blank web page. Many HTML editors will provide a bare-bones structure to a web page that looks something like the following. This structure is the default on Code.org's WebLab, except that a link to a stylesheet has been added on the fourth line. That will be used later.

```
<!DOCTYPE html>
<html>
<head>
<link rel="stylesheet" href="style.css">
</head>
<body>
</body>
</html>
```

- To add the image to the website, first upload the image to the HTML editor or, if working directly from the computer, add the image to the same folder as the HTML document. Then, inside the body tags, add the image tag with the appropriate filename between parenthesis, such as:

  ```
  <img src="greetbot_3000.jpg" alt="greetbot robot" />
  ```

- Once the robot image is showing up on the page, it is time to add a div for the robot's mouth. The robot already has a mouth, which should be quite large. The image, however, is not interactive. To make words appear in the mouth, create an invisible box to hold the words and then position it on top of the robot image. This is the purpose of the div. First, create the box by adding the following HTML code below the image tag:

  ```
  <div id="robotMouth">
  mouth
  </div>
  ```

- The id in the code above is used to connect the box to the CSS file students will create next. CSS allows participants to position the box where they want it and add other styles. The word *mouth* found between the div tags just helps participants see where it is. Without it, the div would seem invisible.
- Next, have students create a stylesheet to position the div over the robot's mouth. In Code.org's WebLab, simply click the purple button that says "Add CSS." A new stylesheet will be created. It will include some bare-bones code that can be deleted. If using Notepad or another editor, create a new file in the same folder as the HTML file and the robot image and save it with the filename "style.css."
- Type the following inside the saved stylesheet. This uses the id robotMouth that is given to the div in the html document. This collection of styles is known as a ruleset.

  ```
  #robotMouth {
  background-color:gray;
  height:60px;
  width:205px;
  }
  ```

- The purpose of the gray background is simply to make the mouth box easier to locate on the screen as participants move it around. The height and width are numbers that will need adjusting to make them roughly the size of the mouth of the robot image. This is trial and error, but when it is the right size, the next task is to position the div over the mouth of the robot image. To do so, the #robotMouth ruleset will need a few lines more styles. When finished, it should look like this:

```
#robotMouth{
background-color:gray;
height:60px;
width:205px;
position:absolute;
top:130px;
left:300px;
}
```

- The position absolute tells the div to position itself regardless of where other elements are on the page. This allows it to ignore and overlap the robot image. Top and Left indicate how far from the top and left of the page the div should appear. This, again, will be trial and error. When done correctly, the gray div box should be roughly the same size and in the same location as the mouth from the robot image. The only thing left to do with the stylesheet, and this is optional, is to change the appearance of the text that will appear. Here are the complete styles that work well with the robot, but experiment and see what works for you:

```
#robotMouth{
background-color:gray;
height:60px;
width:205px;
color:white;
position:absolute;
top:130px;
left:300px;
font-weight:bold;
text-align:center;
font-size:20px;
padding:5px;
}
```

- With the HTML and CSS complete, it's time to move on to the JavaScript that allows the robot to ask users for their names and then give personal responses to each of them. Back in the HTML document, below the </div>, add the following to the body:

```
<script>
var name = prompt("What is your name?");
name=name.toLowerCase();
</script>
```

- Everything inside the script tags is JavaScript. The first line of code creates a variable called "name." Then it makes the browser prompt the user by popping up a box that asks "What is your name?"
- Whatever the user types is stored in the variable "name." The second line takes that name and converts it into all lowercase letters. This ensures that a user who wrote henry or Henry or HENRY or HeNrY would all get the same result.
- Now that the GreetBot is asking for names and converting whatever names it receives to lowercase, it is time to program it to look for specific names. To do that, use a switch statement. It looks like this:

```
switch(name) {
case "henry" :
document.getElementById("robotMouth").innerHTML =
    "Greetings Henry. Can I call you Hen?";
break;
}
```

Here, the switch statement checks to see if the name value is "henry." If so, it finds the div with the id "robotMouth" and then replaces whatever value is inside it with a new value. After checking to make sure that the program is working properly, participants can add as many names and personalized greetings inside the curly braces as they like. For example:

```
switch(name) {
case "henry" :
document.getElementById("robotMouth").innerHTML =
    "Greetings Henry. Can I call you Hen?";
break;
case "ada" :
document.getElementById("robotMouth").innerHTML = "Hey
    Ada! I'm stuck in this computer. Help!";
break;
case "max" :
document.getElementById("robotMouth").innerHTML = "Hi
    Max! Did you know that your name backwards
would be Xam?";
break;
}
```

- At this point, GreetBot should be functioning properly. However, notice what happens when participants type a name that is not included in the switch statement. Nothing happens, and that's disappointing. It is better if the robot responds regardless of the input name, otherwise it will seem broken. To handle any unknown names, add the following right above the curly brace at the end of the switch statement.

```
default:
document.getElementById("robotMouth").innerHTML = "I'm
    sorry. I don't guess I know you yet."
```

- It is worth noting that because Code.org's WebLab and other online editors auto-refresh, the "What is your name?" prompt will pop up repeatedly while the user is trying to code. To avoid this, simply use // to comment out the line of code that includes the prompt. Then delete the // when you're ready to test again.
- In step 4, the instructions said to put the word *mouth* into the div so that you can see where it is. Now that the div is positioned, "mouth" is no longer necessary. Go ahead and delete it. Similarly, in step 6, the instructions added a gray background to the div to help position it. That is no longer needed, so delete "background-color:gray;" from the CSS file.
- You now have a complete Greet-Bot 3000 (or whatever you named it). Below is the complete HTML, CSS, and JavaScript as it might look at the end of the project.

```
HTML File:
<!DOCTYPE html>
<html>
<head>
<link rel="stylesheet" href="style.css">
</head>
<body>
<img src="greetbot_3000.jpg" alt="greetbot robot" />
<div id="robotMouth">
</div>
<script>
var name = prompt("What is your name?");
name= name.toLowerCase();
switch(name){
case "henry" :
document.getElementById("robotMouth").innerHTML =
    "Greetings Henry. Can I Call you Hen?";
break;
case "ada" :
document.getElementById("robotMouth").innerHTML = "Hey
    Ada! I'm stuck in this computer. Help!"
break;
```

```
case "max" :
document.getElementById("robotMouth").innerHTML = "Hey
   Max! Did you know that your name backwards
would be Xam?";
break;
case "amanda" :
document.getElementById("robotMouth").innerHTML = "Hi
   Amanda. Good luck on the election. You've got
my vote!"
break;
case "andres" :
document.getElementById("robotMouth").innerHTML = "Hey
   Whit! Are there any other nationality-based
horns, or is it only French?";
break;
case "jason" :
document.getElementById("robotMouth").innerHTML = "Hola
   hermano!";
break;
case "tayveon" :
document.getElementById("robotMouth").innerHTML = "Hey
   Tayveon! What have you been reading lately?";
break;
default:
document.getElementById("robotMouth").innerHTML = "I'm
   sorry. I don't guess I know you yet.";
}
</script>
</body>
</html>

CSS File:
#robotMouth{
//Size and Position of the Robot Mouth Div
height:60px;
width:205px;
color:white;
position:absolute;
top:130px;
left:300px;
//formatting of text
```

```
font-weight:bold;
text-align:center;
font-size:20px;
padding:5px;
}
```

LEARNING OUTCOMES

Participants will:

- Practice self-expression through project-based learning.
- Work at debugging by finding and fixing mistakes.
- Learn new elements of each language within this project.
- Learn divs in HTML, absolute positioning in CSS, and prompts and switch statements in JavaScript.

RECOMMENDED NEXT PROJECTS

Variations on this project could include anything that students are interested in. A student interested in languages might create a Language-Bot that asks "What language do you speak?" and the robot could respond in the language given. A Career-Bot might ask users what their favorite subject is and then respond with careers in that field. Librarians would appreciate a book Recommend-Bot that can offer patrons book suggestions based on their preferred genre.

48

Player Ready
Making Your First Video Game

LOREN McCLAIN
Administrative Specialist III | Muncie (Indiana) Public Library

PROJECT DESCRIPTION

Game development has grown exponentially over the years, and most recently—in the last decade—more indie content creators have popped up, giving the big studios a run for their money. The amazing thing is, with more independent people in game development, everyone can bring unique experiences and backgrounds into game design.

The more people making games and sharing their experiences and knowledge, the more games and technologies will evolve in exciting new directions. Unbelievably, a youth's own work of art starts now. With the wide range of tools available to the public, the support to start developing tweens' and young adults' own games is within reach.

Age Range

- Tweens (Ages 8–12)
- Young adults (Ages 13–18)

Type of Library Best Suited For

- Public libraries
- School libraries

Cost Estimate

- $0–$300
- Optional choice of program application upgrade

OVERVIEW

Digital game-based learning (DGBL) is a partnership between any educational content and computer game; it was not until recent years that games have been widely accepted as part of an educational system and method for learning. When users are allowed to not only play video games but also create their own content and game logic, they are encouraged through multiple factors and increase their ability to learn outside the realm of game logic.

Software/Hardware Needed

- Computer or Mac running, Windows, iOS, or Linux
- The latest version of Stencyl (currently version 3.4.0) available at stencyl.com
- The Crash Course Kit available at stencyl.com

STEP-BY-STEP INSTRUCTIONS

Preparation

- Download the Stencyl program and the Crash Course Kit.
- Make sure the Stencyl program and the Crash Course Kit are installed properly on the computer before the workshop.

PROJECT INSTRUCTIONS

Getting Started

- When students first open Stencyl explain to them the screen they are seeing is the Welcome Center.
- To create a new game, click the dotted rectangle labeled **"Click here to create a Game."** Explain that the new screen that appears is called a **dialog box.**
- Click on the **Crash Course Kit**, to the left, and then click the **Next button** located at the bottom of the dialog box.

  PRO TIP: Ask students if they see the button with "**Get Sample Games/ Kits**"? Explain that these kits come with everything they would need, pre-made resources, settings, and game-functioning logic pre-installed, but encourage students to make use of the kits when they want to add more personalized characteristics to their games.

- When another dialog box appears, instruct students about setting the size of the game window (in pixels) and how to name their game—it can be as simple or complex as they would like.
  - Explain to students how setting the **width** and the **height** dimensions in the **Screen Size** section determines the size of the game play window

and how the player will see the game. Encourage students to try a width of 640 pixels and a height of 480 pixels.

NOTE: If your institution has purchased an upgraded version of Stencyl, students can create a game and publish it to a mobile device—if that is the case, use 320 pixels for the width and 480 pixels for the height if the game is to be used in landscape mode. Switch the width and height to 480 x 320 for portrait mode.

- Click the **Create** button.
- The next screen students see is the **Dashboard**. They can see and open their game's resources (actors, game logic, graphics, sounds, etc.) from this screen.

Adding Game Resources

- When students are ready to create, explain that anything that moves or can be interacted with is called an **Actor**.
- Click **Actor Types**, located under the tab labeled RESOURCES on the left sidebar.
  - The numbers listed to the right of the labels indicate the total number of actors in the created game so far. Students will start off with 2: Noni and Clown.
  - Double-click the icon for Noni for the **Actor Type Editor** to open.

    Once inside the **Actor Type Editor,** students will be able to customize any Actor's appearance, behavior, and physical abilities properties.

    The **Appearance** page for the **Actor Type Editor** will always open first, by default; just skip over to the **Properties** tab.
  - Have students check to make sure Noni is part of the **Players Group**. Explain that if Noni is not part of the Players Group, there will be no main character.
- **Tilesets** are the collections of rectangle tiles used to build the levels of each game. Each level constitutes a **Scene** within the game. Students will build 1 scene to begin with, but they can always add more later.

Creating a Group of "Enemies"

- Click **Settings** in the toolbar. When a window titled **Game Settings** appears, this is where students can set and change their game settings at any time.
- Point to the left sidebar and click the **Groups** icon and then click on the green **Create New** button.

    - Label the group name **Enemies** and click **Create**.
- Without rules, the game won't work. This is where students get to be creative and make their rule sets for when the enemies interact (or collide) with their players and tiles.
    - Navigate to the section "Collides With" and click **Players** and **Tiles**. When students have selected both options, their respective buttons should turn green. Click **OK**.

Adding Action to Actors

- Explain that just like adding rules to enemies, in order for the game to work properly, each actor needs to have behaviors added to him.
- Select **Noni** from the **Actor Types** tab on the left by double-clicking. (See figure 48.1.)

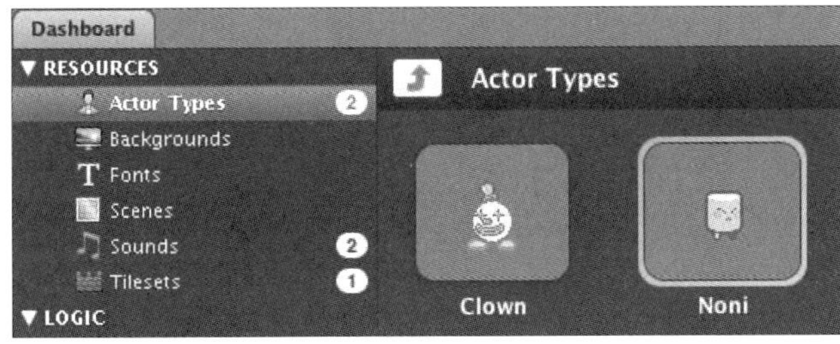

FIGURE 48.1

Make sure you are selecting Noni from the Actor Types tab

- Double-check that **Noni** is part of the **Players Group** to ensure **Noni** interacts with the **Enemies** as intended.
- Click on the **Physics** page at the top of the editing screen. Explain that making Noni rotate will make the game harder. So, for their first time making a game, it's best to make sure that **Noni** cannot rotate. Uncheck the rotation box found under the heading **General**.
- Guide students to the **Behaviors** tab. Here, they can add behaviors to each **Actor**. Click **Add Behavior** in the lower left corner. Another screen will appear.
    - Double-click on **Walking Behavior.**
    - Once added, the Behavior page will be seen again. This time, Walking Behavior is added to the pane on the left.
    - Click **Walking on the left** to open the Attributes window. Set the Move Right Key and Move Left Key to the right and left arrows on the keyboard respectively. It is important that these keys match the arrows, otherwise the movements of Noni will be mirrored!

 - Allow students to choose what type of animation they want for each behavior and encourage them to get creative. To add an animation, click **Choose an Animation** to select the animation style they would like.
- Continue to **Add Behaviors** for each activity they want Noni or the **Enemies** to do. This will take the most time, but it's well worth it!
  - Pro tip: Are the Enemy groups not showing up? Reload the document. Use Ctrl-R on Windows, Command-R on Mac, or going to File > Reload Document.

Creating a Scene

- Students are almost done with their first video game! It's time to add their characters to a scene.
- From the **Dashboard**, click **Scene**. When students are just starting out, they will see a message that says, "This game contains no Scenes. Click here to create one." Click on the message.
- The **Create New Scene** window will appear. Enter a creative name for it.
- Make sure the student's game is set to a width of 20 tiles and a height of 15 tiles. Leave **Tile Width** and **Tile Height** at 32 pixels because any smaller or bigger would throw the entire game out of proportion.
- Select a background color and the style of the coloring they would like. Again, be creative! Mention that sometimes a solid color or a gradient can be a great way to set the mood and scene for their game. Suggest a light blue for a sky background.
- When students are finished, they will click **Create**.
- The **Scene Designer** will automatically open. **Scene Designer** works similarly to other art programs students may have used in the past.
  - Click on the pencil tool located on the left toolbar.
  - Click on the type of tile they would like from the Palette, which is located on the right side of the screen.
  - To place the tile into the Scene, simply left-click on the color background that was created earlier. It is okay to demonstrate this the first time to show students what to expect. Tiles will always be placed on the bottom of the screen.
  - If students would like to place more than 1 tile at a time, all they need to do is click and drag.
- There is no game unless students add in their actors! Click the **Actors** tab in the **Palette** and select **Noni**. **Noni** will be automatically added to the scene

when students click on the **Scene**. Encourage them to click on the scene every time they have selected an actor. Only 1 Noni can be placed in each scene, but students can have as many enemies as they want.

- Do the same thing with the **Enemies**. Encourage students to add a few for a more challenging level.
- Before students complete their game, let them know there is one more thing to do—make sure the game follows the rules of physics! Go to the **Physics** tab. In the **Vertical Gravity** section, add the number 85. Explain that higher numbers mean there is stronger gravity, while lower numbers have a lower gravity (good to know if students are making a scene in space!).

Testing the Game

- Now is the part everyone has been waiting for. Click the **Test Game** button at the top of the screen.
- Students should be able to walk using the left and right arrow keys that they set up earlier. Remind them which actions are connected to which keys.
- Tell students not to worry if they run into an **Enemy** because the screen will just reload. Aim to jump on top of the **Enemy**.
- When they are finished, celebrate because they have done incredible work and have completed designing their first video game!

LEARNING OUTCOMES

Participants will:

- Express their creativity using coding and technology.
- Use basic steps in algorithmic problem solving to design solutions.
- Create meaningful software applications rather than large chunks of isolated code.
- Learn to visualize a process that accomplished a task they have set for themselves.

RECOMMENDED NEXT PROJECTS

- Character creation using Adobe Illustrator
- Thames & Kosmos Code Gamer Experiment Kit
- Bloxels Build Your Own Video Game

49

Partners in Technology

How to Create a Successful Technology Mentorship Program

JULIA CLARK

Library Experience Manager | Evansville Vanderburgh (Indiana) Public Library

PROJECT DESCRIPTION

Libraries are always looking for ways to engage the community and offer new experiences for their patrons. One way to do this is to reach out to and work with the community to create a mentorship program. Engaging mentors, tapping into community knowledge, and creating partners and pairs based on youth interest allow libraries to offer a program specially tailored to each youth participant. Because technology is often an area that is new and occasionally intimidating to library staff, community members working or dabbling in these areas can be invaluable resources to the library and youth participants. Utilizing community volunteers also reduces the amount of staff time needed to run the program. Although the following program, Partners in Technology, focuses on pairs exploring technology such as coding and robotics, this model can be adjusted for a plethora of interests.

Age Range

- Tweens (Ages 8–12)
- Young adults (Ages 13–18)

Type of Library Best Suited For

- Public libraries
- School libraries

Cost Estimate

- $0–$25,000 (depending on equipment and number of participants)

OVERVIEW

Partners in Technology pairs children ages 10–14 years old with an adult mentor from the community who has experience in a technology field or area of study. Partners meet at the library weekly for 1-hour sessions over the course of 8 weeks. Meeting times are chosen based on mentor and participant availability. During these sessions, partners explore coding, robotics, and circuitry/hardware concepts using a variety of free, open-source online and physical resources. This program is designed to help foster computer science and computational thinking skills while encouraging a love of learning and technology exploration. Sessions are led by participant interest and mentor expertise.

One librarian dedicated to the design of the program, recruitment of volunteers, assigning and support of partners and sessions, and upkeep of technologies should suffice. Library staff members assist by checking in partners for sessions and circulating technologies to the partners. Depending on size and available staff, you may choose to limit the number of pairs to 25 or less. This number can fluctuate depending on library size, available staff, interested mentors, and number of youth participants. This program can be scaled to any budget using free online resources as well as low-tech options.

Software/Hardware Needed

Necessary Equipment

- A system, electronic or physical, for mentors and youth to sign up—Google Forms is a good option
- Space for partners to meet—it should be out in the open with a table, chairs, and an accessible electrical outlet
- A way to track session attendance—Google Sheets or a shared Excel document may be helpful
- A list of suggested technologies, websites, and resources for participants to pick from and guided lesson plans for the sessions depending on subjects of interest

Recommended Equipment

- Laptops available for checkout or desktops for partners to use
- Technology available for circulation, including:

- Arduino kits
- Dot and Dash robots
- LEGO MINDSTORM kits
- LEGO WeDo kits
- littleBits
- Makey Makeys
- Snap Circuits

STEP-BY-STEP INSTRUCTIONS

Mentor Recruitment and Partner Pairing

- Make a list of any local businesses, colleges, and universities that may have IT departments or technology affiliations.
- Create an elevator speech describing exactly what kind of commitment the library is asking of volunteers.
- Develop a mission statement for the mentorship program to help communicate to interested parents, participants, and mentors what the library is seeking to accomplish with this program. Although each library must decide its own priorities for the program, it may be helpful to communicate to all involved that the program is intended to help foster interest, confidence, and understanding of different technologies rather than producing youth with an advanced new skill at the conclusion of the 8-week program.
- Create an application for interested mentors and participants. Google Forms is a helpful digital resource because it is easy to use and shareable. This application should include questions about areas of technology interest, level of experience, knowledge of available technology resources, and availability.
- Begin reaching out to potential mentors and participants via e-mail and social media.
- Because mentors are meeting with children, it might be a good idea to run background checks, depending on library policy.
- Using the information from the applications, begin assigning pairs based on availability, area of interest, and level of ability.
- Send e-mails to accepted mentors, participants, and parents making them aware of their partner's contact information and scheduled mentorship time. It is helpful to encourage mentors, partners, and parents to communicate with each other if a session needs to be missed or rescheduled.
- Inform potential participants who could not be admitted into the program and provide them with information about the next session, if known.
- Designate a place for partners to check in before each session. This can also be the place where they may check out any available technology they might need for their session.

- Designate a space for partners to meet, such as in the Children's Department, reserving a few tables each hour. However, the partners could also meet in a designated room depending on space and available staff for monitoring.

Training and Information for Staff, Mentors, Parents, and Participants

- Before beginning the mentorship sessions, it is helpful to have any staff members who may be assisting with the program trained on any available technologies that participants may use. This will help staff better troubleshoot issues that partners may face. Locating or creating basic written guides for the technology is helpful, as is allowing staff time to explore technology on their own.
- Once you have your pool of mentors, it is helpful to offer a few mentor information sessions for any new mentors. This will allow mentors to see what technologies and resources are available, hear from staff about any rules or expectations, and ask any questions they may have about the program.
- It is also a good idea to hold parent and participant information sessions. This will allow staff to communicate with parents and participants, setting the expectations for the program and expressing the library's goals. Parents and participants can also get acquainted with the available resources and technologies and ask questions before the program begins.

Mentorship Sessions

- Check with staff to ensure they are aware of the sign-in procedures and where circulating technologies can be found for checkout.
- For the first week of sessions, it is helpful for the staff person(s) coordinating the mentorship program to be available to greet partners meeting for the first time and make sure they have a plan for what they want to work on.
- If the first meeting is the first time the participant and mentor are meeting, it is a good idea to provide instructions for an icebreaker activity.
- Provide a list of resources, physically or electronically, for groups to give them options for projects and technologies to work through. Keep in mind that some partners may instantly know what they want to work on without your guidance. Others might need a little more assistance. It may be helpful to create a series of learning pathways, including a guide of activities utilizing the circulating technologies and a few suggested lesson plans from Code.org, Khan academy, Scratch, and other free coding sites.

- Monitor sessions by regularly communicating with mentors, participants, and parents through e-mail or quick session drop-ins. Staff may also utilize simple, quick surveys for mentors and participants to provide feedback and let staff know what they are working on each time.
- At the conclusion of the mentorship program, be sure to thank the mentors and participants for their time. Encourage them to participate again in any future sessions and recommend their friends and colleagues who might be interested. Word of mouth is often the best tool for recruiting future mentors and participants. If funds are available, a small thank you gift such as a coffee mug is a good way to show appreciation and retain mentors as future contacts.

LEARNING OUTCOMES

Participants will:

- Gain greater comfort and familiarity with technology by being able to explore in a guided, low-pressure environment.
- Meet positive adult role models who might inspire them to pursue career and study paths they may not have previously considered.
- Increase their problem-solving and critical thinking skills by working through new projects and solving any potential problems that arise with help from a knowledgeable facilitator.

RECOMMENDED NEXT PROJECTS

- You might find that tapping into community knowledge yields community members interested in volunteering and assisting with other technology programs.
- Consider utilizing these community resources to try providing programs such as:
    - Chapter 42: Form a Hacker Club and Hacker Club Jr. by Jessica Franco and Emily Sheehan
    - Chapter 43: Host a Teen and Tween App Development Camp in Your Library by Jessica Franco and Emily Sheehan
    - Chapter 54: Programming Stories: How to Animate with Code by Austin Olney

50

Walk Through My World

Create a Virtual Reality Digital World

LISA O'SHAUGHNESSY
Children's Librarian | East Orange (New Jersey) Public Library

PROJECT DESCRIPTION

Walk Through My World. The magic of virtual reality lies in the ability to be transported from the physical world to a new and exciting virtual space. Users can climb aboard the International Space Station on an educational field trip through Google Expeditions, escape dinosaurs in the popular Jurassic Park VR game, or even become a digital artist using Tilt Brush to paint on their own virtual canvas. The possibilities are endless and can be accomplished with little to no investment.

World building, as any successful author or video game designer will tell you, is an essential part of an engaging project or story. Using CoSpaces, a virtual reality (VR) space builder designed for children, students will create their own digital world. The world will include characters, actions driven by block coding, dialogue, backstory, and more. At the end of class, students will have the chance to walk through their own worlds by using the CoSpaces app and a simple VR headset to demonstrate the project for the class.

Age Range

- Tweens (Ages 8–12)
- Young adults (Ages 13–18)

Type of Library Best Suited For

- Public libraries
- School libraries

Cost Estimate

- $40–$1,000
- This cost estimate assumes you have access to laptop or desktop computers. The software cost to this project is free. There is a pro version of the software, which will give greater access to coding functionality, characters, and objects. Licensing plans can be found at https://cospaces.io/edu/. If you don't already have VR headsets, you can purchase a simple Google Cardboard headset for $3–$10. To keep the cost low, students could bring their own mobile device to class. The class could also share 1 mobile device and 1 VR headset.

OVERVIEW

Using the CoSpaces program, students will create a unique virtual reality world. World building is an important part of digital storytelling. The world must include 2 or more characters, a setting/environment, a backstory, dialogue, and several coded actions. These specific tasks will allow students to become familiar with the different functions of the CoSpaces interface and aid them in creating a more thought-out and engaging project. After creating their world, students will demonstrate their projects for the class.

Using the CoSpaces app and a simple VR headset, students will take turns exploring their projects. The entire project should take about 1.5–2 hours. Keeping the class size small allows you to give more individual assistance. I recommend 10–12 students as the maximum class size. Especially with older students, there should be no problem running this class on your own, although having a teen volunteer or 2 is always helpful.

Software/Hardware Needed (see figure 50.1)

- 10–12 Google Cardboard or more advanced VR headsets. (VR headsets anything from Google Cardboard to a more advanced headset will work and can be found in many places, including Amazon and eBay).

FIGURE 50.1

Materials needed: CoSpaces account, VR headset, and mobile device

- 10–12 laptop/desktop computers
- 1–12 mobile devices able to run the CoSpaces app: https://play.google.com/store/apps/details?id=delightex.cospaces.edu&hl=en_US/
- CoSpaces desktop version (according to the CoSpaces website, a desktop, tablet, or mobile device running an up-to-date browser; see https://cospaces.io/edu/faqs.html#tech/).
- CoSpaces app: https://play.google.com/store/apps/details?id=delightex.cospaces.edu&hl=en_US/
- CoSpaces has a free basic version and a pro version with a licensing plan. See the website for pricing. The pro version offers additional coding functionality and access to a larger library of characters and objects.

STEP-BY-STEP INSTRUCTIONS

Preparation (60 minutes)

- Create a CoSpaces teacher account and copy the classroom code. (CoSpaces allows you to work in a monitored classroom environment. The free version allows up to 30 students and has the ability to create assignments.)
- Download a simple VR game/experience to demonstrate during class.
- Download the CoSpaces app on all available mobile devices.
- Charge mobile devices or have several charging cords ready for students who bring their own devices.
- Create a sample world to show in class.

Project Intro (15–20 minutes)

- Give a brief introduction to virtual reality.
- Demonstrate a virtual reality game with the class.
- Explain the project and requirements:
    - Each student must create a virtual world.
    - Each world must include 2 or more characters.
    - Each world must have several objects.
    - Each world must have a written backstory.
    - Each world should include dialogue between characters.
    - Each world can include multiple scenes, but it is not required.

FIGURE 50.2

Screenshot of sample world within CoSpaces interface

- Show an example of a VR world (figure 50.2).
- Have students create CoSpaces accounts using the classroom code.

Project (40–60 minutes)

- Once everyone has created a CoSpaces account, give an introduction to the CoSpaces interface.
- Show the library, how to pick an environment, and how to choose a character/object.
- Demonstrate the sub menu, which appears when you right-click on a character. This is where you can add actions/mood, change colors (including clothing color, hair color, and skin color), rotate and modify character/object size.
- Demonstrate how to add dialogue.
- Demonstrate how the block coding works. (CoSpaces pro version offers the ability to use JavaScript, which can allow for an advanced version of this project.)
- The naming feature under the sub menu turns on the ability for objects to be coded. Demonstrate how to turn on and off this feature.
- Allow students 30–40 minutes to create their project.
- Walk around to answer questions.

World Sharing (15–20 minutes)

- Depending on your budget and students' access to mobile devices, this portion can work with 1 headset and 1 mobile device for the whole class or as many as 1 per student.

- Have students who have brought their own device download the CoSpaces app.
- Access students' projects through their CoSpaces log-in.
- Load their project on the mobile device through the CoSpaces app.
- Press "play" and select the VR symbol.
- Put on the VR headset and experience each world.

LEARNING OUTCOMES

Participants will:

- Gain a basic understanding of virtual reality.
- Gain an intermediate understanding of the CoSpaces interface.
- Be introduced to block coding.
- Expand their digital storytelling skills through a literacy activity.

RECOMMENDED NEXT PROJECTS

- The CoSpaces website offers a variety of project ideas complete with teacher guide and lesson plans. The website also offers additional teacher resources and an online course: https://cospaces.io/edu/resources.html#special-projects/.
- A community of users is always helpful. Check out the CoSpaces Facebook group: https://www.facebook.com/groups/480579362131541/.
- A simple CoSpace tutorial is available from Instructables: https://www.instructables.com/id/Futuring-With-Virtual-Reality/.
- For those who like a course-driven environment, Aquila Education offers a free CoSpaces class. Although it seems to be more geared for teachers, the class only requires an e-mail to sign up: https://aquilaeducation.thinkific.com/courses/cospacesedu/.

51

Living in Fairyland

Explore Fairy Tales with VR Technology

LISA O'SHAUGHNESSY

Children's Librarian | East Orange (New Jersey) Public Library

PROJECT DESCRIPTION

Fairy tales are a part of everyone's iconic childhood experience. They can impart a moral lesson, warn against dangerous behavior, encourage perseverance, and teach story structure and other literacy skills—all wrapped up with a dash of magic and dragons. Imagine being able to fly on a magic carpet, battle with a magic wand, or swim with merpeople. With virtual reality and the CoSpaces program, all of this is possible.

In the Living in Fairyland project, students will use the CoSpaces program to create a story based on an original fairytale. They will employ characters, dialogue, multiple scenes, and actions to tell their story. One twist applies: They must change the original story in some way. After they have created their tale, they will be given the chance to explore their story using a virtual reality (VR) headset.

Age Range

- Tweens (Ages 8–12)
- Young adults (Ages 13–18)

Type of Library Best Suited For

- Public libraries
- School libraries

Cost Estimate

- $40–$1,000
- This cost estimate assumes you have access to laptop or desktop computers. The software cost to this project is free. There is a pro version of the software. which will give greater access to coding functionality, characters, and objects. Licensing plans can be found at https://cospaces.io/edu. If you don't already have VR headsets, you can purchase a simple Google Cardboard headset from $3 to $10. To keep the cost low, students could bring their own mobile device to class. The class could also share 1 mobile device and 1 VR headset.

OVERVIEW

Using the CoSpaces interface, students will create an original version of a classic fairytale. They will employ multiple characters, several different scenes, text, dialogue, and coded actions to tell the story. Retelling a classic tale will allow students to use their imagination to enhance their digital literacy and storytelling skills. Once completed, students will explore their tale using a VR headset.

The program will take about 1.5–2 hours. Although teenage learners need less support, it is still recommended to keep your class size small (10–12 students) to ensure you have adequate time to spend with each student. It is not necessary to have extra assistants to teach this class, but it would be a great way to incorporate a teen volunteer as your teaching assistant.

Software/Hardware Needed

- 10–12 Google Cardboard or more advanced VR headsets. (VR headsets anything from Google Cardboard to a more advanced headset will work and can be found from Amazon to eBay).
- 10–12 laptop/desktop computers
- 1–12 mobile devices able to run the CoSpaces app: https://play.google.com/store/apps/details?id=delightex.cospaces.edu&hl=en_US/).
- CoSpaces desktop version. According to the CoSpaces website, a desktop, tablet, or mobile device running an up-to-date browser (https://cospaces.io/edu/faqs.html#tech/)
- CoSpaces app: https://play.google.com/store/apps/details?id=delightex.cospaces.edu&hl=en_US/

- CoSpaces has a free basic version and a pro version with a licensing plan. See the website for pricing. The pro version offers additional coding functionality and access to a larger library of characters and objects.

STEP-BY-STEP INSTRUCTIONS

Preparation (60 minutes)

- Create a CoSpaces teacher account and copy the classroom code. (CoSpaces allows you to work in a monitored classroom environment. The free version allows up to 30 students and has the ability to create assignments.)
- Download a simple VR game/experience to demonstrate during class.
- Charge mobile devices or have several charging cords ready for students who bring their own.
- Download the CoSpaces app on all available mobile devices.
- Create a sample fairytale to show in class.

PROJECT INSTRUCTIONS

- Introduction (20–30 minutes)
- Give a brief introduction to virtual reality.
- Demonstrate a virtual reality game with the class.
- Explain the project and requirements:
  - Each story must be based on an original fairytale or folktale.
  - Each story must have more than 1 scene.
  - Each story must have a chosen setting or environment.
  - Each story must include more than 1 character.
  - Each story must have more than 1 object.
  - Each story must include coded actions.
- Demonstrate an example of a VR fairytale/folktale (figure 51.1).
- Have students create CoSpaces accounts using the classroom code.

FIGURE 51.1

Sample digital story using CoSpaces

Project (40–60 minutes)

- Once everyone has created an account, give an introduction to the CoSpaces interface.
- Show the library, how to pick an environment, and how to choose a character/object.
- Demonstrate the sub menu, which appears when you right click on a character. This is where you can add actions/mood, change colors, rotate and modify character/object size.
- Demonstrate how to add dialogue.
- Demonstrate how the block coding works. (CoSpaces pro version offers the ability to use JavaScript, which can allow for an advanced version of this project.)
- Allow students 30–40 minutes to create their project.
- Walk around to answer questions.

Story Sharing (20–30 minutes)

- Depending on your budget and students' access to mobile devices, this portion can work with 1 headset and 1 mobile device for the whole class or as many as 1 per student.
- Have students who brought their own mobile device download the CoSpaces app.
- Access students' projects through their CoSpaces log-in.
- Load their project on the mobile device.
- Press "play" and select the VR symbol.

LEARNING OUTCOMES

Participants will:

- Gain an intermediate understanding of digital storytelling.
- Gain a basic understanding of virtual reality.
- Gain an intermediate understanding of the CoSpaces interface.
- Be introduced to block coding.

RECOMMENDED NEXT PROJECTS

- The CoSpaces website offers a variety of project ideas complete with teacher guide and lesson plans. The website also offers additional teacher resources and an online course: https://cospaces.io/edu/resources.html#special-projects/.
- A community of users is always helpful. Check out the CoSpaces Facebook group: https://www.facebook.com/groups/480579362131541/.
- A simple CoSpaces tutorial is available from Instructables: https://www.instructables.com/id/Futuring-With-Virtual-Reality.
- For those who like a course-driven environment, Aquila Education offers a free class. Although it seems to be more geared for teachers, the class only requires an e-mail to sign up: (https://aquilaeducation.thinkific.com/courses/cospacesedu/.

52

Create and Choreograph Original Music Videos

JESSICA FRANCO
Teen Librarian | Groton (Connecticut) Public Library

EMILY SHEEHAN
Children's and Emerging Technologies Librarian | Groton (Connecticut) Public Library

PROJECT DESCRIPTION

This Music Video Camp is a multi-week series of programs for young adults and tweens. Participants are asked to write their own song using Soundtrap, choreograph robot dances using Ozobots, and work in teams to edit a final video using iMovie. The lesson allows for expression of youth voice, as well as opportunities for teamwork and collaboration.

Age Range

- Tweens (Ages 8–12)
- Young adults (Ages 13–18)

Type of Library Best Suited For

- Public libraries
- School libraries

Cost Estimate

- $100–$1,200
- Ozobots range in price from $100 for a single robot to $1,200 for a classroom set with 12 robots and supporting materials.

OVERVIEW

While hosting a minimum of 5 sessions, the library will teach participants to use sound mixing to write original songs, use block coding to choreograph an

Ozobot dance, and create a music video. Because there are so many intricate layers to this project, having a small class size and 2 instructors is recommended. Often 1 instructor will take on the teaching role, while the other troubleshoots any problems that occur. Each participant's progress will vary, so being flexible with the timetable for each lesson is essential.

Software/Hardware Needed

- Ozobots
- Computers with Internet access
- iPads for filming and editing
- Google or e-mail accounts
- Flash drive

Optional:

- Coloring supplies
- Poster board

STEP-BY-STEP INSTRUCTIONS

Introduction

- Introduce participants to Soundtrap and have participants make a 60- to 90-second song. This lesson can be repeated each week until participants have finished, but most need only 1 or 2 sessions.

PROJECT INSTRUCTIONS

- Open with an overview of the program series; review the ultimate goal of creating a music video and the steps required.
- Discuss what makes a good song—length, genre, beat, etc.
- At Soundtrap.com, have attendees establish accounts, many of which can be connected directly to Google.
- Enter the Studio and explore the various options. Explain how looping works and demonstrate layer sounds to create rhythms.
- Allow the participants to create their own original songs.
- Once the songs has been finalized, download them to a storage device.
- End the session with "Digging Deeper" questions.
- Using an iPad or iPhone, import the downloaded songs into iTunes and create a playlist. Later, this will be used during the editing process.

Digging Deeper

- What did you learn today?
- Was it easier to use a template or write your song from scratch? Why?
- What were some of the editing features that you used?
- Did you use loops, and, if so, how did they work?

Ozobot Dance

Have teens listen to their songs and choreograph a dance. Depending on their experience with Ozobots, this lesson could take 2 or more sessions.

PROJECT INSTRUCTIONS

- Open with a discussion of the successes, challenges, and confusion from the previous session.
- Introduce the Ozobots and discuss or demonstrate their various moves. Give attendees a storyboard template and then have them listen to their songs and sketch out possible dance moves. This should take about 10–20 minutes.
- As they wrap up their storyboards, direct participants to the computer and Ozoblockly.com. Give an overview of the code block available to Level 2 coders (this is the easiest level for new users and this project).
- Allow users to begin coding a dance.
- As each user finishes, demonstrate installing the code (figure 52.1). Ozoblockly will states how long the code takes to install, but not how long the code will run. Once the Ozobot is ready, the completed dance should be timed to ensure that it matches the length of the song.
- Save the dances to a storage device to be used later.
- End the session with "Digging Deeper" questions.

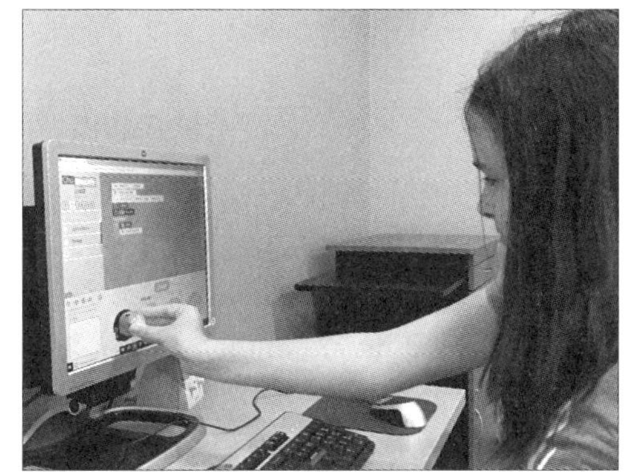

FIGURE 52.1

The code for an Ozobot is installed by holding the robot up to the screen. Flickering lights will install the code in a matter of minutes

Digging Deeper

- What did you learn today?
- Is it easier to code your Ozobot with color or through the computer? Why?
- How many different moves does your Ozobot do?
- Did you use loops? If so, why?

Video Filming

Participants begin filming their videos. This lesson can be added to the end of the choreography session or the beginning of Video Editing. It typically does not take a full session to record the dance.

PROJECT INSTRUCTIONS

- Open with a discussion of the successes, challenges, and confusion from the previous session.
- Give each participant an Ozobot and install the code for their dances.
- Allow participants to create sets and backgrounds.
- Distribute iPads or have participants use their iPhones.
- Record the dances. Take multiple recordings from different angles so participants can incorporate close-up shots or aerial views.
- End the session with "Digging Deeper" questions.

Digging Deeper

- What did you learn today?
- What issues did you run into?
- Was it easy matching the Ozobot dance to your song? If not, why not?
- How many different angles did you film from?

Video Editing and Showcase

Participants will edit their videos and finish with a showcase. This may be finished in 1 session, but larger groups or those with limited iMovie experience may need additional time.

PROJECT INSTRUCTIONS

- Open with a discussion of the successes, challenges, and confusion from the previous session.
- Redistribute iPads.
- Introduce participants to iMovie by demonstrating how to import music, insert, and shorten video clips, manipulate sound, and add a title slide. Some may need to alter the speed of the video or song, both of which can be done in iMovie.
- Allow teens to begin working—provide encouragement and troubleshooting as needed.
- On the last day, celebrate the end of the camp with snacks and showing the finished videos.
- Have teens introduce themselves (name, grade, and school), their video, and their thought process when making it.
- End the session with "Digging Deeper" questions.

Digging Deeper

- What did you learn today?
- What was the hardest part about editing?
- What part of the camp did you like best?
- How can the skills you learned at camp help you in the future?
- Will you make more music or music videos?

Resources

- View some examples of music videos at https://tinyurl.com/yb3h30nq/.
- https://ozoblockly.com
- https://www.soundtrap.com

LEARNING OUTCOMES

Participants will:

- Learn to layer and loop sounds to create an original song.
- Be able to choreograph a dance using a storyboard template.

- Be able to code a robot to perform a dance.
- Be able to record video, utilizing angles and close-up views.
- Learn to use iMovie or other editing software to create a music video.

RECOMMENDED NEXT PROJECTS

- **Mixing It Up:** Having learned the basics of each step, consider going more in-depth. Soundtrap offers users the opportunity to upload sound files. Consider writing lyrics and record participant voices for the song.
- In addition, choreographing a dance for multiple Ozobots would challenge experienced participants.

53

After Scratch

Connecting Teen Patrons with Next Steps

OLIVIA HORVATH

Digital Services Specialist

Prince George's County (Maryland) Memorial Library System

PROJECT DESCRIPTION

A participant in your coding club has mastered Scratch. Hooray! Now what? What's the best way to guide an enthusiastic young learner without becoming overwhelmed at the options? Librarians without a coding background may feel intimidated by the task of bridging the gap between learning languages like Scratch and workforce-oriented coding tutorials aimed at adults. This chapter is a guide to evaluating creative young learners and connecting them with next steps.

Age Range

- Tweens (Ages 8–12)
- Young adults (Ages 13–18)

Type of Library Best Suited For

- Public libraries
- School libraries

Cost Estimate

- $0–$700

OVERVIEW

One of the joys of the coding club model is watching participants learn and grow at their own pace. But when 1 learner outpaces the average skill level of the group, it can be a challenge to support his enthusiasm. If the facilitator does not have significant coding experience past block-based scripting, the challenge is even greater. The following is a strategy for evaluating participants' strengths and reflecting their interests back through a recommended next project. All suggestions are available for free and are supported by robust online tutorials and communities.

This chapter is written as a strategy for a 1-on-1 evaluation within a larger group, but it can be used with multiple participants or an entire coding club. The "Code as Collaboration" section provides a framework for assisting multiple participants with the jump from Scratch to more advanced software.

Of course, there are scores of other options both in this book and beyond. It's important to experiment, research, and reflect before introducing new languages to your learning environment. Avoid overwhelming yourself and your learners by experimenting with these options outside of club time and limiting the number of "next steps" introduced at once.

Software/Hardware Needed

Hardware

Personal computer or laptop with Internet access

Software (Optional)

- Twine 2.0 (free) available at http://twinery.org/
- Sonic Pi (free) available at https://sonic-pi.net
- Python (free) available at https://www.python.org/downloads/
- Pygame (free) available at https://www.pygame.org
- Stencyl (basic subscription free) available at http://www.stencyl.com

STEP-BY-STEP INSTRUCTIONS

Preparation

Do Your Research. If participants are ready to move past Scratch, you will need to be ready to provide at least a basic framework of next options. Experiment with the following offerings so you can provide at least a basic understanding of the scope and function of each. All suggestions provide free introductory tutorials as well as resources for educators.

PROJECT INSTRUCTIONS

Reflect

- Ask participant to give you a tour of their Scratch projects. What kinds of stories are they telling? What problems have been solved using code? What about Scratch is exciting and fun? What is frustrating?
- Are there aspects of Scratch that have still gone unexplored? Before moving on, participants should have experience with advanced Scratch functions such as lists, variables, and conditional statements. Adding a scoring mechanism, inventory system, or additional scene can challenge learners who feel mired in Scratch's more straightforward scripts.
- If participants feel limited or bored by Scratch after giving it a dedicated go, introducing them to a new language can only expand their horizons. This learning path doesn't need to be linear. There is always the possibility of bringing new skills and discoveries back to a future Scratch project.

Imagine

- What are participants' dream projects? Prompt them to think further than just "I want to make a game." Identifying genres, concepts, characters, and examples can help you understand what their motivations are and how best to support their creativity.
- Reflect on the insights you have gained from assessing their work and asking about their interests. With these in mind, assess the following suggestions and pair your learner with a next step.

Explore

Code as Storytelling: Participants whose projects have been narrative animations or Choose Your Own Adventure–style games may benefit from a story-focused game editor with a simple UI. Twine (http://twinery.org) describes itself as "an open-source tool for telling interactive, nonlinear stories." Twine (figure 53.1) is an excellent tool for creating text-based interactive games at any level of code literacy. Beginners can easily create a Choose Your Own Adventure–style game, while advanced learners can incorporate more complex logic systems or customize the look and feel of their game using CSS and JavaScript. They may also benefit from the project featured in Chapter 54: Programming Stories: How to Animate with Code by Austin Olney.

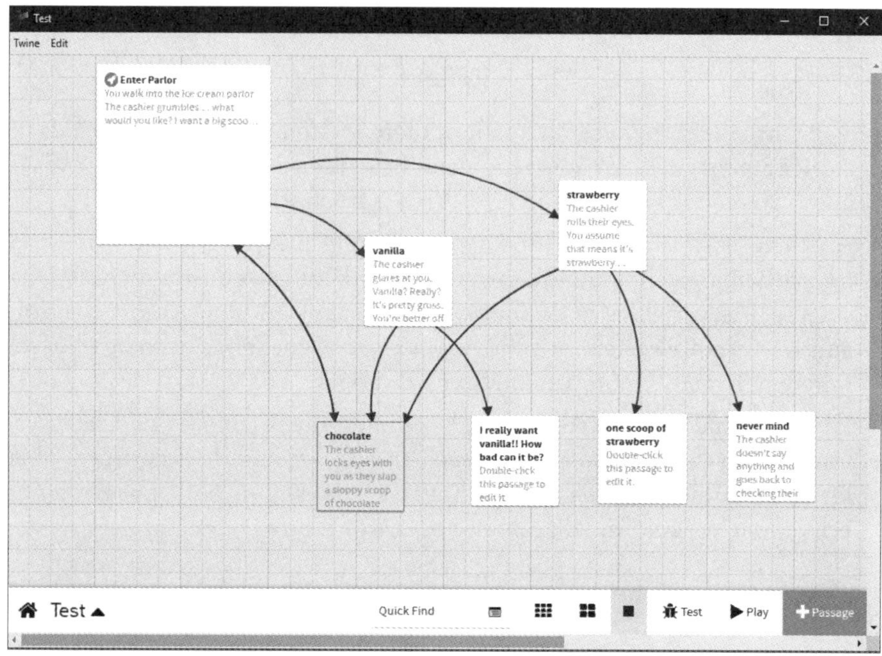

FIGURE 53.1

An example of a simple Twine game

Code as Canvas: Some participants may show more enthusiasm in creating assets (sprites, backgrounds, music) than in scripting. These learners can benefit from keeping code as a tool in their creative arsenal. HTML and CSS are excellent starting points for those looking to express themselves visually. Mozilla offers several introductory web design experiments through its Thimble code editor. The silly and satisfying Build-a-Burger project (https://thimbleprojects.org/mozillalearning/286539/) introduces learners to basic HTML page structure and the CSS class attribute through the manipulation of color and shape. Learners can learn more about coding for the web with the project in Chapter 47: Use HTML, JavaScript, and CSS to Create an Interactive Online Greet-Bot 3000 by David Vance. For those seeking an instantaneous and unique way to synthesize code into art, **Sonic Pi** (https://sonic-pi.net) is a Ruby-based and Raspberry Pi-ready language for live-coding music.

Code as Poetry: Participants who have pushed Scratch's scripting function to its limit are ready to break free from the restrictions of block script. **Python** is a practical, powerful text-based language known for its legibility and used commonly in educational environments. Trinket's excellent

Hour of Python (https://hourofpython.com) includes a blocks to code learning project as a first step. Further experiments in Python exist as chapters in this book, including the projects in Chapter 24: Program a Mad Libs Game with Python by Connor McNamara and Chapter 25: Program a Number Guessing Game with Python by Connor McNamara. **Pygame** (https://www.pygame.org), a Python programming language library, opens up a host of creative avenues for those looking to expand their skills as game programmers.

Code as Collaboration: One challenge of the coding club model is supporting participants in tackling advanced concepts and projects across weekly or monthly sessions. Having a collaborative coding project at the heart of your club can be a way for learners to work at a manageable scale while developing at a larger scope. Using Pixelatto's **1xGDD** (available for download at http://pixelatto.com/, a simple, 1-page visual tool for mapping game design ideas, guides participants in creating a concept and defining the scope of a collaborative game project. The game development tool **Stencyl** (www.stencyl.com/ is a great option for a post-Scratch game project. Stencyl's block-based language and drag-and-drop scene editor (figure 53.2) are designed to be familiar to Scratch users. Because of its focus, game development concepts like inventory systems and collision physics are easier to implement than in Scratch. Guide learners to focus on a single asset or behavior each session—design and animate a walk cycle, define the parameters and exits of a room, or define the properties of an object. At the end of each session, experiment as a whole with combining solo work and interacting with the collaborative piece.

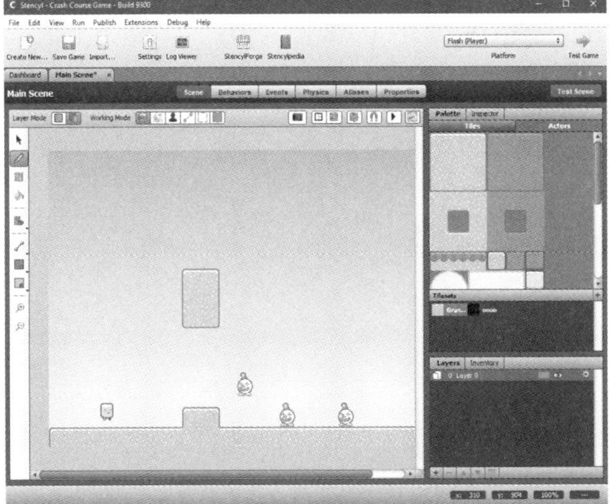

FIGURE 53.2

Stencyl's drag-and-drop scene editor

LEARNING OUTCOMES

Participants will:

- Reflect on and expand previous Scratch projects.
- Identify what interests and what challenges them as a learner of code.
- Create connections between computer science concepts learned in Scratch and their applications in other languages.
- Experiment with new coding languages, expanding their creative horizons.

RECOMMENDED NEXT PROJECTS

The recommendations in this chapter mostly revolve around web and computer-based game development, but these are far from the only options available to you and your learners.

- Move to mobile development with Chapter 43: Host a Teen and Tween App Development Camp in Your Library by Jessica Franco and Emily Sheehan.
- Expand into physical computing with Chapter 44: Host an Escape Room with a Robotic Twist by JoAnna Schofield.
- Explore new dimensions with Chapter 51: Living in Fairyland: Explore Fairy Tales with VR Technology by Lisa O'Shaughnessy.
- To support participants taking their skills in a diversity of directions, consider Chapter 49: Partners in Technology: How to Create a Successful Technology Mentorship Program by Julia Clark.

54

Programming Stories
How to Animate with Code

AUSTIN OLNEY
Digital Media Specialist | White Plains (New York) Public Library

PROJECT DESCRIPTION

Advanced programming algorithms is not something kids typically get excited about. Not surprisingly, many librarians face obstacles when trying to capture the interest of children toward coding. Although there are plenty of teaching resources available, many of these tools are geared for a particular group of users who are mainly interested in video games. An alternative approach is to show patrons how to program animations, potentially capturing the attention of a more artistic crowd. It can provide a learning "hook" that fosters creativity and, at the same time, opens a window into the programming world. The following lesson will dissect this approach, helping you to teach coding in a nontraditional way and ideally capture the attention of non-gamers everywhere.

One of the main advantages of a creative programming class is that it attracts a diverse audience. Linking programming and art presents a fresh perspective on computer science and attracts a nontraditional crowd. The stereotypical image of a computer programmer as a "math geek" is being replaced with a more realistic view of a digital artist.

Age Range

- Tweens (Ages 8–12)
- Young adults (Ages 13–18)
- This program can be adapted to work for older teenagers as well.

Type of Library Best Suited For

- Public libraries
- School libraries

Cost Estimate

- $0
- This estimate assumes the library has computers available for instruction. The software application to be used is free.

OVERVIEW

Many children are natural storytellers, and it is possible to direct this creative energy into a basic programming environment through the digital scripting of stories. Librarians can break down the specific processes of storytelling into understandable parts and gently guide children to create a virtual world and express themselves through programmed animations.

The application used in a class such as this is Alice 2 from Carnegie Mellon University. It is an intuitive learning environment, targeted for those not familiar with development software. Although Alice 2 has not received the level of international attention as programs such as Scratch (https://scratch.mit.edu), it is nonetheless a great initial step for programming within a 3-D environment and learning advanced concepts. The application uses simplified object-oriented programming (OOP), which is a form of coding that uses various "objects" as representations of elements and organizes it as such. In Alice 2, one is literally adding graphic "objects" to the story and manipulating and commanding them directly.

The physical setup of the space is a typical computer lab setup, with a set of computers for patrons and a main computer for the librarian instructor. If you have fewer computers available than the attendee target amount, you can feasibly share a computer between every 2 patrons, effectively doubling the available class capacity. Another factor is the ability to be able to project the screen of the librarian's computer so the class can observe various demonstrations and video content. Finally, it may be helpful to have a volunteer or another staff member present to help facilitate the class and provide individual support.

Software/Hardware Needed

- Projector that can display the librarian's screen and audio
- Projector screen

- Teacher computer, connected to the projector
- Class set of computers with Internet connection. The number of computers needed depends on the desired amount of attendees, usually 5–15 people.
- Alice 2 installed on computers: https://www.alice.org/get-alice/alice-2/

STEP-BY-STEP INSTRUCTIONS

Preparation

There are some basic skills every librarian interested in teaching with Alice 2 should learn beforehand. Fortunately, the software is equipped with preinstalled interactive tutorials to train users how the application functions. It is highly recommended that librarians complete the 4 tutorials, located on the initial splash screen when the application is opened. In addition, there is a helpful section on the official website for beginners at https://www.alice.org/resources/alice-2-how-tos/.

PROJECT INSTRUCTIONS

Demonstration

- Emphasis on the creative aspect of storytelling should be paramount during the coding class, almost as if it were a creative writing class. Discuss the components of a good story, specifically looking at essential parts. Explore concepts such as characters, exchanges, or events involved within an interesting story. Perhaps point out a popular show they may know and use it as a reference. The goal is to incorporate examples from the discussion into features of a project they can create.
- Showing examples of what participants will be creating is helpful in setting expectations. A quick search on YouTube (www.youtube.com) for Alice 2 projects will result in interesting content that can inspire. Examine these videos beforehand to ensure there's no violence or inappropriate content.
- An example of a video to display is Final Project- Alice Programming: Curse of the Mummy v13. at https://www.youtube.com/watch?v=cXtmBtFAhTw. It demonstrates the basic capabilities of Alice 2 through a simple animation. Once you show the video, ask participants about what they watched and discuss the different aspects of the story. Ask about the objects and the movements they made and require the class to be very specific. Ask them exactly what kinds of movements the characters made and how that

is possible. Explain that it is possible because of different transformations of shapes and axes based on programmed commands by a human artist.

- Direct participants to the front screen and explain that they should look at the main computer for the time being for a demonstration; there will be plenty of time for them to create their own projects afterward. It may be helpful to point out that if they pay attention, they won't have as many questions later on. When you first start up Alice, a window appears that allows you to choose 1 of 6 world options. Proceed through the following steps, explaining to patrons along the way.
- Ask the class which world you should choose and impartially select the first one you hear called out. When the world is selected, explain the basic layout of the program and how the various parts work (figure 54.1). Explain that the World Hierarchy panel (1A) is the object hierarchy where everything in the virtual story they will be working with is listed here; the center panel (1B) is the View panel, a window into the created environment where the purple arrows control a virtual camera and objects are added in; (1C) is the Events panel, which controls the general code methods (for the purposes of this project, will leave this panel alone for now); the World's Details panel (1D) is where code commands are found; and, finally, the bottom right Method panel (1E) is where code commands are placed.

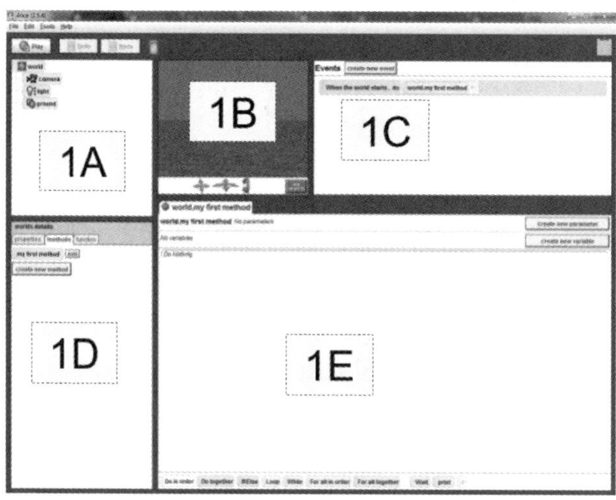

FIGURE 54.1

Main layout of Alice 2

- To add objects into the project, click the Add Objects button within the View panel (1B) to open up a new window shown in figure 54.2.

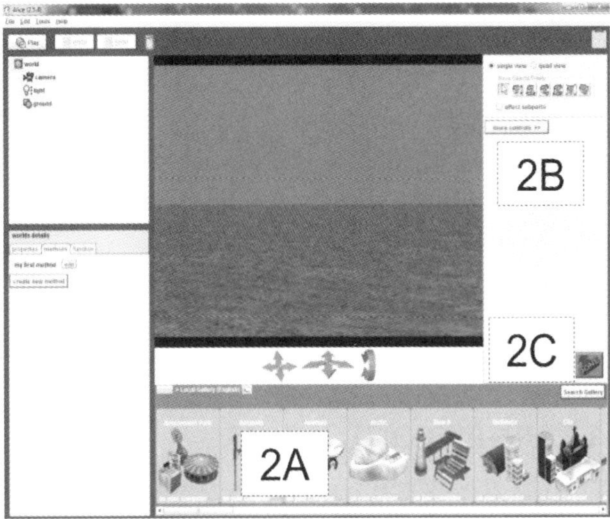

FIGURE 54.2

Add Objects window button

- In the Local Gallery panel (2A), select a character, manipulate it with the options in the transform panel (2B), and click the Done button (2C) to insert the object into the project.
- With an object inserted in the scene, select it in the World Hierarchy panel (1A), drag in a command from the list displayed in the World's Details panel (1D), and press the "Play" button at the top left corner of the screen to see the result. A new window will open and read the chosen command block and execute it. A fun command block within the "World's Details panel (1D) is the Say block, which creates an editable speech bubble for the object.
- Explain that the command blocks represent lines of code. When they are associated with an object, it will execute like someone following instructions.

Programming the Story

- When you have demonstrated to the class how the application works, allow patrons to begin working on their own projects. Have them start by adding objects by clicking the Add Objects button within the View panel (1B). As they work, walk around the room and assist with any inquiries from patrons. It is also helpful to look at the projects and encourage participants to do better.
- Instructor guidance is very important, and having an assistant on hand is helpful. Many times students have questions, relevant to their specific project, and 1-on-1 guidance is essential. Sometimes a word of inspiration or an

idea or small praise keep children motivated. Common issues are getting lost in the Add Objects module, whereby an instructor can point them back to the Local Gallery button.

- While patrons are working it is often helpful to ask if anyone has something interesting to show. This encourages participation and motivates them to work on something for a potential audience.
- To save the project, click the File button, click Save Project As, give it a name, and click Save. The project can be shared via e-mail and viewed from an installed Alice 2 application.

LEARNING OUTCOMES

Participants will:

- Obtain familiarity with Alice 2 application.
- Understand basic story, animation, and coding concepts.
- Create their own animation.

RECOMMENDED NEXT PROJECTS

- When the class is over, there are a number of subsequent directions that patrons can go. One of the best programs to use after Alice 2 is Alice 3 (www.alice.org/get-alice/alice-3/). There is a great guide available online to get started with the program (http://www.alice.org/wp-content/uploads/2017/05/Alice-3-HowToGuide-Complete.pdf). It offers the same basic setup of Alice 2 but offers many new features.
- For patrons looking for more advanced programs, plenty of free or inexpensive software is available. To design digital models, they can use an online resource called Blender (www.blender.org). To practice using a professional object-oriented programming language such as Java, they can use an integrated development environment called "IntelliJ Idea" (www.jetbrains.com/idea/). To create more complicated interactive 3-D projects, they can use a game engine called Unity (www.unity3d.com).

PART IV

PROGRAMS FOR ADULTS

55

Scratch Coding for Adults

Creating a Collectible Game

KARLENE TURA CLARK

Coordinator of Circulation Services and Student Employment

Chester Fritz Library, University of North Dakota, Grand Forks

PROJECT DESCRIPTION

It's Going Swimmingly

Many adults have apprehension for coding. Scratch, originally developed by the Massachusetts Institute of Technology Media Lab in 2007 for ages 8–16, encourages digital citizenship and fundamental computational concepts and practices. Scratch has aided adults in transitioning to more traditional text-based programming languages after gaining the foundational understanding. Scratch is open-source, shared software, designed to encourage remixing of projects.

This project creates a game with a cartoon octopus that moves, collects fish, and avoids a crab moving around the screen. Coders are also taught how to add points and make the animals talk.

Instructors may request a "classroom" to help manage the projects of a group or across multiple "classrooms" at https://scratch.mit.edu/educators#teacher-accounts. Instructors use their own e-mail for all student accounts in the group. Ask adults to get their information to you before the first day of class so they can be added and see each other's work for inspiration.

Age Range

- Tweens (Ages 8–12)
    - Recommendation for this group is to have at least 1 other instructor available to circulate and attempt it only after foundational projects like *Dinosaurs at the Movies*
- Young adults (Ages 13–18)
- Adults

Type of Library Best Suited For

- Public libraries
- Academic libraries
- School libraries

Cost

- $0
- Libraries already have the necessary equipment, as listed under "Software/Hardware Needed." The only cost is librarian time in preparation and teaching.

OVERVIEW

The use of Sensing (touch reaction), Control (conditional statements), Operators (>, <, =, etc.), and Data (variables) blocks in addition to the foundational blocks are used to create a point collection game. Most of the blocks are used in the creation of a little octopus that collects fish while avoiding a crab. The octopus is controlled by the player and the others are set to move in a pattern across the screen. Both a "you win" and a "game over" screen are created.

Software/Hardware Needed

- Computer with speakers
- Network connection;
    - the Chrome Internet browser is recommended
- Method of projecting the instructor project during the lesson
- Current version of Adobe Flash Player

STEP-BY-STEP INSTRUCTIONS

Preparation

- Create a classroom account ahead of time, if desired.
- Create usernames at https://scratch.mit.edu.
- Have students log in to their accounts.

Demonstration

- Show students https://scratch.mit.edu/projects/154781453/ and https://scratch.mit.edu/projects/155828528/. Both are creative collectible games created by some of the author's former students, shared with their permission.
  - This demonstrates a few of the many ways collectible games can be created.
- The instructor demonstrates on a screen, letting students follow along with the steps to create a mid-level project: collecting for points.
- Start by clicking Create in the upper left corner of the screen, next to the Scratch logo. The coding screen (currently empty) will appear on the right, with coding blocks in the center and their first sprite, Scratch Cat, in the center of the left window.
- At the bottom of the screen, the sprite is outlined in blue. Right-click and delete the cat.
- To choose a new one, click the little figure next to New Sprite. Some of them will have only 1 image and some will have multiple costumes. For this project, choose "Octopus."
  - Click the Costumes tab at the center top. You'll see she has 2 different costumes. Let's use her!
- She's going to need a backdrop. At the bottom left, click on Stage, and notice the blue box around it—this means it is the active item.
  - New backdrops can be added at the top center or under Stage.
  - Just under the words *new backdrop* are images of mountains, a pen, a folder, and a camera. For now, use the mountain portrait to choose a backdrop from the library.
  - Choose "underwater1."
- Drag the octopus to the upper left corner. Her sprite box should now be outlined in blue again so we can work with her.
- Click the Scripts tab again.
  - To make anything happen, we need an Event (brown) to get things started. Specifically, choose "when green flag clicked."
  - Motion (blue) allows movement, sets locations, and determines graph coordinates. To make the octopus always start where she was moved to, now choose the block "go to x: O y: O." The numbers in the coordinates will be different for each person, depending on where the octopus is resting.

  - Drag the block over to the right pane and attach it under the Flag.
  - We also want her to always be there at the start of the game, so go to the purple Looks blocks and find "show."
  - Place that under the "go to" block.
- Because we want her to have room to move around the screen, we need to make her smaller.
  - Above the green flag and red stop sign, there are editing tools.
  - Choose the one with the arrows pointed inward, then click the sprite as many times as you like to make her small enough. This can be further adjusted later. But for now, she has space to move.
- We also want her to be able to move not only left and right, but also up and down.
  - Go to the Control (yellow) tab and drag over a "forever block" under the blue "go to" block.
  - Under the same tab, you will need 4 of the "if . . . then" blocks.
  - Place these one under the other, inside the forever block.
- Next, we'll need to add blocks that tell us what happens in the "if . . . then" conditions. That happens under Sensing (light blue).
  - There are a number of fun things that can happen in this area. We'll come back to some of them later, but for now, we need to move the "key space pressed?" into each of the empty hexagons between the "if" and "then."
  - Notice that they have a dropdown. In order, go down the 4 and change "space" to right arrow, left arrow, up arrow, and down arrow.
  - This is telling our game what keys on the keyboard will control her movements.
  - But we still have no answer to "then." To provide motion, go back to the blue Motion tab.
  - You want to drag a "change x by 10" under the first 2 "if . . . then" sections.
  - Try starting your game by pressing the green flag above the play screen and move her to the right. You'll see that 10 steps move very quickly!
  - Try changing the number from 10 to something smaller like 8. Try the game again. Much better! However, she's still going only 1 direction.
  - In the "left arrow" section, change x to -8. Try the game again. She should now be going back and forth.
- Back in school we had to learn graphing and coordinates. Here's where to put it to use. X is your horizontal line and Y is your vertical line. In other words,

X is your back and forth and Y is your up and down. For the last 2 sections
    - Drag over the "change y by 10" blocks.
    - Do as you did for the X coordinates; change it to 8 and -8.
    - When you press the start flag, she should now move in all 4 directions.
- She also had a second costume.
    - Go to the Looks tab (light purple) and place a "Next costume block under each of the change blocks. Now she can swim!
    - However, it's extremely fast. We want to control that, right? To the yellow blocks!
    - "Wait 1 secs" will allow you to slow down how fast she's moving.
    - A full second is too slow; try .25 or .20.

Congratulations! Your first part of the project is complete. The next step is to create sprites to collect and sprites to create trouble.

- Go back to New sprite and find Fish2.
    - Remember to shrink it down smaller than the octopus.
    - Add a brown Event for "when the flag is clicked."
    - Add a blue Motion for "go to x: O and y: O" (after placing the fish where you would like it).
    - Add a purple Looks block to "show."
    - We need the fish to move. This involves yellow Control again. Specifically, a "forever" loop.
    - Inside that, we need our blue Motion again.
    - This time we want
    - "move 10 steps" (change it to 3)
    - "if on edge, bounce."
    - Press the green flag and see what happens!
- Let's get another sprite. This time, Fish3.
    - Shrink it down, pick a spot on the screen (not close to the octopus), and . . . (Pause and see if they remember at this point. They should be getting used to the concept of needing "when the flag is clicked" and "go to.")
    - Don't forget a purple Look to "show" him!
    - We'll need another "forever" loop from . . . (pause to let them fill in yellow Control).
    - Blue motion and get a "move 10 steps." Experiment on speed.

  - Now another Control block.
  - "If . . . then" allows us to set parameters. Put this inside the "forever" loop.
  - Just like the other fish, we need a light-blue Sensing block now.
  - This time, we want the fish to leave the screen and reappear on the other side. To do this, we need
  - "touching mouse-pointer" and change the dropdown to "edge."
  - Now, move your fish to the far left side of the screen. Get him as close to the edge as you can without his tail fin touching it.
  - Add another "go to x:O y:O."
  - Change your Y to match the Y in your first instance under your Event block. This will allow your fish to stay in a straight line.
- Try pressing the green flag again. You should now have 1 fish bouncing back and forth and 1 scrolling across the screen.
- Press the stop button to halt the movement.

We're going to add one more sprite—the enemy. If the octopus touches him, the game is over.

- Go back to the New sprites and choose Crab.
  - Place him at the bottom of the screen.
  - Add your Event and Motion blocks to set his location.
  - Add a Look block to keep him visible and shrink his size.
  - We're going to Control his movements with a Forever loop. Randomly move the crab to a new location.
  - Drag a "glide 1 secs to x:O y:O."
  - Repeat this 6 or 8 times, ending up near the place he started.
  - When you press the green flag, he should now be moving in the pattern you set for him.

Break Time

This is a natural spot to stretch, look away from the screen, or break for the day, depending on the frustration level of participants or the amount of time it took to create so far. At this point, they can see that something is happening and that they have created the first level of coding: a moving cartoon. If adults are comfortable, continue. If not, they can pick up here the next day.

Back to Coding

- If starting over on a new day, review the blocks used the previous day and how they work.
- Now, we're going to add orange Data. This involves bouncing back and forth quite a bit between the blocks and the sprites. It's not too bad though!
    - Click Make a Variable."
        - Name the variable "Points" and leave it set "for all sprites."
        - We have to set up all sprites to understand what they need to do with the points, starting with a reset of points at the beginning of the game.
        - Let's go back to the octopus. At the start of the game we always need . . . (by now they should know "when the flag is clicked"). Let's move that over!
            - Back under orange Data, move "set Points to 0" under the new event header.
            - Another "when the flag is clicked" is needed for the octopus. This will set up the win conditions.
                - To make that happen, we need Controls.
                - Just like the first row of coding on the octopus, we need a "forever" loop and an "if . . . then" block inside of each other.
                - This time, we're going to use a green Operator. Take the one that looks like 2 squares with an equal sign between them and place that inside the "if . . . then" block.
                - Go back to orange Data. Drag the oval that says "points" into the first square.
                - Because we have 2 fish to collect right now, we want it to say "if points = 2, then," so in the second square, type 2.
            - Next, we'll need to have a winning response. For the game to understand this, we need to "broadcast." (Give them a few minutes to explore and see if they can find it.)
                - Under brown Events, attach a "broadcast message1." To make this more specific, use the dropdown to make a new message that says "you win."
- When the octopus touches the fish, we want the fish to disappear.
- Starting with Fish2, we need "When the flag is clicked" (brown Event) and "if . . . then" (yellow Control) wrapped by "forever."

  - Our condition is when the octopus is touching the fish, so that would be under . . . (give them a minute to look) light-blue Sensing: "touching mouse-pointer."
  - In the dropdown, change it to "octopus."
  - Our "then" reaction is to have it hide. (Again, give them a minute to see if they can find it.)
  - Purple Looks, and "hide."
  - We also need to add Data (orange): "change points by 1."
- The other fish is also going to need these same conditions, but let's simplify our work.
- Click/hold and carefully drag that series of blocks on Fish2 over Fish3 and let go.
  - It will bounce your coding back to the right side, but (show them the coding on Fish3) there it is!
  - It copied over, but be careful not to let go over the center coding blocks—that will erase your work on the current sprite!
- The crab is a little different.
- You can copy the coding from Fish2 over but then take out the "hide."
- We want him to broadcast a different message from Events.
  - Drag over a "broadcast you win" where "hide" had been.
  - Create a new message to say "game over."
  - Surround all of this by a "forever" loop".
- Back to the broadcast "you win" we created on the octopus, we need the others to receive the message.
- Starting with Fish2, under brown Events, we want "when I receive you win."
- Again, we want the sprite to "hide" (under purple Looks).
- Drag this to Fish3 and Crab to duplicate your coding.
- For the octopus, now create another "when I receive" block with "hide" attached.
  - Make sure the received message is "game over" now.
  - Drag this to both fish.
- Because the octopus and the crab will be our sign for winning or ending the game, we need them to do something special.
- For the octopus, drag over a "when I receive you win" and a "when I receive game over."

- We'll do the second one first.
    - If "game over," then simply add a "hide" under this Event.
    - But for the fun part, when she wins, move her to the top right of the screen.
    - Let's have her always move to this spot on winning and always change color.
    - We're going to need a Motion (go to x:O y:O) and a Looks under the "when I receive you win."
    - Now add a "change color effect by 25."
    - Again, we don't want it there at the beginning, so under "change size by -20" add "set color effect to 0."
    - The last thing for the winning octopus: If you want the color to keep changing once winning has happened, it will need a Control factor.
    - (Let them look—by now they should figure out . . .) A "forever" loop! Be careful to only go around the color change block.
- We're almost done! The crab needs to do something if the game is over.
- Drag a "when I receive game over" (brown Event) over to the coding section.
- There are 2 options for purple "say."
    - Change the "hello" to something silly like "I'm too fast for you!"
- Under yellow Control, we need the crab to wait before he speaks.
    - Take the second option that has no seconds attached so it will stay on the screen.
    - Now add at the bottom a Next Costume block.
    - Control this "forever" by placing the yellow block around the costume.

To Have a "You Win" Show up on the Screen

- Go to New sprite options.
    - Only this time, click on the paintbrush.
        - Find the capital T (for text) on the editing side and click on it.
            - Click in the editing screen and type something like "You win!"
                - You can use the edit tools at the top to make it bigger (just like we made the other sprites smaller).
                - The area with your other sprites should show an empty blue box labeled Sprite1. Click in it and the words should appear.
    - You can now drag the words in the game window down toward the bottom.

- Go back to the Scripts tab for "you win." We're going to need just a few things:
  - "When the flag is clicked" (brown Event)
  - "hide" (purple Looks)
  - "When I receive you win" (brown Event)
  - "show" (purple Looks)
- Follow the same instructions to make a "Game Over" sprite.
- Then try playing the game again. You may need to go back and adjust the speed for either the crab or the octopus.

Final Step

- Click See Project Page at the top right of the screen.
  - In the "Instructions" box, tell your players how to play. This can be something simple like: "Use arrow keys to move the octopus. Collect the fish, but avoid the crab!"
  - In the "Notes and Credits" section, you may list other examples that provided inspiration.
  - Give it a name, and don't forget to click the "share" button so others can play it. That's it! Have fun playing your new game. Figures 55.1 and 55.2 show what the coding should look like.

Check out the complete animation at It's Going Swimmingly: https://scratch.mit.edu/projects/238290452/.

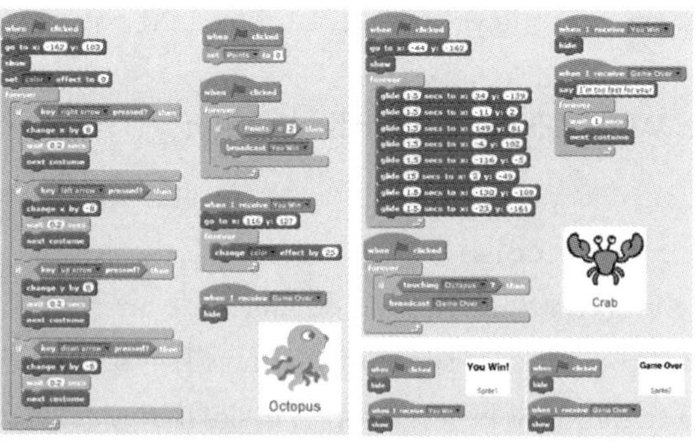

FIGURE 55.1

What the code should look like

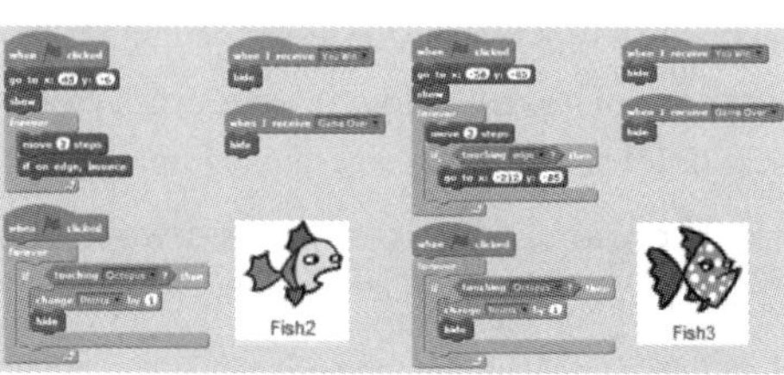

FIGURE 55.2

What the code should look like

LEARNING OUTCOMES

Participants will:

- Learn to utilize the Scratch coding language to create a collecting game.
- Be able to create data for point collection.
- Be able to use Operator and Conditional blocks to set circumstances for actions and reactions.
- Use technology to creatively express themselves.
- Improve their computational thinking skills by learning how to layer and nest coding for maximum abilities.

RECOMMENDED NEXT PROJECTS

- "Level up" your game.
    - Add more point collecting.
    - Have the sprites interact with colors.
    - Add music.
    - Use additional backdrops to show on "you win" or "game over" conditions.
- The collectible project is a more advanced game to create and can be done on its own. But doing a project like Chapter 22: Scratch Coding for Tweens: Creating Cartoons by Karlene Tura Clark builds a stronger foundation and aids in building confidence for those who have never coded before.
- There are numerous types of collectible games to create.
    - A next step would be to create falling "cloned" items that originate in different spots and disappear once touching the bottom of the screen.
    - Tutorials are available on YouTube to assist in navigating the steps to create such a game.
    - Readers are also invited to view other projects by the author under the Scratch user name of Realityjumper1.

REFERENCES

Brennan, K., Balch, C., & Chung, M. (2014). Creative Computing. *Harvard Graduate School of Education*. http://scratched.gse.harvard.edu/guide/files/CreativeComputing20141015.pdf.

ISTE. (2018). ISTE standards for students. *International Society for Technology in Education*. http://www.iste.org/standards/for-students/.

Scratch. (2007). https://scratch.mit.edu.

56

Learn with Lynda.com
An Introduction to JavaScript

JOANNA SCHOFIELD
Branch Services Librarian-Generalist | Cuyahoga County (Ohio) Public Library

PROJECT DESCRIPTION

Have you considered using your library to meet the professional development needs of your community's teen and adult workforce? In today's economic climate, many workers often cannot afford to go to trainings or other professional development opportunities to build their "toolbox" of skills. Informal learning environments for teens are even harder to locate. Enter Lynda.com. Lynda.com is a professional development database that has classes on a wide variety of topics, such as advanced computer coding, 3-D design, photography, Photoshop, and Illustrator. Position your library as a go-to place for technology training by using classes in Lynda.com to help teens and adults learn basic computer programming skills in JavaScript. Start patrons on the path to becoming developers for websites, mobile apps, desktop apps, and games.

Age Range

- Young adults (Ages 13–18)
- Adults

Type of Library Best Suited For

- Public libraries
- School libraries

Cost Estimate

- $0 (this estimate assumes you have a subscription to Lynda.com)

OVERVIEW

Lynda.com (figure 56.1), a learning database featuring asynchronous classes on a wide range of topics, offers a learning program called Programming

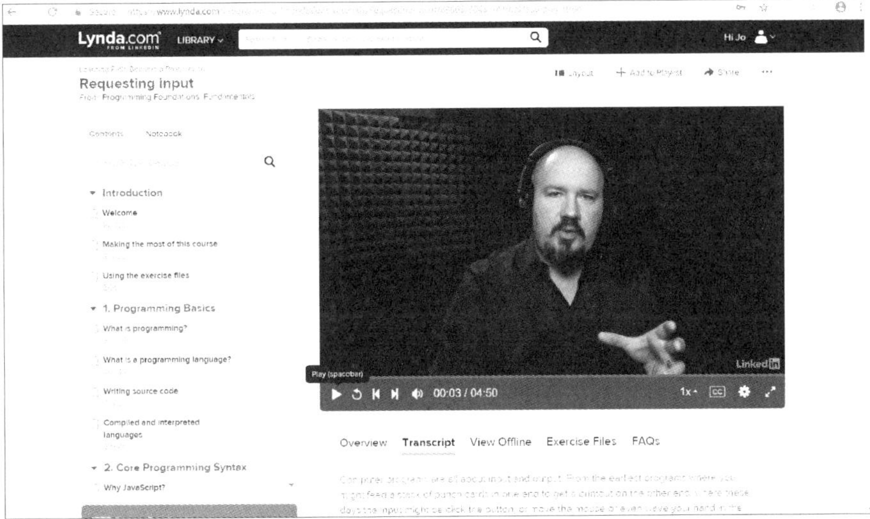

FIGURE 56.1

Lynda.com screen

Foundations: Fundamentals. Participants will take this course as a cohort to learn together, problem solve, and experience the content in a group setting. The facilitator serves as a guide throughout the process (not as an expert) and helps participants navigate the videos and exercises. In the end, participants will gain a better understanding of JavaScript and programming basics. They will also learn how to access the content on their own time.

The number of participants for this program depends on your space. The appropriate number of participants is 10–15 students, although the program will still be effective with a smaller number of participants. This program is designed to be a 4-week series lasting 1 hour each week.

One benefit of Lynda.com is the ability to pause videos as you watch them. The facilitator can pause videos during basic code introduction to help explain how the code will run and answer questions along the way. The facilitator's main duty is to ensure all participants understand videos and supplement the videos through direct instruction and review.

Software/Hardware Needed

- Computer
- Projector
- Lynda.com subscription

Materials List

- Module worksheet (a sample is included at the end of this chapter)
- Writing utensils

STEP-BY-STEP INSTRUCTIONS

Preparation

- Obtain a subscription to Lynda.com through your library.
- Visit Lynda.com to select the training video set you will use for the program. For mine, I used Programming Foundations: Fundamentals.
- Watch the entire module to gain a feel for the scope and depth of information presented.
- Rewatch the module and create a note-taking, fill-in-the-blank, or short answer worksheet. A short sample note-taking worksheet is included at the end of this chapter.
- Become familiar with the downloadable exercises available through Lynda .com. Incorporate these exercises into your worksheet.

During the Program

- Set up the room in a classroom-style design with all chairs and tables pointing toward the screen where you will be projecting.
- Access the Lynda.com database module on the computer and project onto the screen.
- As participants arrive, greet them and give them a copy of the worksheet and a writing utensil.
- When everyone has arrived, explain that Lynda.com is a database generously purchased by the library and filled with training videos on a wide variety of subjects. Show them how to access Lynda.com and remind them they can access this resource at home by using their library card.
- Discuss the worksheet and describe how it is to be used to direct note-taking efforts. Extra notes can be added to the page as well as questions to be asked at the end of each section.
- Watch each section of the video. At the end of the section, stop to answer questions, discuss the topics covered, and help fill in any answers on the note-taking worksheet. This will help ensure comprehension.

- Have a selection of programming books in all formats available for checkout. This will help boost circulation and showcase how participants can further their skill building with library resources.

LEARNING OUTCOMES

Participants will:

- Be able to write basic code in JavaScript.
- Be able to debug a JavaScript program.
- Gain exposure to other programming languages.
- Be more aware of and comfortable using library resources.

RECOMMENDED NEXT PROJECTS

After this program, participants will be able to take additional Lynda.com courses in a variety of related areas, including JavaScript Essentials, Android App Development, HTML Essential Programming, and many others.

SAMPLE WORKSHEET

Introduction to Computer Programming (Day One)

With these exercises, you will

- Gain an understanding of programming languages.
- Be able to write basic code in JavaScript.
- Be able to debug a JavaScript program.
- Be more aware of and comfortable using library resources.

You will be able to answer all of the questions while watching the Lynda.com videos:

Every computer program is a set of ______________________________.

Computers will do exactly what you tell them to do so the instructions better make sense.

A statement is ____.

The only thing that a chip understands is machine code or machine language. True or false? ______________

____________________ try to bridge the gap between us as human beings and the computer hardware.

What is source code? ______________________________________

Programming language source code is written in __________________.

You don't want to write code in a word processor. ☐ True ☐ False

A Programmer's Text Editor is a ____________ text editors with some extra features like line numbers, more powerful Find and Replace, and color coding.

__________________ will let you know if it finds a problem with your code as you are typing it.

____________________________________ (IDE) are professional-level text editors.

A ____________________ creates an executable file.

An____________________ converts the file on the fly.

An ____ is a partially compiled machine code that is then finished using an interpreter.

Core Programming Syntax

______________________________ is a language that works with and manipulates web pages.

______________________________ are more limited programming languages that are embedded inside another program.

JavaScript works inside which application? ______________________________

____

JavaScript is a case-sensitive language. ☐ True ☐ False

JavaScript is a C-based language. ☐ True ☐ False

HTML is not a programming language. It is a markup language.
☐ True ☐ False

A ______________________ is a bucket that can hold some data so you can use it on the next line.

Code you'll be using:

```
Alert ["Hello World"];
var name = prompt ["What is your name?"];
alert ["Hello" + name];
```

Variables and Data Types

Variables are containers that hold data.

To create a variable in JavaScript, use______________ and then name the ______________.

The name for your variable must be one word with no spaces and consist of letters, numbers, the dollar sign, and the underscore.

The__________ sign sets the variable.

Working with Numbers

The most common types of values in computer programs are ______________.

What does var a mean in JavaScript? ______________________.

```
var a;
a = 5;
a = 1000000
a = 123.654
a = -500
alert(a)

var b = 123
var c = "123"
```
WHEN PUT IN PARENTHESIS, 123 BECOMES A STRING AND BEHAVES DIFFERENTLY.

The equal sign assigns a value. It is called the ________________________.

If I want to make a negative number in JavaScript, I just put a negative sign in front of it.

Using Characters and Strings

Examples of strings: characters, words, sentences, e-mail addresses

When you see words contained in a set of____________, you are dealing with strings.

```
alert ("Hello World")

var message = "Hello World";
alert (message);
```

You cannot mix double and single quotes when writing out strings.

```
var phrase = 'Don't mix your quotes.'; Incorrect
var phrase = "Don't mix your quotes." Correct
var phrase = "He said "that's fine," and left." Incorrect
var phrase = "He said \ "that's fine, \" and left."; Correct
```

```
var phrase = "This is a simple phrase.";
alert (phrase.length);
```

Working with Operators

__________________ Operators: +—* /

```
var a = 100;
var b = 50;
var result = a + b;
var result = a - b
var result = a * b
var result = a / b
```

Operator precedence: order of operations applies!

`score = score + 10;` **is the same thing as** `score += 10;`

You can also use -=, *=, and /= as operators.

Increment operator: To add one to the value use the shorthand ++. Example: `a++;` **adds 1 to the value a.**

Decrement operator: to subtract one from the value use the shorthand --. Example: `a--;` **subtracts 1 from the value a.**

57

Meetup.com and Libraries

Programming Partnerships to Teach Adults

ESTHER JACKSON

Public Services Librarian | New York Botanical Garden, the Bronx

RASHAD BELL

Collections Maintenance Associate | New York Botanical Garden, the Bronx

PROJECT DESCRIPTION

This project involves collaborating with local developer communities to teach programming skills to adults. More than a specific recipe for an individual language or programming concept, this project will help you use your local resources to bring in expert instructors from the tech industry and teach adults new and valuable skills. Users will have the opportunity to learn many different programming languages with this model.

`result = 5 + 5 * 10;` **The multiplication would be done first so the answer would be 55.**

`result = (5 + 5) * 10;` **The information in parenthesis would be calculated first so the answer would be 100.**

Age Range

- Adults

Type of Library Best Suited For

- Special libraries
- Public libraries

Cost Estimate

- $0–$100
- In theory, this can be done at no cost other than staff time. If you have a bank of computers, or if attendees can bring their own, there should be no technology cost. The culture of Meetup.com dictates that, when possible, the hosting organization provide some sort of food or refreshments for participants. If you're not able to do this, don't worry! It's not necessary to feed attendees, but do communicate with the Meetup group about food and refreshments. There is a good chance that you may need to purchase some supplies, if only name tags and water bottles. Does the library provide you with a budget, or will this come out of pocket? Additionally, some Meetup groups are able to provide branded "swag" for attendees. If you would like attendees to have a small takeaway, such as a sticker or pin with the group's name, don't be afraid to ask the Meetup group if this is something they would like to or are able to provide.

OVERVIEW

So, you've decided that you want to offer a coding workshop to adults. That's great! Coding skills are in demand and useful in a variety of professions—they are not just for programmers. However, if you haven't taught coding classes before, it can be intimidating to know where to start. This is where you should use your local resources to find help from organizations and individuals who regularly teach programming to adults. You might find that such collaborations aren't essential as you move forward—perhaps you will feel comfortable teaching by yourself. However, collaborating with other organizations as you get started—in this case, Meetup.com groups—will help you learn to teach programming effectively and develop relationships between the library and local tech communities.

Every Meetup group has its strengths and weaknesses. Libraries in urban areas will have more opportunities for in-person collaboration than libraries in more rural areas. However, many nonprofits that are dedicated to teaching coding skills to groups traditionally under-represented in tech (women, nonbinary coders, people of color) will be willing to offer you guidance even from a distance. Many Meetup groups that regularly offer classes will have their own curriculum that they can teach to your library's population; some instructors are also willing to work with you to meet your specific curriculum needs.

The best place to start is to sign up for a Meetup.com account and see what types of Meetup groups are geographically close to you. As with many things in life, making a good first impression is important. If you have the time and ability to go to an event or class that a Meetup group is hosting prior to making your overture, you will likely have better success. However, contacting a group sight unseen is also a viable option, and perhaps it's your only option if you are in a very rural area. Here are some national organizations that are education-minded and collaborative:

National Groups

Girl Develop It—https://www.girldevelopit.com

Girl Develop It is a nonprofit organization that exists to provide affordable and judgment-free opportunities for women interested in learning web and software development. Through in-person classes and community support, Girl Develop It helps women of diverse backgrounds achieve their technology goals and build confidence in their careers and everyday lives. Available curricula is geared toward beginners with courses such as Intro to Web and Programming Concepts, Intro to HTML & CSS, Intro to JavaScript, etc.

Hour of Code—https://hourofcode.com/us/

The Hour of Code is a global movement reaching tens of millions of students in 180+ countries. Anyone anywhere can organize an Hour of Code event. One-hour tutorials are available in over 45 languages. No experience is needed.

PyLadies—www.pyladies.com

PyLadies is an international mentorship group with a focus on helping women become active participants and leaders in the Python open-source community. Its mission is to promote, educate, and advance a diverse Python community through outreach, education, conferences, events, and social gatherings.

RailsBridge—www.railsbridge.org

RailsBridge workshops are a free and fun way to get started or level up with Rails, Ruby, and other web technologies. Their events focus on increasing diversity in tech so that people of all backgrounds can feel welcome and comfortable in the industry.

ScratchED—http://scratched.gse.harvard.edu/

Scratch is a programming language that makes it easy to create interactive art, stories, simulations, and games—and share those creations online. ScratchED is the online community based around Scratch.

Additional Noteworthy Curricula for Libraries to Utilize without a Meetup Group

The Beauty and Joy of Computing—https://bjc.berkeley.edu

This is a free, introductory computer science curriculum developed at the University of California, Berkeley as a CS Principles course.

The Carpentries—https://carpentries.org

The Carpentries teach foundational coding and data science skills to researchers worldwide. Geared toward academic researchers and librarians, the curricula for Software Carpentry, Data Carpentry, and Library Carpentry are all open source and available online.

CS50's Introduction to Computer Science—https://www.edx.org/course/cs50s-introduction-computer-science-harvardx-cs50x/

This is Harvard University's introduction to the intellectual enterprises of computer science and the art of programming for majors and non-majors alike, with or without prior programming experience. It is a well-known and well-respected course.

Even though there are a few groups that have many chapters throughout the United States, the fact of the matter is that for libraries in very rural settings, it may be quite difficult to find local collaborators. Don't be deterred! It doesn't hurt to reach out to a group even if it is not extremely close geographically. Although the group may not be able to provide an instructor, they may be able to connect you to someone who is local, or even offer some other form of support such as remote instructor training or a monetary donation for snacks for attendees. If a Meetup group has developed curricula for teaching programming courses, it may be open source or creative commons licensed, and they may be able to share the workshop content with you even if they are not able to provide an instructor.

For the sample project, we will look at a course in the Girl Develop It curriculum and outline how you would implement this course in your library. The example course would take place during 4 evenings over the course of 2 weeks. However, you could easily amend this model to have a workshop that is 2 hours, 4 hours, 6 hours, or 8 hours over 1 or several days. You will need as many staff as your library typically does to stay open, which means if you are thinking about running a program during hours you would otherwise be closed, you may need to pay for staffing. Ideally, you will want as many staff as you can spare participating in the workshop as they will also be able to learn the content and assist students; a ratio of at least 1:5 for instructors/TAs to students is advised. Typically, these events are most successful with 7–15 students; the class size can be as large as you would like, provided that you or the Meetup group has provided enough instructors and TAs to assist students. Keep in mind whether your facility has additional requirements, such as paying for additional security or maintenance related to hosting an event.

Time/Location

Think through when and where you will host your Meetup. It is important to keep in mind that while a location may be convenient for you, that may not be the case for your potential attendees.

A few questions you should ask when selecting a Meetup location:

- Is the location easily accessible from multiple parts of town?
- Is it easy to find?
- Is it in an area people feel comfortable going to?
- Is it a time when people are free and able to attend?
- Will there be conflicting events at the location?
- Can this Meetup be held at multiple locations?

If you are thinking of hosting a Meetup in your home branch, you won't have to think too much about location. However, if you are planning programming throughout a library system or if you have to host the event on a different site because of things like technology or accessibility requirements, these are important questions to answer.

Staffing

This is very simple but very important. Confirm that you have enough staff to handle your Meetup event. As with any other job or project, it is a good idea to make sure that your collaborators have clearly defined roles to guarantee that your needs and your attendees' needs will be met.

- Will library staff be instructing or assisting with the course as teaching assistants (TAs) or in some other way? (For example, checking students into the building, setting up/breaking down food services, and directing people to the classroom building.)

- Will you need an outside instructor? (Because you are interested in having a Meetup group offer a class, this is probably something you will want. But perhaps you would prefer to use curriculum from a Meetup group and teach the course yourself.)
- Will you need volunteers? (Again, although different Meetup groups offer support by way of instructors, TAs, and organizers, you may still need help from your own organization to handle practical details of the event, such as food and security.)

It's always a good idea to include as many staff as you can spare, at least for a first event. Not only will this help the event run more smoothly, but staff will have the chance to learn the curriculum from a professional, if you have an outside instructor. This will be beneficial if you host the event in the future and would like for internal staff to teach the program.

Software/Hardware Needed

- Projector and screen to display the instructor's computer so students can follow along
- Computers for attendees (encourage participants to bring their own)
    - It's nice to have computers available at the library for people to use, but depending on the complexity of what they will be learning, they may need to have access to things like the command line or bash. For workshops like this, people should plan to bring their own devices. If you're not sure whether or not people should bring their own devices, ask your Meetup collaborators. There are many online websites that allow for people to practice coding different languages without installing anything on their computers. If your users don't have access to their own computers, you may want to teach a course for which there is a good online editor.

STEP-BY-STEP INSTRUCTIONS

Preparation

- Be sure that you have everything you need before you commit to the event. Communicate clearly with the Meetup group to find out if they have any expectations related to available technology. Does your instructor require a specific kind of projector or screen? How will you accommodate someone who might have an accessibility request, such as a special microphone that connects to a hearing aid? Do you have the capacity in your Wi-Fi network to host the number of attendees you are expecting? Items such as extra computers, projectors, and screens may need to be requested from another department in advance. It is a good idea to take stock of what you have versus what you need and then determine what is available to you.

- Make a Meetup.com account.
- Identify a Meetup group or groups that you would like to work with and reach out to them. Even better, go to an event that they are hosting. Don't be afraid to reach out to a few groups. If you are specifically interested in hosting a class, be sure to mention that as well as the language or curriculum you are interested in if you have something specific in mind.
- Make sure that you and your collaborator clearly understand your roles in the event. Will you provide food? TA assistance? Most people who organize Meetups are pretty organized themselves, which is nice.
- The Meetup group will make a Meetup event page for your workshop. Work with them to make sure all of the details are correct, including number of attendees, cost for attendees, if any, instructions for attendees, required equipment and technology, such as software to install ahead of time, etc.
- Confirm with your collaborator, TAs, and attendees 1 week ahead of time. Your Meetup collaborator should be able to e-mail the workshop attendees through Meetup.com, making this step fairly simple.
- Confirm again with instructors, TAs, and attendees 2 days before.

PROJECT INSTRUCTIONS

- Identify a Meetup group that you would like to collaborate with.
- Identify what kind of class you would like to offer, such as Introduction to HTML/CSS, Introduction to Python, etc.
- Plan an event with a Meetup group, such as a class. Below is an example class with an example curriculum. Note that different Meetup groups may have their own curricula that they are able to teach.
- Sample class:
  - Introduction to HTML/CSS curriculum from Girl Develop It is a great beginner workshop. Each session is taught in a 2-hour session. The curriculum can be taught over 4 evenings or 1 full day.
    - **Class 1**—Introduction to HTML (http://girldevelopit.github.io/gdi-featured-html-css-intro/class1.html)
    - **Class 2**—Introduction to CSS (http://girldevelopit.github.io/gdi-featured-html-css-intro/class2.html)

  - **Class 3**—HTML, beyond the basics (http://girldevelopit.github.io/gdi-featured-html-css-intro/class3.html)
  - **Class 4**—CSS, layouts and formatting (http://girldevelopit.github.io/gdi-featured-html-css-intro/class4.html)
- Assess the success of your event, and plan your next one.

LEARNING OUTCOMES

Participants will:

- Be introduced to coding through a language of your choice.
- Enjoy an inclusive atmosphere with instructors expressly focused on teaching adults.
- Be inspired to continue learning in-demand skills both through the library and independently.

RECOMMENDED NEXT PROJECTS

- If your collaboration is successful, you can work with the Meetup group to host another one. If you don't have the ability to offer a more structured class, even offering the library as a meeting place for study groups may be a model for you to explore. This may also be a way for you to interact with new Meetup groups without the pressure of planning a full class.
- Whether or not you collaborate with a Meetup group more than once depends on many things, not the least of which is resources. In many cases, Meetup groups are volunteer run and don't always have the resources to come and give a program every week or every month. If there is a Meetup that you really like working with, find out how possible it would be for you—or maybe a library school student—to teach their curriculum. Many groups, such as Girl Develop It, have open-source curriculum that can be used and adapted.

58

MakeCode with Circuit Playground Express

Physical Computing for Adults

CHAD CLARK

New Media Services Manager | Highland (Illinois) Park Public Library

PROJECT DESCRIPTION

This project is designed to introduce adults to the world of physical computing, showing them how easy it is to create systems that respond to, and control, part of the physical world using computer programs. This project focuses on Circuit Playground Express and Microsoft's MakeCode. Circuit Playground Express, created by an open-source hardware company called Adafruit Industries, is a small microcontroller that houses a wide variety of baked-in sensors. Circuit Playground Express serves as a solid introduction to physical computing that can be coded with Microsoft's MakeCode, CircuitPython, or the Arduino IDE.

Age Range

- Adults

Type of Library Best Suited For

- Public libraries
- Academic libraries

Cost Estimate

- $125 for 5 Circuit Playground Express boards

OVERVIEW

One of the beautiful things about Circuit Playground Express is that it can be programmed using MakeCode, CircuitPython, or Arduino IDE. This versatility allows librarians to lead physical computing learning sessions that can be tailored to fit different programming language skill sets and levels of experience (including no experience at all!). This project is intended for absolute newbies, so we will focus on MakeCode. MakeCode (figure 58.1) is a web-based code editor for physical computing. It provides a block editor, like Scratch or Code.org, and a JavaScript editor for more advanced users. MakeCode doesn't rely strictly on users' knowing extensive specific syntax, but instead it allows participants to build applications by stacking commands together in a drag-and-drop interface.

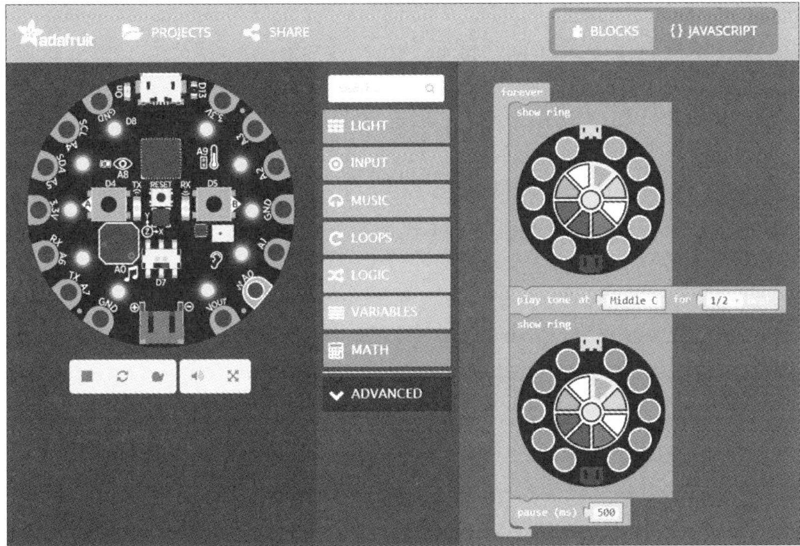

FIGURE 58.1

MakeCode interface

Participants will use MakeCode to make simple programs that can sense and respond to the analog world utilizing the sensors on Circuit Playground Express. Here are some of the great goodies baked into each Circuit Playground Express:

- Motion sensor
- Light, temperature, and sound sensors
- Proximity sensor
- 10 RGB LEDs (NeoPixels)
- 8 input/output pins for connecting additional hardware, which can also be used as capacitive touch sensors. This enables Makey Makey–style projects without the need for a ground connection.
- Mini-speaker

Software/Hardware Needed

- Circuit Playground Express
- Computer or laptop (USB ports required) with Internet connectivity

STEP-BY-STEP INSTRUCTIONS

Preparation

- The block editor is the best way to get started with MakeCode and Circuit Playground Express. MakeCode does not require any software installation; it works on any computer with a web browser. Drag and drop blocks from the category list. Each time a change is made to the blocks, the simulator will automatically restart and run the code. Programs can be tested in the browser.
- A good way to learn how MakeCode works is by building a simple program that blinks the 10 awesome NeoPixels. Creating a blink effect is done by setting all the ring LEDs to red, pause for a little, then turn them off, pause for a little, and then repeat forever. The blocks needed to convert the description above into blocks that Circuit Playground Express can understand and run are:
    - **forever** runs blocks in a loop with a 20ms pause in between.
    - **show ring** block sets the color on the 10 NeoPixels at once.
    - **Pause** blocks the current thread for 100ms. If other events or forever loops are running, they can run at this time.

Demonstration

- Demonstrate this Blinky block program in action for participants who may follow along. Point out how the blocks are "slotted together." Clicking the question marks on the box will pop up a comment to explain what the block does.
- Ask participants what they would do if they wanted to select or change colors. The show ring block has a built-in color picker. Select the color from the color wheel to select a color, and then click 1 of the 10 NeoPixel rings to modify its color.
- Challenge them to disable a NeoPixel. The gray dot in the middle of the color wheel indicates that the pixel is off. Select the gray from the color wheel and then click the NeoPixel ring.

Downloading and Flashing

Instruct participants how to get their code into Circuit Playground Express. This is very easy with MakeCode. They do not need to install any software on their device and the process takes 2 steps:

STEP 1

Connect the board via USB and enter bootloader mode

- Connect the board to the computer via a USB cable. Press the reset button once to put the board in bootloader mode. When Circuit Playground Express is in bootloader mode, all the LEDs will turn red briefly, then green. Verify your status LED is also pulsing red. Your computer should show a new removable drive called "CPLAYBOOT."

STEP 2

Compile and Download the .uf2 file into the board drive

- MakeCode has a built-in simulator that reloads and reruns code when restarted. This is an easy way to both ensure that the code compiles and simulates it before moving it onto the board. The refresh button reloads the simulator with your latest version of block code. If the board is working in the simulator, it's time to download it to the actual board! Click the Download button. It will generate a .uf2 file and download it to the board drive. UF2 is a file format designed to flash microcontrollers over USB.

View Other Examples

When this is completed successfully, head over to the MakeCode examples web page at https://makecode.adafruit.com/examples/ and experiment with example programs that employ different sensors. These examples are great because they illustrate all the blocks necessary to run the program as well as provide background on why particular blocks are arranged as they are and to what end. The projects, also on this page, demonstrate several ways Circuit Playground Express can be incorporated into craft projects. Librarians can mix and match these examples and projects any way they want to provide a fun and rewarding introduction to physical computing.

LEARNING OUTCOMES

Participants will:

- Learn definitions for physical computing.
- Understand the possibilities of physical computing and coding.
- Experience hands-on opportunities with Microsoft's MakeCode.

RECOMMENDED NEXT PROJECTS

- CircuitPython for Circuit Playground Express
- Arduino IDE for Circuit Playground Express

PART V

CREATING CIRCULATING COLLECTIONS

59

Rotating Kits for Easy STEM Programming

KELSEY HUGHES
Adult and Teen Services Specialist
Prince George's County (Maryland) Memorial Library System

PROJECT DESCRIPTION

Reinvigorate your STEM programming and inspire confidence in your library staff who might be new to STEM programming by creating a series of pre-made kits. These kits can rotate throughout your library system or simply be readily available when a programming need arises. Projects contained in the kit can range in cost and complexity based on your budget and familiarity with STEM.

Age Range

- Tweens (Ages 8–12)
- Young adults (Ages 13–18)

Type of Library Best Suited For

- Public libraries
- School libraries (especially if the school librarian rotates through multiple libraries)

Cost Estimate

- $20–$2,000
- The cost can be scaled up or down based on the budget and materials already available that could be repurposed.

OVERVIEW

The purpose of this project is to develop a continuous system by which you can rotate high-quality STEM programming ideas and resources to your library branches or among staff within a branch. Each kit includes at least 1 STEM lesson plan and the materials necessary to carry out the program. It is recommended that lesson plans employ an inquiry learning model in which students make predictions, experiment, and assess outcomes to develop new knowledge with instructors' support. As a result, instructors don't need to have a lot of background knowledge on the scientific subject at hand because they are learning and experimenting alongside students.

The benefits of employing a kit model are manifold. For one, library staff may be intimidated by STEM programming and might not know where to start should they have to come up with a program from scratch. By creating these kits—and including a very specific and detailed lesson plan that is designed for the instructor to learn via inquiry model alongside students—some of the intimidation factor is removed. Additionally, these kits can be helpful for last-minute or impromptu large groups or programming needs because they can be quickly pulled out and set up with little preparation time.

There are many different methods by which the kits can be rotated, based on your programming needs and capabilities, but an effective method is a monthly rotation schedule. Each month, staff at each branch would receive a kit, and at the end of the month, they would send it along to the next branch on the schedule. Another method would be to have the kits available for staff to check out from a central location when they identify a programming need. At regular intervals (after a set time or at the end of a full rotation), all kits are checked and replenished with all needed materials.

Figure 59.1 shows the schedule we use to circulate our kits around the north half of the county. We have a second identical schedule for the south area. A copy of the schedule is available on our staff intranet and placed in each kit.

Software/Hardware Needed

Materials needed will vary based on the project, but our library's kits are listed to give you inspiration. Most kits can be purchased from a company with all the required materials for basic projects. For those that cannot be purchased as a pre-made set, the materials needed for the kit are listed. All of the projects and corresponding lesson plans can be found by looking through books just like this one, as well as consulting online resources and STEM librarian

STEM Kit Routing Apr 2018--Dec 2018 (If a branch is closed, kits will be sent to an alternate branch. MB is not in rotation) Kit__________________

- Kits should be rotated on the last workday of each month. **Do not send the kit prior to the last day of each month.**
- Date and legibly write your name in the box under kit title when ready for delivery. This signifies that kits are complete and in good condition.
- If replacement items are needed contact

Branch	Apr 1-30	May 1-31	Jun 1-30	Jul 1-31	Aug 1-31	Sep 1-30	Oct 1-31	Nov 1-30	Dec 1-30	Jan
HY	1 Brain Flakes	9 Straw Struc.	8 Squishy Circ	7 Magnets	6 Snap Circuits	5 Keva Planks	4 Esc the Rm	3 Flat/Flex Circ	2 Fairytale Eng	
BL	2 Fairytale Eng	1 Brain Flakes	9 Straw Struc.	8 Squishy Circ	7 Magnets	6 Snap Circuits	5 Keva Planks	4 Esc the Rm	3 Flat/Flex Circ	
NC	3 Flat/Flex Circ	2 Fairytale Eng	1 Brain Flakes	9 Straw Struc.	8 Squishy Circ	7 Magnets	6 Snap Circuits	5 Keva Planks	4 Esc the Rm	
SB	4 Esc the Rm	3 Flat/Flex Circ	2 Fairytale Eng	1 Brain Flakes	9 Straw Struc.	8 Squishy Circ	7 Magnets	6 Snap Circuits	5 Keva Planks	Send To AO
BW	5 Keva Planks	4 Esc the Rm	3 Flat/Flex Circ	2 Fairytale Eng	1 Brain Flakes	9 Straw Struc.	8 Squishy Circ	7 Magnets	6 Snap Circuits	
LA	6 Snap Circuits	5 Keva Planks	4 Esc the Rm	3 Flat/Flex Circ	2 Fairytale Eng	1 Brain Flakes	9 Straw Struc.	8 Squishy Circ	7 Magnets	
BV	7 Magnets	6 Snap Circuits	5 Keva Planks	4 Esc the Rm	3 Flat/Flex Circ	2 Fairytale Eng	1 Brain Flakes	9 Straw Struc.	8 Squishy Circ	
GR	8 Squishy Circ	7 Magnets	6 Snap Circuits	5 Keva Planks	4 Esc the Rm	3 Flat/Flex Circ	2 Fairytale Eng	1 Brain Flakes	9 Straw Struc.	
MR	9 Straw Struc.	8 Squishy Circ	7 Magnets	6 Snap Circuits	5 Keva Planks	4 Esc the Rm	3 Flat/Flex Circ	2 Fairytale Eng	1 Brain Flakes	

Branch	Date	Write First and Last Name Legibly	Notes
HY			
BL			
NC			

FIGURE 59.1

Circulation schedule

forums. They may then be adapted to fit your library's needs. Coding-based kits are marked with an asterisk (*).

- Strawbees
- Arduinos*
- Makey Makeys
- Snap Circuits
- LEGO WeDo*
- littleBits*
- Ozobots*
- Brain Flakes
- Keva Planks
- Squishy circuits: modeling clay, Play-Doh, circuit wires, batteries, battery connectors, LEDs
- Magnets: various strength and shapes of magnets and various magnetic and non-magnetic materials
- Flat and flexible circuits: circuit wires, conductive tape, scissors, construction paper, LED lights, batteries, scotch tape, markers
- Storage boxes and labels for kits

STEP-BY-STEP INSTRUCTIONS

Preparation

- Think about what kind of budget you have and how the kits would be best utilized in your library. This will affect what kinds of items you purchase and how you set up your rotation. Remember to consider the long-term maintenance costs for kits with items that will need to be replaced as the programs take place.
- Establish your rotations.
    - Take into account the variety of patrons you serve and the unique programming needs of each branch. Who is your target audience: Elementary? Middle school? High school? A mix? Some kits and projects can apply to multiple groups and some can be scaled up and down based on the individual's ability level and prior knowledge, but some will only work for a certain group. Arduinos, for example, tend to work best with older teens or children who already have some experience with circuits and coding.
    - Consider physical locations and distances. Could you use a continuous circuit, or would it be more feasible to create a checkout system for borrowing on demand from a central location? A hybrid approach may also work, where some kits are rotated regularly and some are only checked out centrally.
    - Examine the needs of your staff and the available space. Where will the kits be stored? How long should the kits stay at each branch, if rotating?
- Survey what materials you already have and what lesson plans you and your staff already have been using. Can any of these be turned into ready-made program kits?
- Scan programming websites and other library and teacher resources to identify what other projects you could turn into a kit.

PROJECT INSTRUCTIONS

- Purchase needed materials.
    - You will need a storage box and label for each kit.
    - Depending on the size of your library system and the estimated use the kits will get, you may want to purchase duplicates.

  - You'll also want to purchase enough of the consumable items for the kit so that it will be able to complete the whole rotation (or last for whatever predetermined time works best for you) without needing to be replenished.
- Assemble the kits. Each kit (figure 59.2) should contain all needed materials along with a packing list (including images when necessary), a lesson plan, and, if rotating, a schedule so users know when and where to send it next. All paper materials should be laminated or placed in a clear plastic protective folder. It is helpful to make available a digital version of each document as well.

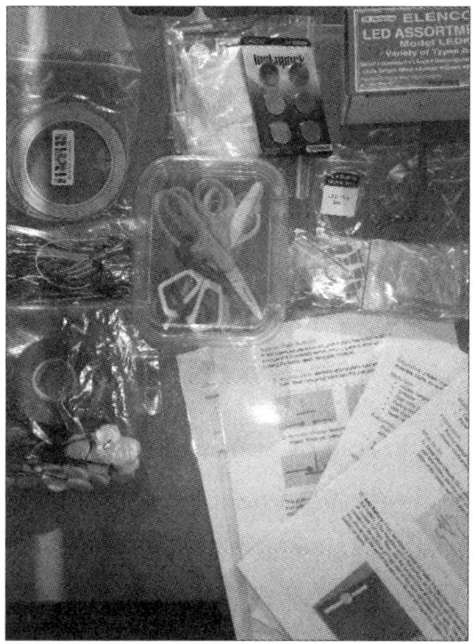

FIGURE 59.2

Contents of a Flat and Flexible Circuits Kit

- Hold a training so staff know what to expect when the kits arrive, how to use the materials, and how they should be incorporated into programming.
  - To familiarize staff with the materials and facilitate the incorporation of the kits into programming, host a maker fair where all the kits are set up on various tables around the room. After an introduction to the purpose of the kits and description of how they would be used and rotated, staff are encouraged to visit each table and spend some time simply playing with each kit. One experienced staff member should be stationed at each exhibit for guidance. The goal is to have staff receive hands-on experience with the kits and see for themselves that the gadgets and projects are not intimidating but fun!
- Start using the kits. Check in regularly to make sure they are moving from branch to branch as expected or are being used often if you employ a staff check-in and checkout system. Also keep in touch with staff, not just to make sure the kits retain all their pieces as they move around, but also to find out whether the kits are working as programming tools.
- After a full rotation or a certain time period of checkouts or uses, recall the kits to make sure they still work and have all needed pieces. This is also a good time to assess the system you've set up and make any necessary changes before sending the kits back out or adding more kits into rotation.

LEARNING OUTCOMES

Staff participants will:

- Be able to set up highly effective STEM programming with minimal preparation.
- Develop confidence in leading STEM programming.
- Be able to guide students through STEM learning.

Based on the Next Generation Science Standards as a guide for developing learning objectives for each lesson, student/library patron participants will:

- Ask questions (for science) and define problems (for engineering).
- Develop and use models.
- Plan and carry out investigations.
- Analyze and interpret data.
- Use mathematics and computational thinking.
- Construct explanations (for science) and design solutions (for engineering).
- Engage in argument from evidence.
- Obtain, evaluate, and communicate information.

RECOMMENDED NEXT PROJECTS

- **Scale Up Your Kits:** If you focused on one age group, add lesson plans so the materials can be used for different ages. Or, add extra lesson plans for beginner, intermediate, and advanced activities.
- Read other chapters in this book for kit inspiration, including Chapter 60: Creating a Tech-Related Circulating Collection by Michael P. Sauers, for more ideas about how to make circulating kits work for you.

60

Creating a Tech-Related Circulating Collection

MICHAEL P. SAUERS
Director of Technology | Do Space, Omaha, Nebraska

PROJECT DESCRIPTION

Not sure what to do with tech in your library? Looking for a special activity to engage patrons? Why not create a circulating collection of Tech Activity Kits that can be checked out by patrons. Patrons can check out one of these kits to learn and explore technology on their own. Filled with tech toys from robots to mini-programmable computers, these kits are intended to be interactive for use by 1 person, a couple, or a whole group. Designed to be with played with on their own, these kits include how-to instructions and ideas to encourage patrons to become hackers of the kits and tech inside.

Age Range

- Kids (Ages 3–7)
- Tweens (Ages 8–12)
- Young adults (Ages 13–18)
- Adults

Type of Library Best Suited For

- Public libraries
- Academic libraries
- School libraries

Cost Estimate

- $50–$10,000
- Costs will vary significantly based on the technology being offered. A library can start with a single item and then scale up, or make a significant investment in a collection of items and roll out a larger more marketable program.

- There are a number of choices for containers for the materials for each kit. The Hefty 3.75-Gallon Clear Tote with Latching Lid is recommended. Although these totes still can break, they last much longer and are more durable than any other brand of tote.
- 1 Avery Mini Durable View Binder for 5.5" × 8.5" Pages, 0.5 inch Round Ring for each kit at $7 each.
- Laminator for binder pages at about $50. (If you don't laminate the pages, the instructions won't last more than a single use or 2.)
- Internal signage and promotional materials will also be needed, but costs can be as little as virtually nothing for internally printed signs and website updating to hundreds of dollars for professionally printed signage and printed marketing and promotion of the new program.

OVERVIEW

Tech Activity Kits are an ongoing program as part of your library's traditional collection. You may want to limit the number of kits that patrons may check out at a time and/or the length of the checkout in hours instead of days. Also consider whether you will allow these kits to be taken off site or if they will be for use in the library only. (At Do Space, we do not allow any of our equipment to leave the building.)

From a staffing perspective, as with most items added to a library's collection, cataloging and processing staff will need to be involved to make the kits ready for circulation. Staff will need to create basic instruction manuals for each kit, and front-line staff will need to be at least minimally familiar with the operation of each kit as patrons will ask questions about the kits.

As previously mentioned, the size of your collection is up to you. However, we've found that the process for each item in the collection is the same. Therefore, I have only included instructions using 1 of our Tech Activity Kits as an example. Repeat as necessary.

Software/Hardware Needed

- Tubs
- Binders
- Laminator

STEP-BY-STEP INSTRUCTIONS

Preparation

- The first thing you'll need to do to prepare is to evaluate which technologies you wish to create kits out of. Feel free to use Do Space's list of existing kits at the end of this chapter as a great place to start. Keep in mind the following: age range you're looking to attract, cost of the kit, durability of the technology involved, and number of pieces included. For example, littleBits (https://shop.littlebits.com) are extremely interesting and popular. However, they contain many small parts that are easily broken or lost. On the other hand, Snap Circuits (https://www.elenco.com/brand/snap-circuits/), while more simple in their design and what they teach, can accomplish the same learning goals while having larger more durable pieces. Not every kit you create will end up being popular nor stay functional as long as you would like. Some kits will be extremely popular, but you'll find yourself reordering missing or broken parts pretty consistently. Don't be afraid to experiment and try something new and then deaccession it if the hassle of keeping it in the collection or the cost starts to outweigh the benefits of the experience to patrons.
- Step 2 is to procure the technology you wish to turn into a kit.

PROJECT INSTRUCTIONS

- For this project, I'm going to use our Cubelets Tech Activity Kit as the example. Cubelets (https://www.modrobotics.com/cubelets/) are a collection of magnetic cubes that can be assembled in a nearly infinite combination to create machines and robots that perform various tasks or interact with their environment. Different cubes perform different functions and responses varying from drive, brightness, blocking, and inverting. Think of them as a sort of "robotic LEGO," but they are significantly larger and less complex than such systems as LEGO WeDo. LEGO adapter pieces are also available for connecting Cubelets to any LEGOS you have. Although no programming skills are needed, there is an app through which you can directly program the cubes via a bluetooth connection. Cubelets come in several differently sized collections ranging from 6 to 20 cubes priced from $129 to $499. Individual cubes are also available for purchase should you wish to slowly grow your collection or need to replace a particular cube. Lastly, educator kits (figure 60.1) are available for purchase complete with lesson plans. (See the Cubelets website for details.)

FIGURE 60.1

Cubelets Kit

- Once you have the Cubelets in hand, spend some time with them to learn how they work. The Cubelets themselves come with a collection of project cards that provide straightforward instructions for assembling various types of robots based on the number of cubes in your collection. Additional projects can be found on the Cubelets website. Although you may not spend time with members walking them through a kit as the kits are designed for self-discovery and learning, it is best to have available staff who have a basic understanding of how the kit work and to be able to troubleshoot common problems. (For example, is the power cube charged and turned on?)
- Next, create a basic set of instructions that would allow users to not only get a sense of what can be done with the kit before checking it out, but also enough to get them started once they have it in hand. In the case of Cubelets, not only have we included our own set of basic instructions, but we've also included the project cards provided from the company. The instructions you create should include the following:
    - Brief description of the kit
    - Age and experience level of the intended audience
    - Approximate minimum amount of time to set up and create something with the kit
    - Full parts list
    - 1 project to get users started
- When the instructions are written, print them in a 5.5" × 8.5" booklet format. Laminate the pages, hole punch, and assemble in the binder. Include a cover sheet for the binder.
- Each kit requires 2 storage tubs. The first contains the technology included in the kit. This tub should be stored in a staff-only access area. Label the tub with the name of the kit. (This becomes very important as you add more kits to your collection.) The other tub should contain the instruction book for the kit,

but none of the tech. Keeping the on-floor tubs empty ensures some security over the potentially high-cost equipment and ensures that patrons need to check out the kit. This also helps you acquire much-needed usage statistics. You may want to design an insert for each tub that includes a photo of the kit's main piece of technology, the name of the kit, and instructions to bring the tub to the circulation desk for checkout. You can use the services of a local printing company to print and laminate the inserts. (They may be way too long for a standard office laminator.) The inserts are then attached to the inside walls of the tub using clear packing tape.

- Catalog and barcode the kit. Place the barcode on the tub displayed on the floor. Follow whatever local cataloging rules and procedures your library has for this step.
- Display the (empty) kit on the floor. How you will display the on-floor kit will obviously vary based on the number of kits you have and the available space. If you're short on space, you could reduce display needs to something as simple as a notebook at the circulation desk containing a page for each available kit that patrons can choose from. Of course, this would make availability much less obvious and have a negative impact on circulation numbers.
- When member want to check out a kit, they browse the available collection and pick their kit. Once they choose a kit, they bring the empty barcoded tub to the circulation desk. At this point, the kit is checked out to the member following standard procedure. Staff take the kit parts from the bin in the staff area and put all of the parts into the barcoded tub. In the case of Cubelets, this is the cubes themselves, the project cards, and the power cube that's been plugged in to charge. The filled tub is then given to the member. In some cases, kits also include other parts that need to be handled a bit differently. For example, some kits include a tablet or laptop. Tablets and laptops, like the power cube, should be stored separately for charging and are reimaged after each use. Raspberry Pi kits may also include a monitor and keyboard, which are also stored separately because they will not easily fit in the bins.
- Once a kit is returned, staff will not only need to follow standard return procedures but also be sure that all of the kit's pieces have been returned and all tech is in working order. Management will need to establish procedures for what to do in regard to missing or damaged equipment if they don't have them already. Staff should also consistently evaluate the condition of the tub, insert, and notebook as these will experience normal wear and tear and need to be cleaned or replaced periodically. Staff will then need to move the pieces back into the storage tubs and put

the empty tub back onto the floor. For equipment that needs to be recharged, reshelving may need to be delayed to ensure that the next borrower receives a fully charged kit.

LEARNING OUTCOMES

Participants will:

- Gain exposure to new technologies.
- Learn to explore through self-guided learning.
- Depending on the kit, parent and child can work together as part of the learning process.
- Evaluate new technologies for possible home purchase.

RECOMMENDED NEXT PROJECTS

- As previously mentioned, the steps for putting together a Tech Activity Kit do not depend on the kit's contents. But the kit's content is what offers all of the possibilities. Below is a list of other kits that Do Space currently offers or has offered in the past. A list of all of Do Space's current Tech Activity Kits can be found at https://www.dospace.org/tech-activity-kits/.
    - Arduino
    - Bee-Bot
    - Code-a-pillar
    - Cubetto
    - Da Vinci Mini Maker 3-D printers
    - Dash and Dot
    - iPad Pro with Apple Pencil
    - littleBits
    - Makey Makey
    - Nintendo Switch
    - Oculus Go
    - Osmo
    - Sphero BB-8
- Staff should also constantly gather feedback from borrowers about their experience with the kits and suggestions for other kits. Such feedback may lead to both removing and adding kits to your collection. Another thing to consider is how to improve the overall process for staff and experience for patrons.

Resources

HARDWARE

Arduino—https://www.arduino.cc

Dash Robot—https://www.makewonder.com/dash/

Code-a-Pillars—https://www.fisher-price.com/en_CA/brands/think-and-learn/products/Think-and-Learn-Code-a-Pillar/

Bee-Bots—https://www.bee-bot.us

Ozobots—https://ozobot.com

LEGO Robots and LEGO WeDo Kits—https://education.lego.com/en-us/shop/

KIBO Robots—http://kinderlabrobotics.com/kibo/

SPRK Sphero Robots—https://www.sphero.com/sphero-sprk-plus/

Finch Robots—https://www.finchrobot.com

Finch Robot Loan Program—https://www.finchrobot.com/finch-robot-loan-program/

Micro:bits—https://microbit.org

Cubelets—https://www.modrobotics.com/cubelets/

Circuit Playground Express—https://learn.adafruit.com/adafruit-circuit-playground-express/overview/

SOFTWARE

Scratch—https://scratch.mit.edu
ScratchJr—https://www.scratchjr.org
PencilCode—https://pencilcode.net
Blockly—https://developers.google.com/blockly/

Blockly Games—https://blockly-games.appspot.com
Thonny: Python IDE for beginners—https://thonny.org
Made with Code Projects—https://www.madewithcode.com/projects/
GROOVECODERS—https://groovecoders.com
Bloxels—http://edu.bloxelsbuilder.com
Thunkable App Builder—https://thunkable.com/#/
MIT App Inventor—http://appinventor.mit.edu/explore/
Code.org's WebLab—https://code.org/educate/weblab/
CoSpaces, VR Space Builder—https://cospaces.io/edu
Soundtrap Online Music Studio—https://www.soundtrap.com
Twine Interactive Story Creator—http://twinery.org
Sonic Pi Music Coding App—https://sonic-pi.net
Python—https://www.python.org/downloads/
Pygame—https://www.pygame.org
Stencyl Video game creator—http://www.stencyl.com
Alice 2—https://www.alice.org/get-alice/alice-2/
Lynda.com—https://www.lynda.com

LEARNING RESOURCES

Libraries [Ready to Code]—http://www.ala.org/tools/readytocode/
Codecademy—https://www.codecademy.com
Code.org—https://code.org
Coder Dojo—https://coderdojo.com
Girl Develop It—https://www.girldevelopit.com
Hour of Code—https://hourofcode.com/us/
Microsoft MakeCode—https://www.microsoft.com/en-us/makecode/
ScratchED—http://scratched.gse.harvard.edu

Index

C

M

N

O

S

T

U

V

W

Y